BUSINESS AND PRICES

THE BRITISH LIBRARY OF BUSINESS STUDIES

EDITORS: MICHAEL P. FOGARTY, RALPH GLASSER

Monograph series
THE COMPUTER AND THE CLERK
ENID MUMFORD AND OLIVE BANKS

Textbook series
MARKETING AND MARKET ASSESSMENT
J. L. SEWELL

BUSINESS AND PRICES

by

LÁSZLÓ SONKODI

LONDON

ROUTLEDGE AND KEGAN PAUL

First published in 1969
by Routledge & Kegan Paul Ltd
Broadway House, 68–74 Carter Lane
London, E.C.4
Printed in Great Britain
by Butler & Tanner Ltd
Frome and London
© *László Sonkodi 1969*
No part of this book may be reproduced
in any form without permission from
the publisher, except for the quotation
of brief passages in criticism
SBN 7100 6543 4

CONTENTS

v

CONTENTS

CONTENTS

INTRODUCTION

Prices are hard, inescapable facts which affect the general public and the businessman alike. Correct pricing policy can make or break a company. Despite its importance, it is still one of the fuzziest areas of all executive decisions. It has been well stated: 'Most well-managed manufacturing enterprises have a clear-cut advertising policy, product policy, customer policy and distribution channel policy. But pricing decisions remain a patchwork of *ad hoc* decisions. In many otherwise well-managed firms pricing policy has been dealt with on a crisis basis!'[1]

The object of this book is to survey the problems of pricing, to shed light on the logic of price-making and on the many and various aspects which influence this field of business activity. The problem will be examined from three standpoints. First, attention will be given to the business firm as a decision-making unit; secondly, to the issues of public policy and, finally, to the position of the consumer in relation to market prices.

The first of the book's fifteen chapters will be given over to explaining certain basic economic concepts which must be understood before attempting to formulate properly the principles of price formation. Various market structures are surveyed as a background to pricing and special attention is given to oligopolistic markets because of their prominent role in the contemporary economic scene.

The various pricing objectives and actual pricing methods are then examined against economic theory.

Modern business organizations devote considerable expenditure to discovering what the consumer wants and how much he is prepared to pay for it. Therefore, as a preliminary to pricing policies, the findings of these researches into consumer reaction to prices are surveyed.

[1] Joel Dean, *Managerial Economics*, Englewood Cliffs, N.J., 1961, p. 401.

Because of the different nature of industrial and retail price-setting, actual pricing policies of manufacturers and retailers are discussed separately.

Coming to more specialized issues, the nature and economic effects of price agreements are considered in the light of the findings of the Restrictive Practices Court and the Monopolies Commission.

The analysis proceeds with an exposition on the issue of resale price maintenance, which has recently aroused much public controversy, leading to special legislation in 1964. After the abolition of resale price maintenance the importance of price recommendation as a distinct form of price policy has grown. This pricing practice is considered in detail.

The questions of discounts and rebates, which are often applied in order to make price systems more flexible, are examined with particular attention to the question of aggregated rebate schemes as a form of restrictive practice.

Ex-works and delivered pricing methods are also taken into account.

Commodity exchanges, which deal with agricultural and mining products, are explained in terms of their characteristic features, both as price-regulators and insurers against the risk of price fluctuation.

No book on prices can be complete without reference to the special pricing problems facing the management of nationalized industries. The penultimate chapter is devoted to this topic.

In conclusion, the discussion is rounded off with a description of the main issues inherent in the prices and incomes policy and the role of the National Board for Prices and Incomes in modern business.

Chapters 9 and 10 are based partly on the author's articles published in the July 1963 and July 1964 issues of *Cartel*. I am grateful to the International Co-operative Alliance for permission to use this material.

CHAPTER 1

Markets and competition

Business transactions take place in the market where the prices of goods and services are determined by the interaction of suppliers and buyers. The most outstanding feature of a market is the degree of competition among sellers, and economic theory classifies it according to this characteristic. Three main types of market are distinguished: perfect competition, monopoly and imperfectly competitive.

A perfectly competitive market is where competition operates to the full without any impediment among a large number of sellers. A monopoly market is characterized by the absence of competition, where the production of a commodity is in the hands of a single producer. A market which contains the elements of both is called an imperfectly competitive one and is the result of the trend of business since the end of the last century.

Perfect competition

The commodities offered on a perfectly competitive market must be homogeneous and therefore capable of being substituted for other units of the same kind. Perfect product uniformity exists where there is no physical difference between the individual units and a sense of complete interchangeability is established in the mind of the buyer. Physical uniformity in itself does not necessarily ensure product homogeneity in an economic sense. If the buyer, for any reason, thinks that some units are superior to others he will have a preference for them and product uniformity will not prevail. Two physically identical articles marketed in different packages, for example, are different commodities if buyers discriminate between them.

Perfect markets have an atomistic structure. A large number of sellers and buyers are in touch with each other, each representing a

3

negligible part of the total supply and demand. Therefore, any of them can enter the market or withdraw from it without affecting the existing market price to any extent. The presence of dominant buyers or dominant sellers is a sign of market imperfection. In a perfectly competitive market, price emerges as a result of bargaining between numerous buyers and sellers, the conditions of supply and demand will exclusively set it. It is important to observe that once the price has been determined all dealings will take place at this single price. No seller could obtain more and, if he tries to charge more, buyers will turn to his competitors for supply. Further, he will have no inducement to cut his price, as he will be able to sell his stocks at the market price.

The next essential feature of perfect markets is a perfect communication system. Buyers and sellers must be in a position of permanent contact and have up-to-date information about the conditions of supply and demand. This contact need not be one of geographic unity since close links can be maintained by telephone or teleprinter between operators in various parts of the country or even different countries. A constant flow of information ensures that changes in market conditions are always reflected in prices.

Individual preferences do not exist in a perfect market, not only in respect of different lots of commodities but also as far as operators are concerned. Neither buyers nor sellers will have any preferences in dealing with people and any possibility of influencing market prices by 'rigging' is non-existent. The human element is excluded from the perfectly competitive market.

An efficient transport system, able to move stocks with the minimum delay and cost, freedom of labour to move to any industry, the flow of capital without restrictions and the marketability of land are further refinements of a perfectly competitive market. High transport costs limit the size of the market and the mobility of the factors of production is both desirable and essential. Government control of investments, licensing, rationing and price-control are all inconceivable on a perfect market.

Perfect competition is, of course, only an abstraction and cannot be found in real life in its purest form. But if one compares various industries, they will exhibit the characteristics of a perfect market to different degrees. Some industries approach the perfectly competitive market structure to a larger extent than others. A marked change has taken place in this respect in the course of the last hundred years or so. Many industries could be classified as perfectly competitive ones in the last century.

In the nineteenth century, when the classical system was taking form, agriculture contributed a considerably larger share of the national product than at present. Moreover, the burgeoning cotton industry, coal-mining, metal and metal-working industries of England of the time were all shared by numerous producers. The production of each was small in relation to that of all. None could much influence the common price. Finally, in England of the day, sellers were exposed to prices that were made in the markets of the world at large. The kind of competition that was implicit in the pioneering designs of the classical economists of the nineteenth century was not unrealistic. It described a world that existed; those who formulated the theory were practical men.[1]

The structure of British industry has changed substantially in this century. Large-scale industries have developed and introduced mass-production methods. The optimum size of plant for the production of certain goods is so large that only a handful of manufacturers can be accommodated within the national market. At the same time, concentration has taken place on the buying side. Powerful buying organizations have emerged who are able to negotiate a price with manufacturers from a position of strength. A recent study on concentration in British industry concluded that trades accounting for only about one-quarter of the total employment in this country had a market structure even approaching the perfectly competitive type.[2] Conditions similar to the pattern of perfect competition can be found, for example, in the wool, cutlery, and pottery trades and in certain branches of the building industry.[3] The cutlery trade consists of about 190 manufacturers and only ten of these employ more than a hundred people. For ordinary patterns of knives in the medium-price range, for example, a recognized price exists and the individual producer has no choice

---

[1] John Kenneth Galbraith, *American Capitalism*, London, 1952, p. 16.
[2] Richard Evely and I. M. D. Little, *Concentration in British Industry*, Cambridge, 1960, p. 11.
[3] *The Structure of British Industry*, edited by Duncan Burn London, 1958, vol. 2, p. 429.

but to accept this price or give up production.[4] The Stock Exchange, the organized commodity markets and foreign exchange markets provide further examples of near-perfect markets. In commodity markets a large number of buyers and sellers deal with homogeneous goods and the flow of market information is unhindered. (This is dealt with in Chapter 13.)

Monopolies

The second type of market is characterized by the total absence of competition as supply is concentrated in the hands of a single seller, the monopolist. Whilst on a perfect market the price is given and cannot be influenced by any producer, the monopolist is free to choose the price he wants to charge. He may sell a larger volume at a lower price or a smaller quantity at a higher one. When deciding which price policy to follow he will take into account the elasticities of the demand of his buyers. (Elasticity of demand expresses the change in the quantity bought in response to a change in price. The demand for certain goods remains practically the same at various prices within pretty wide limits. The demand for table salt is, for example, inelastic. Consumption is hardly influenced by price changes. In certain other cases demand is elastic, a small drop in price brings about a relatively large increase and vice versa.)

Once again, pure monopoly is much more an economic concept than reality. It rarely exists in actual life. Competition is nearly always present to a certain extent. Most of the goods have a close, or more remote, substitute, and, if the producer charges a high price, consumers will switch to a substitute product. Production of coal, electricity and gas are all monopolies in Britain yet they compete with each other on the domestic-heating market and their relative share is very much influenced by their prices. Many goods produced by monopolies are not prime necessities of life and consumers may decide to go completely without them. In a sense all goods and services available compete for the consumer's income and the monopolist cannot pitch his prices to an unreasonably high level.

Markets are often international and competition may come from

[4] Harry Townsend, 'Economic Theory and the Cutlery Trade', *Economica*, August 1954, p. 229.

6

abroad and whilst tariff restrictions may mitigate this competition they do not eliminate it completely. The price of the foreign product, plus transport costs, plus Customs duties paid, form an upper limit beyond which the monopolist cannot go.

Another limitation on the pricing freedom of the monopolist is the potential entry of new competitors in his field. High prices and high profits induce other firms to produce the same article or to produce competing products. Du Pont discovered nylon 66 in 1935. This stimulated research into other man-made fibres and terylene was developed by the Calico Printers Association in 1940.

Finally, the monopolist will be wary of charging an exorbitant price lest adverse public opinion brings about state action to curb his powers. Potential abuses of monopolies are constantly watched by governments and many countries have some sort of legislation to control them.

The monopolist, therefore, when formulating his price policy will take into account all these factors: demand elasticities, potential substitutes, latent competition, import possibilities and public reaction.

Monopolies are often attacked because they may permit irresponsible private power, may be slow in adopting new methods of production and may result in lower economic efficiency and output with higher costs, prices and profits than would prevail under competition.

Imperfect competition

Until the 1930's economic theory distinguished only between perfect markets and monopolies. By that time it was realized that actual market conditions did not conform to these models and most markets exhibited certain features of competition and certain aspects of monopoly side by side. In 1933 E. H. Chamberlin, in the United States, and Mrs. Joan Robinson in this country published the results of their investigations and founded a new market theory which they called 'imperfect competition'.[5]

[5] E. H. Chamberlin, *The Theory of Monopolistic Competition*, Cambridge, Mass., 1933, and Joan Robinson, *The Economics of Imperfect Competition*, London, 1933.

This new theory is that in modern economy, particularly in the field of manufactured consumer goods, product differentiation is the rule and homogeneity the exception. The individual manufacturer endeavours to produce goods with distinct features for which no perfect substitute is available. He develops consumer loyalty for his product by branding, packaging and advertising. To a certain extent, each manufacturer is a monopolist because his particular brand is different from other products. At the same time he is in intensive competition because some other brands are often close substitutes. Prices of competing products are interrelated though they are not necessarily identical. By virtue of his brand monopoly the individual producer can pursue an independent pricing policy and is free to fix his prices between certain limits.

There are other features also which distinguish the imperfect market from the other two. The number of suppliers is usually not large and some of them command a considerable market share. These producers are able to influence market prices. Concentration often takes place on the buying side too and large buyers may command considerable market power.

Further, buyers and sellers often act upon insufficient information about the market. The collection and evaluation of market data is costly and time-consuming and the large variety of existing products, their changing features and price movements demand considerable attention. In an engineering plant, for example, where several thousand items are stocked, detailed executive attention cannot be given to all raw materials and components. There will be a tendency to concentrate on the important lines and to form groups of minor items instead of giving them separate attention. Knowledge of competition and buyers is also limited. The prices of competitors are known but not the secret discounts given to some buyers. The measurement of demand at different price levels is also difficult.

Price and quality are not the only buying considerations. It is obvious that individual preferences do exist in practical business life. Reliability, special attention and delivery on time may be more important than a small price differential, and old-established business relationships are not broken because prices of the regular supplier are temporarily slightly higher. Transport costs often break up the market, especially in the case of bulky goods. Government restrictions, like planning regulations, licensing, patent law, etc., may hinder the perfect mobility of factors of production. The terms 'perfect' and 'imperfect' competition are somewhat unfortunate in that they suggest approval and disapproval. In fact, imperfect competition is not an undesirable market structure in comparison with the perfect model. Under modern conditions imperfect competition is the only possible business behaviour in many fields. There are industries where economies of scale can be exploited only by a limited number of firms which, by the application of large-scale production and marketing methods, achieve low costs and prices. Product differentiation and the widening of the choice of goods available on the market also serves the interests of the consumer.

Depending on the number of competitors in an imperfect market one can speak either of monopolistic competition or of oligopoly. In the former, a large number of firms sell non-standardized differentiated products, each supplying a relatively small part of the market with a variety of designs, qualities, etc., at different prices.

Oligopolies

Where a small number of large firms dominate an industry, whether producing homogeneous (like steel or cement) or differentiated products, the market structure is called an oligopoly.

In an oligopolistic situation the producers of differentiated products have a certain degree of freedom in setting their prices. If the consumer thinks that a certain article has favourable features as compared with others he will be ready to pay a higher price. Equally, a price-cut may elicit a higher demand for a certain article. However, observation has shown that oligopolists are very careful in exercising their pricing freedom and particularly careful when deciding on price-cuts. Price-cuts once made are not easily reversible and the oligopolist tries to avoid retaliation from his competitors. Naturally enough, no producer will remain inactive when his share of the market dwindles as a consequence of a price-cut by a competitor. The relatively small number of important competing producers makes it easy for them to watch carefully each other's business policy and to counteract any move intended to upset the *status quo*. It may easily happen that a price reduction triggers off a series of competitive price-cuts and, though the initiator may reap some short-term benefit, in the long run the sharing of the market remains essentially unaltered and each company makes a lower profit. This is why in an oligopolistic situation competition tends to concentrate less on price than on product design, quality, service and large-scale advertising. The threat of price competition by new entrants is mitigated by the fact that large initial investment is often necessary to enter the field, the technical know-how is not easily obtainable, patent rights protect existing products and substantial advertising is necessary to establish a new product. Self-restraint in competitive pricing among the firms operating on an oligopolistic market can be so marked that they act in a way as though there was a price agreement among them. Such situations are sometimes described as 'oligopoly quasi-agreements'. (Price agreements are discussed in Chapter 8.)

Price leadership

Apart from non-price competition, oligopolies often lead to price leadership and price following. The essence of this practice is that some companies do not exercise a pricing policy of their own but follow the prices of their competitors. This is particularly so in industries producing standardized products but it can also be found elsewhere. The price leader usually leads only when there is a rising tendency of prices. When the market slackens, often the previous followers initiate price-cuts.

The price leader is sometimes the oldest firm in the field, in other cases the largest one. The General Motors Corporation is, for example, the undisputed price leader of the American car industry. Competitors set their prices close to those established by General Motors. If the competitors' prices were much higher, General Motors would profit by it and they cannot afford to be much lower because of their lower efficiency.[6] The Monopolies Commission found that Dunlop Rubber Limited was the price leader in the pneumatic tyre industry in the early 1950's. Its share of the original equipment market was 72 per cent of motor car tyres, 38 per cent of commercial vehicle tyres and 99 per cent of

[6] *The Economist*, April 11, 1964, p. 140.

bicycle tyres in 1952.[7] Dunlop was also the price leader in practically all lines of rubber footwear.[8]

An example of oligopoly and price leadership is provided by the
soap and detergent market in this country. The industry is domin-
ated by two large companies: Lever Brothers and Associates Ltd.,
and Procter and Gamble Ltd., both of which are members of large
international groups. Lever Brothers belong to the Unilever
Group while Procter and Gamble is owned by its American mother
company of similar name. Together they command 85 per cent
of the hard soap market and over 95 per cent of the soap flakes,
soap powders and synthetic powders market. In these products
competition takes place mainly among the two market leaders. The
competitive effort of other firms is not strong and the market share
of these has fallen over the last few years. Lever Brothers alone
produces over 40 per cent of toilet soaps. The rest of the toilet soap
market is shared by three large organizations (Procter and Gamble
Ltd., Colgate-Palmolive Ltd. and Cussons Group Ltd.). Competition in toilet soap is generally confined to the more expensive
quality products. In the synthetic liquids market the competitive
impact of other firms is marked but the two market leaders still
supply over half of the demand.

When the Prices and Incomes Board investigated prices in the
soaps and detergent industry in 1965 it was found that prices, in
general, moved in step. When conditions changed, such as prices
of materials used, a price increase introduced by one company was
regularly followed by the other, even if it had a better chance to
absorb it than its rival. As demand for these products is fairly
inelastic a lower price does not increase brand sales to a large
extent unless the cut is very substantial. Since a reduction in price
may lead to decreased profitability, prices are more likely to follow
costs upwards than downwards. Price competition sets in only
under exceptional circumstances, such as a major product innovation. This happened in the 1950's when Hedley's, in co-operation
with Procter and Gamble, marketed the first white synthetic
powders and rapidly gained sales. Lever Brothers followed suit
with a similar product and, later, the same game was repeated with

---

[7] 'Report on the Supply and Export of Pneumatic Tyres', 1955, paras.
401–411.
[8] 'Report on the Supply of Certain Rubber Footwear', 1956, paras. 268–
275.

blue synthetic powders. After a period of sharp price competition and shifting market shares the position of both companies was stabilized and parity of prices restored in 1957. Otherwise price competition in the industry is confined to short-term localized special offers to distributors; extensive price-cutting does not take place.[9]

Price leadership is not necessarily confined to one company within a given industry. An American study shows that the price of primary aluminium ingot was changed nine times between 1950 and 1956. During this period three organizations acted as price leaders: Alcoa five times, Kaiser Aluminum twice and Reynolds Metals once. On one occasion the three leaders changed the price on the same day.[10]

An example of temporary price leadership in this country is provided by the Rolls-Razor case. A fast expansion of the washing-machine market took place between 1958 and 1960 (deliveries of domestic washing-machines were about £28 million in 1958 and £51 million in 1959). Hotpoint was the most expensive washing machine at that time. Rolls-Razor entered the market in 1959 offering a comparable washing-machine for about £30 less and rapidly gained sales. With a complete reversal of its marketing policy Hotpoint came out with a low-price machine in the autumn of 1962.[11]

The price leadership of a company may be restricted to certain products only and need not be general throughout the industry. In the dyestuffs market, for example, ICI produced about twice as many dyes as the other fifteen companies in the industry in the late 1950's. Although broadly covering every section of the market, there were many dyestuffs which were specialities of the other companies, often protected by patent rights. ICI was the price leader for the industry in general, but not for every particular sub-section of the market.[12]

[9] 'Report No. 4, National Board for Prices and Incomes, Prices of Household and Toilet Soaps, Soap Powders and Soap Flakes, and Soapless Detergents', Cmnd. 2791, 1965, pp. 3, 9–10.

[10] William H. Peterson, 'Divergent Views on Pricing Policy', *Harvard Business Review*, March–April 1963, p. 30.

[11] J. B. Mayers, 'Management and the British Domestic Electric Appliance Industry', *Journal of Industrial Economics*, November 1963, pp. 20–32, and T. A. B. Corley, *Domestic Electrical Appliances*, London, 1966, p. 89.   [12] Duncan Burn, op. cit., vol. 1, p. 249.

It is frequently presumed that price leadership is linked with tacit or open collusion among competitors. This is not necessarily so. Identical prices may be only a sign that the products are standardized or close substitutes. Each company may be acting independently when following the price leader. They operate in the same environment, costs and demand situation. Often the price leader only carries out what has already become inevitable because of changed circumstances. Sometimes the leader possesses superior management and better economic research staff and is able to recognize changes sooner than the others and habitually acts first. The price leader is successful in raising the price only if he hits on the correct change that will be accepted by his rivals. If he misjudges the situation it can be a painful and expensive error. In the early 1960's, in the American chemical industry, companies in some cases had to reverse their price increases because they were not followed by their competitors.[13]

Administered prices

As price changes tend to upset an oligopolistic market, minor fluctuations in market conditions are usually not registered by price changes. It often happens that companies do not alter their prices despite higher or lower demand. When demand exceeds the available capacity of the industry, long order-books are often preferred to high prices. Equally, when demand is slack, the manufacturer may prefer to carry higher stocks instead of cutting prices. The general tendency is to change prices infrequently and then only to take into account substantial changes in raw material or factor (labour, capital) prices. This is why it is often stated that oligopoly prices are rigid as they are not fixed by market forces but are set by the administrative action of producers. They are 'administered prices'.

The term 'administered prices' was originally coined in America by Gardiner C. Means in 1935, and was not meant to apply only to oligopolies. In its widest sense it refers to all prices not reflecting supply and demand conditions, but set and held stable for a period of time by a company or a public enterprise. According to this definition the majority of prices are administered.

[13] Jules Backman, *Chemical Price, Productivity, Wages and Profits*, Washington, D.C., 1964, p. 8.

Senator Kefauver's subcommittee on Anti-trust and Monopoly investigated administered prices, especially in respect of the steel, drug and auto industries, and found that they were likely to be in excess of a reasonable relation to costs.[14]

Attempts have been made to measure the difference between the average level of prices in concentrated and non-concentrated industries in America. A study showed that industries in which the eight largest companies were responsible for over 70 per cent of the value of production between 1936 and 1940 earned a higher profit than other industries. Their average rate of profit, after income tax, as a percentage of net assets, was 12·1 per cent, while the average for the others was 6·9 per cent. The study concluded that this difference was less than expected by those who considered monopoly as a major evil and considered it unimportant for the performance of the economy as a whole.[15]

Another private investigation in America confirmed the findings of the previous study concerning the year 1954, one of the years of the official Census of Manufactures. On this occasion the industries considered concentrated were those where half or more of the total labour force was employed by the four largest firms. The amount of monopoly profit in the economy was calculated by taking the difference between monopolistic and competitive prices in relation to the total output. It was found to be 1·6 per cent of the national income and considered to be relatively small.[16]

Workable competition

Since the inception of the theory of imperfect competition many economists have tried to refine and develop it. A group of them has developed the theory of workable competition. The term was introduced by Professor Clark in 1940.[17] The concept is still fairly

[14] U.S. Senate, 'Hearings on Administered Prices', 85th Cong., 1st Session, July 1957.

[15] J. S. Bain, 'Relation of Profit Rate to Industry Concentration: American Manufacturing, 1936–1940', *Quarterly Journal of Economics*, August 1951, pp. 293–324.

[16] David Schwartzman, 'The Effect of Monopoly on Price', *Journal of Political Economy*, August 1959, pp. 352–362 and 'The Effect of Monopoly on Price: A Correction', *Journal of Political Economy*, October 1961, p. 494.

[17] J. M. Clark, 'Toward a Concept of Workable Competition', *American Economic Review*, June 1940, pp. 241–256.

fluid; one author mentions eighteen different sets of criteria to be found in the literature.[18] The reason for the development of this theory was the recognition that characteristics of perfect competition could not serve as a basis for appraisals of actual market situations. A need was felt that theory should postulate realistic norms to indicate socially desirable and practically attainable goals whose fulfilment can promote public interest.

The Restrictive Practices Court has made use of the concept of workable competition. The Mining Rope Association recommended fixed common selling prices to its members. The Court held the view that the restrictions brought about higher prices than would have prevailed under 'workable competition'. The Court defined 'workable competition' as a market situation where a reasonable number of sellers and a reasonable number of buyers operate and no restrictions exist on either side of the market.[19]

Countervailing power

Professor Galbraith of Harvard University has developed the theory of countervailing power, according to which oligopolies and monopolies are often confronted with balancing groups on the opposite side of the market. Trade unions play this role on the labour market. The excessive power of giant industries is also curbed by large-scale buying organizations, like co-operatives and chain-stores. They are ready to seek out alternative sources of supply or go into production themselves when they think that excessive prices are charged by suppliers.

> While the classical economists had their eyes fixed on competition – on other participants on the same side of the market – power was being countered from across the market. Those who were subject to economic power had a powerful incentive to organize or otherwise to win bargaining power to protect themselves. This countervailing power, as I have called it, is a self-generating regulatory force – as indeed competition was presumed to be. Power on one side of the market both creates the need for, and proclaims the existence of,

---

[18] Stephen H. Sosnick, 'A Critique of Concepts of Workable Competition', *Quarterly Journal of Economics*, August 1958, pp. 380–423.

[19] 'Agreements of the Mining Rope Association, the Wire Rope Manufacturers' Association and the Locked Coil Manufacturers' Association', 1964, L.R. 5 R.P. 146.

rewards to be captured by countering action on the other side of the market.[20]

An American study, based on interviews with the rubber-tyre industry, concluded that, in spite of the clearly oligopolistic character of the industry, prices reflected competitive conditions. The market power of large producers was effectively blunted in major sub-markets by the countervailing force of large buyers, such as car manufacturers, private label buyers and other large-scale distributors.[21] Chapter 8 shows how some industries tried to justify restrictive agreements by reference to concentration among buyers before the Restrictive Practices Court.

In spite of the tendency towards non-price competition, price leadership and administered prices it would be incorrect to presume that oligopolistic situations are always characterized by the absence of competition. Intensity of competition is not primarily determined by the number of competitors in an industry:

> Dazzled by the platitudes of 'perfect' competition, many economists have failed to see what the practicing competitor knows painfully well, i.e., that it is not necessary to have a great number of firms to ensure vigorous competition. They need only be numerous enough or divergent enough to make collusion break down. This may mean only three or four if they are different enough to foil the similarity of interest that might foster collusion.[22]

No generalization is valid about the efficiency of oligopolistic industries. Some of them are restrictive by nature, they keep prices high, economies of scale are sacrificed in the absence of price competition and there may be opinions that they indulge in excessive advertising. There are, on the other hand, progressive oligopolies doing extensive research, producing at a low cost and quoting reasonable prices.

[20] John Kenneth Galbraith, 'Economic Power and the Survival of Capitalism', in Shigeto Tsuru, *Has Capitalism Changed?*, Tokyo, 1961, p. 177.
[21] Robert L. Know, 'Competitive Oligopolistic Pricing', *Journal of Marketing*, July 1966, pp. 47–51.
[22] Joel Dean, 'Competition – Inside and Out', *Harvard Business Review*, November–December 1954, p. 71.

CHAPTER 2

Pricing objectives

It is sometimes felt that economics cannot grasp the complexities of real life situations and that there is a dichotomy between economic theory and practical business. When a large number of factors are at work simultaneously the theorist cannot do anything else but isolate certain of them and keep others constant or disregard them altogether if their influence is negligible. Analysis would be impossible otherwise, although such an approach inevitably gives the impression of simplification as compared with the diversity of real life.

Profit maximization

The same thing applies to the question of pricing goals. Economic theory gives an unequivocal answer to the question of the pricing objectives of the firm. Business organizations are presumed to exist to make profit on the capital invested and as much as possible. They pursue the single pricing goal of profit maximization. Without the unifying supposition that the major aim of every business is to make optimum profit, the logical structure of economic theory could not have been built up. On the other hand the actual pricing policy of a firm is formulated with an object in mind depending on its general business philosophy. When dealing with actual situations allowance should be made for the fact that a particular firm may have more than one pricing objective. Critics have often pointed out that the assumption of profit maximization as the single pricing goal is unrealistic in actual life. It is sometimes emphasized that the entrepreneur receives not only financial reward but also 'psychic income' for his work and he may be more interested in the latter than in the former. He may also appreciate the value of leisure and may prefer an easier life to the hard work involved in keen competition and maximum profit. A scholar of the

17

Graduate School of Business Administration at Harvard University writes:

Why do graduate students, by applying what they avow are sound analytical tools learned in college, often arrive at naïve solutions to the problems in business cases? I have finally concluded that the trouble stems from the assumption in most college economic texts and college classrooms that the objective of a business is to maximize profits. Unhappily, this assumption is not confined to the campus. Countless writers of fiction and non-fiction have seemingly taken it for granted that management's purpose is to maximize profits. Lawyers, labour union spokesmen and government officials often indicate that they share the same belief. Moreover – as if to confirm that what all these other people think is true – businessmen themselves say they operate on this assumption. ... If one assumes profit maximization, a complete and completely consistent package of rules for operating a business can be devised, rules that can be expressed precisely in equations and illustrated by graphs, rules that provide correct answers to classroom problems, and rules which, when they do not work in practice, can always be explained by 'other things being equal'. The usefulness of such an all-inclusive package for teaching purposes, for the exploration and extension of theories and as a device for communicating to one's colleagues, should not be minimized.[1]

Because it is not always easy to get to know the real pricing objective or objectives of a firm, the question of research into the actual pricing goals of companies is made difficult. Some business executives may act according to the corporate spirit of their organization but find it difficult to rationalize about it. Moreover, some companies are reluctant to talk about pricing objectives and others may not have a clear-cut objective at all. Yet, in other cases, company top executives disagree on their pricing goals. An American study states about the giant United States Steel Corporation: 'Company officials differ in their views on what constitutes pricing policy, not only on the level at which pricing of an individual product is determined but also on the level of company-wide decision. ...'[2] The McKinsey study also describes a similar state of affairs in the American food trade:

---

[1] Robert N. Anthony, 'The Trouble with Profit Maximization', *Harvard Business Review*, December 1960, p. 126.
[2] A. D. H. Kaplan, Joel B. Dirlam, Robert F. Lanzillotti, *Pricing in Big Business*, Washington, D.C., 1958, p. 167.

... many operators are unable to talk with conviction about pricing. Many cannot state very clearly just what their pricing policy is. In other companies a pricing policy is thought to exist but only the president seems to be aware of it. For example, some organizations claim to be price leaders but in fact are not, or they indicate they match competition but market basket studies show that they do not (in some large distributor organizations, approaches to pricing, presumably reflecting company policy, are defined differently by different executives).[3]

Empirical investigations show that profit maximization is rarely the sole pricing goal in actual business life. A variety of other objectives are also pursued by business organizations. When more than one pricing objective is set by a firm, profit maximization is often not considered as the principal objective and sometimes not even included in the list of objectives at all.

Price stabilization

The stabilization of prices and margins is one of the alternative pricing goals. This policy attempts to keep prices stable, within broad limits, despite variations in sales volume. Minor changes in raw material prices and wage rates may also not be followed immediately with a price change, but the cumulative effects of a number of changes are taken into account at spaced-out intervals. It has been mentioned previously that in an oligopolistic situation firms are often reluctant to change their prices independently because of fear of upsetting the market. But stable prices are considered advantageous not only because of competitive reasons. Forward planning of turnover, production, labour requirements, stocks, investment and finance is also facilitated by the absence of frequent price fluctuations.

It has been shown that between 1950 and 1961 prices in Britain were not responsive to short-term changes either in market demand or in labour productivity. Rises in wages and costs of materials were taken into account in the prices of industrial products, but not the changes in the volume of output per worker. Firms based their price policy on the long-run trend of costs and tended to disregard movements in actual costs. They did not raise

[3] 'The Economics of Food Distribution', *McKinsey – General Foods Study*, October 1963, p. 14.

or lower prices in response to changes in demand but let profits bear the burden of fluctuations. Long-term considerations took precedence over short-term pressures.[4]

Another study arrived at a similar conclusion based on the pricing policy of a small sample of manufacturers. The general pattern was that when demand was heavy, output was stepped up but prices remained unchanged. The two reasons for this policy were partly the fear of damaging the firm's goodwill because a price rise would have been difficult to justify and partly the fear of prejudicing the future growth of the market. When demand fell it was generally preferred to step up sales efforts, or to curtail output or even to change quality, than to resort to price-cutting. The general conclusion of the investigation was that output was very responsive to changes of demand whilst price was not.[5]

Maintenance of market share

Pricing policy can also be a means to achieve or maintain a certain share in the market, and optimum profit may be considered secondary to this objective. Reputable organizations are more concerned with steady growth, as future profits are largely dependent on the volume of business, than to reap all the benefits of a temporary situation. A further powerful reason for this attitude stems from what is often described as the divorce of ownership and control in modern business. Large-scale organizations are usually controlled by a professional team of executives who may own only a negligible portion of shares. Consequently, their main income is their salary and they are little affected financially by the dividends the company pays. They are, of course, interested in profits but not as a source of personal income. They often prefer to retain profit to finance future developments of the company than to distribute it among the shareholders. The actual power and salary level of top executives depend much more on the size of the organization than on the level of profits. The prestige of the firm is also more closely linked with its market share than its net earnings, and executives like to be associated with well-known, reput-

---

[4] R. R. Neild, *Pricing and Employment in the Trade Cycle*, Cambridge 1963, pp. 50–55.
[5] R. H. Barback, *The Pricing of Manufactures*, London, 1964, p. 165.

able organizations. Therefore, management may sacrifice the present level of profits to the idea of increasing the market share of the firm.

There are recent tendencies which strengthen the interest of management in the profitability of companies. Cash bonuses rising with profits have been introduced in some cases and share-purchase options granted in others. In the United States some corporations have extended their stock-purchase plans to all employees to increase their loyalty and efficiency.

Target return on capital

A special investigation found that the pricing objective most frequently mentioned in American industry and trade was a predetermined target return on capital investment.[6] A survey of the pricing goals of twenty large-scale United States organizations shows that companies who follow this objective set a percentage return figure on capital and formulate their prices with this target in mind. The calculation of the target can be made in various ways: based on own capital or it may also include loan capital; and profits can be considered as before or after the deduction of tax. Naturally, the targets are set according to the individual positions of firms. General Electric and General Motors, for example, specified a 20 per cent return on capital after tax, while the United States Steel Corporation had to be satisfied with a mere 8 per cent.[7] Lever Brothers stated before the Monopolies Commission that the company regarded 5 per cent on sales value and $12\frac{1}{2}$ per cent on capital employed, in both cases after tax, as a normal return for its soap and detergent business. The company also stated that its ultimate objective was to achieve the greatest long-run profits on these products.[8] The pricing objective of the British subsidiary of Kodak Ltd. can also be regarded as a variation of this policy. Kodak stated before the Monopolies Commission that its pricing policy can only be considered in the context of its financial policy as a whole:

[6] A. D. H. Kaplan, Joel B. Dirlam, Robert F. Lanzillotti, op. cit., p. 128.
[7] R. F. Lanzillotti, 'Pricing Objectives of Large Corporations', *American Economic Review*, December 1958, pp. 921–940.
[8] 'Report on the Supply of Household Detergents', 1966, p. 17.

Its aim is to earn such profits on its total sales as will enable it (1) to finance not only 'a progressive programme of research and development' and the additional cost (over and above that provided by depreciation calculated on historic cost) of replacement of fixed assets at current prices but also the expansion of its business, and (2) to remunerate the capital invested in the business by its parent company. In the view of a finance director an overall average profit of seventeen to eighteen per cent on sales has been desirable to achieve these purposes. . . . [9]

Satisfactory profits

Many firms do not aim at making maximum profits but are set to achieve what are described as satisfactory profits. This, of course, is an elusive term and needs further definition in the light of the specific circumstances of each company. It is unlikely that any business enterprise would consider a profit satisfactory which is lower than the preceding year's profit or lower than that generally considered as the standard profit of the respective branch of industry or trade. Furthermore, regular small advances in profits are generally preferred to substantial jumps upwards. Unusually high profits are often deliberately avoided as they may prejudice public opinion and legislators as well as labour relations. The yardstick to satisfactory profits may also be profits earned by competitors. In a declining industry, or during a recession, for example, a modest profit may be thought satisfactory if it is above the profits earned by competitors. [10]

Ethical pricing objectives

Moral considerations often colour the pricing goals of firms anxious to create a favourable public image. Part of this attitude is to co-operate with the government in carrying out its economic policy. When prices are raised most companies pay attention to public opinion to preserve their goodwill. The Chairman of Unilever said about morality in business:

> Naturally anyone investing in business . . . sees as its primary object the making of profits. All too often, I am afraid, many people who are

---

[9] The Monopolies Commission, 'Colour Film, A Report on the Supply and Processing of Colour Film', 1966, para. 159.

[10] George Katona, *Psychological Analysis of Economic Behaviour*, New York, 1951, p. 202.

not themselves engaged in business take the profit motive to be synonymous with avarice. This is simply untrue. The fact that profit plays a fundamental role in all business decisions does not mean that we try and make our profits in a moral vacuum. The morality of businessmen varies, but businessmen as a whole are no less moral or patriotic than anybody else. They do not set out to engage in sharp practice, to mislead, to cheat, or to grind the faces of their employees in order to increase profits. They do not set out to take decisions deliberately harmful to the countries in which they operate. Indeed, any of these things could lead to disaster, and enlightened self-interest, if nothing else, will keep them from straying down these murky ways.[11]

It has been stated that most American business organizations have changed from 'classical' to 'managerial' objectives and they are not any longer exclusively interested in profits but in good public relations, the interests of employees, suppliers, distributors, local communities and national objectives. According to an estimate, chief executives of American corporations spend at least 40 per cent of their time with problems of governmental and community relations, philanthropy and education. Critics have pointed out that American business leaders pay too much attention to their alleged responsibility to society instead of to making profits.[12]

That pricing policy is interwoven with ethical considerations is illustrated by the price pattern of nylon in the early days of its career. Throughout the late forties and early fifties there was an extraordinarily high demand for nylon. Prices could have been fixed at almost astronomical levels. The actual price was certainly quoted on a quasi-ethical view of a fair price, taking into account the heavy capital expenditure required to produce nylon. It has also been demonstrated that the prices of natural and man-made fibres tended to move together. Still, when natural fibre prices were at an extremely high level, as in the years of 1950-2, man-made fibre producers kept their prices down. They preferred to earn moderate profits rather than to face charges of having squeezed the consumer when natural fibre prices were high.[13]

The foregoing enumeration of pricing objectives has not been

[11] *Financial Times*, May 3, 1967.
[12] Michael Ivens, 'In Search of a Business Philosophy', *British Industry*, December 12, 1966, p. 21.
[13] Douglas C. Hague, *The Economics of Man-made Fibres*, London, 1957, pp. 99 and 295.

exhaustive. Other goals may also be set by firms, such as the steady working of plant, the retention of skilled labour, or the maintenance of a comfortable liquidity position.

Multiple pricing goals

The existence of a single pricing goal for a firm is more the exception than the rule. The above-mentioned American survey on the pricing goals of twenty large-scale organizations found that all of them specified one or more collateral aims in addition to their principal pricing objective. Goodyear's major goal was, for example, to meet competition besides maintaining its position and stabilizing prices. Esso (Standard Oil of New Jersey) was mainly concerned with getting a fair return while maintaining its market share and stabilizing prices. Standard Oil (Indiana), on the other hand, wanted primarily to maintain its market share while achieving a target return on investment as well as stable prices.[14] Many boards of directors feel that their overriding goal is not to promote the interests of the shareholders only but that a fair participation in incomes by all interested parties (shareholders, employees, consumer) should be aimed at.

Once more we can quote the Chairman of Unilever:

> Why do we spend time, and money, and energy in trying to meet and to anticipate the consumer's needs? Assuredly, to make a profit. But it is far from being the truth that your Board thinks, or can think, only of profit and nothing but profit. As I said earlier, your own interest as shareholders requires us to consider the interests of employees, of consumers, and of the nation, as interpreted by its government. But in the end all of these, as well as the shareholders, would suffer if we were to forget that the real purpose of business is closely tied to profits.[15]

The president of an American chain-store has put the same idea in a different way: 'With the grocery industry under Government scrutiny, our pricing policy should be designed broadly to keep our companies and our industry healthy, replace equipment, reward stock-holders, pay higher wages and be creative in discharging our marketing responsibilities.'[16]

[14] R. F. Lanzillotti, op. cit., pp. 924–926.
[15] *Financial Times*, May 3, 1967.
[16] *The Grocer*, May 23, 1964, p. 50.

The selection of more than one pricing objective may lead to a conflict between the various goals. A rigid adherence to a specified market share target may, for example, require the sacrifice of the target rate of return on capital. Or, the steady working of the plant may also not be compatible with the predetermined rate of return, particularly in a period of slack demand.

Finally, it should be noted that a particular firm may not have the same pricing objective or set of objectives over the whole range of its activity. Multi-product firms produce a variety of goods. According to their competitive position on the various markets, they may vary their pricing objectives. For example, it is conceivable that a company which is the market leader in one field playing the role of the price leader should, at the same time, be an unimportant producer in another market and be a price follower. Similarly, any one company may follow different objectives concerning its new and established products. Du Pont's case serves as an illustration. Its general pricing objective was a certain target return on investment, but in respect of new products 'an exceptionally good return' was sought to recoup initial investments as soon as possible.[17]

[17] A. D. H. Kaplan, Joel B. Dirlam, Robert F. Lanzillotti, op. cit., p. 153.

CHAPTER 3

Pricing methods

The pricing objectives of a firm provide the framework within which actual pricing decisions take place. There are various methods by which the businessman can arrive at the actual selling prices, and these can be classified into two main groups. One of these considers costs as the principal factor governing price determination, whilst the other recognizes the dominance of the market in pricing. The former method is known as full-cost or cost-plus pricing and the second method is usually referred to as marginal pricing.

Full-cost pricing

Full-cost or cost-plus pricing, in its extreme form, is based on the view that prices are determined by average costs. In the case of a multi-product firm the strict application of the full-cost principle requires that the price of each product should reflect all the costs involved in its production and distribution, and each product should earn a proportional part of total profits. According to this doctrine, if a product cannot be sold at full-cost price it should be discontinued or the order not undertaken. Conversely, even if demand places a higher value on the article it should, nevertheless, be sold at its cost-based price, which will be lower.

Under the full-cost system the actual price determination takes place in successive steps. Aggregate costs are first divided into two groups, variable and fixed. The first category comprises costs that vary according to the volume of production, such as cost of raw materials, power and a large proportion of wages. Fixed costs, on the other hand, are those which are constant between wide limits of output, like depreciation of buildings and machinery, rates, and a large part of salaries paid. The costs which are considered for this type of calculation may be those recorded in the previous accounting period, or a standard cost derived from past average figures, or they may be forecasted figures.

The depreciation of fixed assets is an important element of full costs, particularly in capital-intensive industries. Under the full-cost system each product turned out during the active life of a fixed asset should contribute proportionately towards its replacement. By the time a fixed asset wears out, the firm has built up an accumulated reserve for this purpose. Full-cost pricing makes no distinction between costs currently paid for, like wages, and costs representing actual expenditure five, ten or twenty years ago, as in the case of machinery and buildings. In order to arrive at the cost-determined price, the unit cost of the product needs to be calculated. Single-product firms simply divide total costs by the number of units produced. Multi-product enterprises face, however, a more complicated task of cost allocation. When calculating unit costs, variable and fixed costs are separately treated. Variable costs associated with a certain product can be accurately calculated. Fixed costs, on the other hand, can only be distributed in an approximate way based on various assumptions. The usual assumption is that these overheads are fairly allocated among various lines produced if each individual product carries a charge in proportion to direct labour costs, direct working hours, or machine hours. Such an assumption, naturally, is always somewhat arbitrary and one can arrive at different results by using different bases for cost allocation.

Having arrived at the unit cost of production, the next step is to consider marketing costs. These can either be accounted for as an additional item to production costs, or may be accommodated as part of the gross profit margin. The profit itself is sometimes a conventional percentage mark-up added to costs. For this reason full-cost pricing is sometimes referred to as 'normal mark-up pricing'. In other cases an overall profit target is first set and this is then divided among the various products and added to the costs. In yet other instances a fixed return on investment is looked for and prices are set to achieve this target (rate of return pricing). Finally, mention should be made of the so-called 'conversion cost' variant of full-cost pricing, where profits are related to the 'value added' by the firm. Such pricing has been used in cotton-spinning, non-ferrous metals, aluminium-casting and gold- and silver-refining industries.[1] The average production and marketing cost per unit, together with the net profit margin, gives the price.

Even in the most rigid full-cost pricing, the entrepreneur has to pay attention to the state of market demand and competitors' prices. Cost of production and marketing per unit depends on the total quantity sold. Therefore, when calculating the price determined by full costs, the manufacturer already has an estimate of expected demand for his product. As a basis of comparison, information on the prices of competing products is also necessary. When the full-cost price is too high, as compared with prices of similar goods on the market, production will not be undertaken.

The merits of full-cost pricing lie in its administrative simplicity and in its apparent fairness. A link is established between prices and the actual costs incurred by the producer, and, where a reasonable profit is added, no accusation can be levelled against the firm of unethical conduct, such as exploiting temporary shortages on the market by over-pricing. It sounds acceptable that costs govern price and price based on costs appears to be the 'just price'. Knowing this, businessmen often state that their prices are based on costs, even when a closer inquiry reveals that allowance is also made for the state of demand.

The main line of criticism against full-cost pricing is that it disregards demand. It is a mechanical pricing method and, in terms of profitability, the price arrived at is not necessarily the best. Employed dogmatically, the firm can make maximum profit only by chance. Buyers are sometimes prepared to pay a higher price for the product than the one fixed on a full-cost basis. A firm may produce some more attractive product at a lower cost than its rivals because of its better management and more efficient production. Such a firm could earn a higher profit if it departed from full-cost pricing and this would be a reward for its superior efficiency. It is also sometimes a wise policy to adjust prices of various products in the light of market requirements and thus earn different rates of profit from them. By this method a higher total profit may be achieved.

This point has been made concerning British shipbuilding. After the 1952 Korean War there was a boom in this industry. As rising costs led to losses on fixed-price contracts, shipbuilders

[1] M. Howe, 'Variations on the Full Cost Theme', *Manchester School*, January 1964, pp. 43–57.

changed to cost-plus pricing. Though they had the opportunity of charging 'what the market bears', they preferred not to increase their profit margins but to accumulate long order-books, with the prospect of continued employment for some years ahead. The wisdom of this price policy was questioned. An industry particularly prone to fluctuations in demand may be able to achieve a more even production by charging more in boom years and by making reductions when the market is weak.[2]

Critics of full-cost pricing also maintain that it is a mistaken policy to refuse every order where the price offered is below the full-cost price. Fixed costs have to be met by the firm regardless of the volume of production. By accepting an order at a price not covering full costs, but above variable costs, the firm still earns something towards meeting fixed costs, and this is preferable to keeping the plant idle. Other considerations like the retention of skilled labour in a depressed period may also justify this policy. No firm can, of course, continue to be in business for long if full costs are not covered, but insistence on full-cost price under any circumstances is likely to be harmful to the long-term interest of the firm.

Generally speaking, full-cost pricing operates smoothly in industries where historical margins are applied, the cost of production of the different firms is roughly in line, and a tacit agreement exists among the producers not to upset an existing equilibrium by competitive pricing.

Marginal pricing

The alternative to full-cost pricing is marginal pricing. Theoretical economics is based on the assumption that the overriding aim of pricing is to achieve the maximum of profit, and the way to achieve it is by the marginal method. For this the entrepreneur has to think in terms of infinitesimally small increments in costs and revenues. Each additional unit produced, which will bring an additional revenue, entails an additional cost expended to produce it, and the logical practice will be to extend production up to a point where marginal revenue will just cover marginal costs. Below this there will be some profit on every additional unit sold but

[2] *The Structure of British Industry*, edited by Duncan Burn, Cambridge, 1958, vol. 2, p. 126.

beyond it an increase of production would result in a loss. Production should therefore be stabilized at this point for the firm to earn optimum profit.

To understand clearly the implications of the marginal approach to pricing we should refer back to the distinction between perfect and imperfect markets described in Chapter 1. In a perfect market the firm must sell at the ruling market price. Its volume of production is such a small fraction of the total supply that extension or contraction will have no influence on the market price. It follows that each additional unit will be sold at the same price in a perfect market. The marginal revenue derived from the sale of each additional unit will always be equal to this price. Only cost considerations will stop further production. Because of rising costs, net profit earned on incremental units will decrease after a certain point until marginal cost reaches the level of marginal revenue. It is at this point where a firm, operating in a perfect market, will secure its maximum profit.

In an imperfect market the position is entirely different. The entrepreneur is free, within limits, to choose his selling price. He can sell a larger quantity at a lower price or a smaller quantity at a higher one. In the language of the marginal approach, it means that the marginal revenue is not constant but decreases as the volume sold expands. The marginal revenue will be smaller and smaller after each price drop, not only because of the lower price of each additional unit, but because of the price reduction on all the previous units. So, whilst in a perfect market marginal revenue and price are always equal, in an imperfect market the price is always above marginal revenue. The firm will be confronted with two sets of figures – one of marginal costs and the other of marginal revenues. The marginal cost curve may show either a rising or a decreasing tendency, or it may be constant within certain limits, as the volume of production expands, but sooner or later the cost curve meets the marginal revenue curve and, at this point, the firm will have produced the optimum profit.

Under the marginal system, the marginal costs govern pricing decisions and orders will not necessarily be rejected on the ground that the price obtainable is below average cost. The difference between total revenue and total marginal costs is considered as a fund to cover fixed costs and profit. Every order paying more than the marginal cost may be a welcome contribution to this fund, if other considerations do not rule out its acceptance. Again, if the market places a value well in excess of marginal and average costs of the firm's product, the price may be set at this level. In other words, the firm will charge as much 'as the market will bear'.

Marginal costs, as a rule, represent variable costs since fixed costs are incurred regardless of the level of production. But if additional fixed costs arise, in connection with a new order, they should also be charged against the anticipated revenue.

It is sometimes alleged that marginal pricing cannot be widely applied in practice, as many businessmen have not even heard of the terms 'marginal cost' and 'marginal revenue'. As one commentator stated: 'It is a little difficult to picture a typical dairy farmer carefully calculating his marginal cost and deciding to feed his cow another hundred pounds of grain as a result.'[3] However, the difficulty may lie more in the terminology than in the understanding of the concept itself. The businessman may not be able to answer the question: 'Do you equate marginal cost with marginal revenue?' because he does not understand the terms used, not that he is ignorant of the principle. Without using the terms, the businessman may judge the profitability of a new order by asking himself the question: 'How much more will I earn on it than it will cost me?' which reflects a marginal-cost way of thinking.

An American professor referred to the problem:

> To ask a businessman about the 'elasticity of demand' for his product is just as helpful as inquiring into the customs of an indigenous Fiji Islander by interviewing him in the King's English. But with a little ingenuity it is possible to translate ideas from the businessman's language into that of the economist and vice versa. Questions such as 'Do you think you might sell more of this product if you cut the price by ten per cent?' or 'How much business do you think you would lose if you raised your price by ten per cent?' will evoke intelligent answers in most cases. ...[4]

The difficulties of practical research in this field were shown by an interview with the management of a large engineering company. When asked how prices were determined, it stated 'according

[3] Leonard W. Weiss, *Economics of American Industry*, New York, 1961, p. 58.
[4] Fritz Machlup, 'Marginal Analysis and Empirical Research', *American Economic Review*, September 1946, p. 537.

to costs'. The second question, about a hypothetical situation when, owing to a new invention, the company became a low-cost producer able to undercut everyone and having two years' worth of orders on its books that it could not possibly complete, was whether they would turn down further orders or put up prices. The respondents admitted that they would depart from costs in this case.[5]

Another line of attack on marginal pricing stresses the administrative difficulties in the way of its practical application. Marginalism requires the businessman to estimate future demand and future costs at various price levels in an accurate way and such forecasts cannot be made with precision. Companies usually have only a dim idea about the demand curve of their products. Past records of changes in demand in response to an increase or a decrease in price may help, but in many industries prices do not change frequently and the experience is not available. But, even if they are at hand, past figures cannot be extended into the future uncritically, since a number of changing factors shape the demand curve. The future is bound to remain elusive to some extent and special research into the problem can, at best, only decrease the margin of error, not eliminate it. The forecasting of future costs embraces the problem of estimating input prices, such as wages, raw material and component prices at various production levels. As in the case of demand forecasting, such estimates always contain some inaccuracies.

As revenues and costs cannot be precisely forecast, there is often a discrepancy between planned and actual figures and, consequently, profits are not maximized, and when the firm discovers that forecasts are not realized it may attempt to change existing prices to reap a higher profit. Such change may be made only after a certain time-lag, when information on actual figures has been processed for the use of management. Further, in some industries the change in price itself may present difficulties. Buyers may dislike frequent changes and prefer stable prices, particularly if it is customary in the industry concerned to keep prices stable for long periods. A price-cut may unsettle the market and there may be counteraction from competitors. Again, it may prove to be particularly difficult to put up prices after a previous decrease.

[5] I. F. Pearce, 'A Study in Price Policy', *Economica*, May 1956, pp. 124–125.

No firm can earn a good reputation by putting up prices in periods of temporary shortages. High prices may also invite new entries into the industry. Some critics, therefore, emphasize that marginal pricing is essentially a short-run policy which may conflict with the long-term interests of the firm.

A further point against the application of marginal pricing can be made by reference to the administration costs of operating such a system. Undoubtedly, marginalism involves machinery for estimating demand elasticities and forecasting sales, and the cost of these, by a firm producing hundreds of different items, may be prohibitive. Frequent price changes may also be costly in their application. Because of its less complicated nature, the administrative cost of full-cost pricing is less than that of a marginalist system. Marginal pricing is also attacked on the ground that it may lead to losses, as overheads are not covered. This view asserts that only full-cost pricing ensures the replacement in time of fixed assets.

These criticisms have some validity but the difficulties should not be overstressed. It is true that demand and cost forecasts cannot be precise, but absolute accuracy should not be expected from any pricing method. Even with imperfect forecasting the firm may benefit from marginalist pricing in many cases. The prospect of frequent price changes may be disturbing in some trades but not in others. When buyers are used to long-standing unchanged prices, obviously their reaction should be taken into account. Again, the application of marginal pricing should be kept within reason and the number of price changes within acceptable limits. It is true that the cost of operating a marginalist pricing system can be greater than that of full-cost pricing, but marginalism does not involve demand and cost estimates for dozens of different prices concerning a given product. The area of movement in price-setting is usually not too wide, often not more than 10–15 per cent around the price of competing goods. The benefits to be derived from marginal pricing may often justify the additional administrative costs involved. The view that marginal pricing leads to losses comes from the misconception that marginal cost is always below average cost, whereas in fact it may equal or exceed the average cost and so produce profit.

It is a more flexible method than the full-cost system. When setting its prices the firm is confronted with three guide-posts:

33

an upper limit of price – what buyers are prepared to pay for the article, a lower limit – the variable costs incurred to produce the article, and in between the price determined by full costs. Full-cost pricing clings only to this middle guide-post; the marginalist moves up and down between the upper and the lower limits. A rigid application of full-cost pricing can lead to marketing disasters. Marginal pricing is market-oriented and more competitive. It is a mistake to refuse an order because the price does not cover the full cost of production, including the depreciation of fixed assets. The replacement of buildings and machinery depends on the total profit of the company, and total profit is increased by accepting an order below the full price when the plant would not be working to capacity otherwise.

But marginal pricing should be applied with caution. Overheads must be covered in the long run. A firm will naturally refuse an order at a price below average cost if it can reasonably expect another order coming in to bring a higher return. Similarly, no company will enter into a long-term contract, engaging a considerable part of its capacity, if overheads are not covered. But it could still accept a smaller order for the same price, and by doing so make some contribution towards fixed costs. The important thing to realize is that marginalism is a valid theory and should not be excluded dogmatically as a possible way of pricing. The two main pricing methods can reinforce each other: the marginalist should watch average price when deciding whether to accept an order and full-cost pricing should be modified by paying attention to the state of demand.

Empirical studies of pricing methods

The usefulness of marginal pricing in practice has been hotly debated by economists during the last few decades. As only a limited amount of empirical research has been carried out here and in America, it is not possible to obtain an overall picture of the extent of this method in actual business. Some of the empirical studies show the predominance of full-cost methods, others conclude that marginalism is widely applied and yet others speak of the marriage of the two pricing systems.

One of the first empirical studies into actual pricing policies in this country was based on data supplied by thirty-eight entrepreneurs in 1939, and the general conclusion was that most firms did not aim at maximizing their profit by the equation of marginal revenue and marginal cost. The overwhelming majority of entrepreneurs thought that a price based on full average cost was the 'right price'. This conclusion was reached in spite of the fact that a few firms admitted that they might charge more than average full-cost in periods of exceptionally high demand, and a greater number stated that they might lower their prices in periods of depressed demand.[6] The conclusion of this study was challenged on various grounds. Since the majority of entrepreneurs reacted to demand elasticities, and departed from the full-cost price under exceptional demand conditions, and margins added to average costs varied from firm to firm, and within firms from period to period and from product to product, it can be interpreted that the firms concerned showed marginalist tendencies.[7] Another critic pointed out that the findings of this study, made in the doldrums of the inter-war years in an economy with widespread restrictive practices, were not necessarily valid in the more competitive climate of the post-war decades. The mail questionnaire technique of the survey was also attacked, because what businessmen actually do is more relevant than what they say they do.[8] A more recent investigation into the pricing policies of seven medium-sized manufacturing firms found no trace of marginalist thinking. These companies were found to aim at a comfortable level of profit and not at a maximum. There was no tendency towards marginalism; all the firms examined first fixed their prices upon some non-marginalist principle and then tried to sell as much as possible at the fixed price. They had very little knowledge of the elasticity of demand for their products and were much more concerned that the volume of sales might fluctuate at any given price than by the fluctuations at various prices.[9]

Statements on full-cost pricing are often linked with the assumption that conventional margins are generally applied. The

---

[6] R. L. Hall and C. J. Hitch, 'Price Theory and Business Behaviour', *Oxford Economic Papers*, May 1939, pp. 12-45.

[7] Fritz Machlup, op. cit., pp. 545-546.

[8] James S. Earley, 'Marginal Policies of "Excellently Managed" Companies', *American Economic Review*, March 1956, p. 67.

[9] R. H. Barback, *The Pricing of Manufactures*, London, 1964, pp. 160-163.

conventional margin hypothesis assumes that profit margins are determined by historical factors – that is, that firms charge traditional profit. A special investigation into the inter-war price and cost structure of selected British industries found that the actual variations of gross margins were so great that the conventional margin hypothesis was insupportable. In the cement industry, for example, gross margins varied from £0·46 to £0·72 per ton in 1935. In the tinplate industry the corresponding figures were £2·30 to £3·20 per ton.[10]

An American survey probed into the pricing policies of 110 leading firms, selected out of 217 rated by the American Institute of Management as 'excellently managed'. The survey found that most companies did not base their prices on full costs, but exhibited marginalist attitudes. A compromise of short-term and long-term considerations was discernible mainly in consequence of the rapid pace of innovation in these industries, since new products, especially, were priced according to short-term demand elasticities. The majority of these companies did not conceive short-run versus long-run profitability as inconsistent goals but tried to maximize their long-run profits by increasing their current profits. Whilst these companies cannot be considered as typical of American industry they are, however, leaders in the use of new management techniques and likely to have an influence on future business practices of American industry as a whole.[11]

Elements of both full-cost and marginal pricing can be found in the women's outerwear industry. The usual practice is that manufacturers first calculate the total production and then the selling costs per unit. The costing method used by many small firms in the industry is often not more than a rule-of-thumb estimate of full costs based on past experience. Demand is taken into account by varying the profit margin added to costs. The average profit margin varies from about 5 per cent for cheaper garments and non-fashion lines to over 100 per cent for the highest grade of 'wholesale model' production.[12]

A Danish inquiry into the pricing methods of industrial firms concluded that the dividing line between full-cost pricing and the

[10] L. Rostas, *Productivity, Prices and Distribution in Selected British Industries*, London, 1948, pp. 22 and 44.
[11] James S. Earley, op. cit., pp. 44–70.
[12] Margaret Wray, *The Women's Outerwear Industry*, London, 1957, p. 296.

marginal is often blurred. Full-costing is more usual but often modified in a way which brings it into line with the marginal theory. The inquiry concludes that:

It is conceivable that a descriptive price theory may be propounded in which the distinctive features would be that, on the whole, businessmen determine their prices on the basis of the full-cost principle, but in consideration of the reaction of consumers and the behaviour of competitors, etc., an adjustment to the prices which fulfil the conditions of the marginal theory takes place – even though this adjustment may quite possibly be imperfect.[13]

[13] B. Fog, *Industrial Pricing Policies*, Amsterdam, 1960, p. 224.

CHAPTER 4

Consumers and prices

Economic theory rests upon a few general assumptions, and one of these is the rationality of the consumer. It is assumed that among the large selection of goods offered on the market with various characteristics, qualities and prices, his choice will be a rational one. Some critics point out the weakness of this fundamental tenet of economic theory:

> Traditional economic theory postulates an 'economic man', who in the course of being 'economic' is also 'rational'. This man is assumed to have knowledge of the relevant aspects of his environment, which, if not absolutely complete, is at least impressively clear and voluminous. He is assumed also to have a well-organized and stable system of preferences, and a skill in computation that enables him to calculate, for the alternative courses of action that are available to him, which of these will permit him to reach the highest attainable point on his preference scale. Recent developments in economics, and particularly in the theory of the business firm, have raised great doubts as to whether this schematized model of economic man provides a suitable foundation on which to erect a theory – whether it be a theory of how firms do behave, or of how they 'should' rationally behave.[1]

It would be unreasonable to say that the otherwise rational man is completely irrational when acting as a consumer but it cannot be denied that he has, apart from a rational judgement, whims, fancies and irrational preferences. The assertion of the irrationality of the consumer should not, however, be carried too far.

It is more difficult for the present-day consumer to make a rational choice than it was for his counterpart a century ago. Then the range of consumer goods was limited and most of them were simple enough for quality to be assessed fairly accurately. Today's consumer is no longer an expert buyer. The selection of goods has multiplied and grown enormously in complexity. The comparison

[1] Herbert A. Simon, 'A Behavioral Model of Rational Choice', *Quarterly Journal of Economics*, February 1955, p. 99.

of sizes, prices and qualities is difficult even in respect to fairly simple articles. With technical goods, which have become everyday necessities for a large number of people, it is even more so. In this market the consumer may rely more on the reputation of a brand name, the retailer's advice, the outer appearance of the product or, as we shall presently see, accept the price as an indicator of quality. The greatly bewildered consumer cannot exercise a truly rational choice. The difficulties of modern shopping have led to the setting up of consumer associations in many countries which conduct product tests on an objective and scientific basis and publish reports for the information of consumers. The help they are able to give is subject to serious limitations but they, nevertheless, undoubtedly contribute towards widening the horizon of the consumer. If consumers were completely rational their market behaviour could be predicted in many respects. For example, a reduction in price should bring about a rise in demand but under actual circumstances this is not always so and the entrepreneur cannot make assumptions about the future without prior investigations when embarking on a certain price policy. Consumer reactions can be researched and tested in advance.

A convenient start to this research would be to ascertain the consumer's buying habits. A useful distinction can be made, first of all, among the various goods according to the attitude of the various groups of consumers towards them. This distinction has implications affecting business pricing.

Consumer goods are often classified into three groups: convenience, shopping and speciality. The American Marketing Association suggested the following definitions:

'Convenience Goods: Those consumer's goods which the customer purchases frequently, immediately, and with the minimum of effort.'[2]

'Shopping Goods: Those consumer's goods which the customer in the process of selection and purchase characteristically compares on such bases as suitability, quality, price and style.'

'Speciality Goods: Those consumer's goods on which a significant group of buyers characteristically insists and for which they are willing to make a special purchasing effort.'[3]

[2] Definition Committee, American Marketing Association, Report of the Definition Committee, *Journal of Marketing*, October 1948, p. 206.
[3] Ibid., p. 215.

Convenience goods

Convenience goods are, in general, those household items which are bought frequently, like food, newspapers, cigarettes, electric bulbs, toiletries and cleaning materials. The type of shop selling convenience goods is usually the food store, hardware store, tobacconist and sweet shop. The consumer gets to know these articles and their prices quite well, develops certain preferences for qualities, tastes and brands, and perhaps has a clear-cut idea about acceptable substitutes if he cannot find his favourite line. Unit prices of convenience goods are fairly low and, therefore, rarely induce consumers to shop around, as the possible gain would not perhaps justify the extra time and trouble spent on looking for bargains. This is mainly the field where purchases are not necessarily planned but may be made on impulse.

Impulse buying

An American study suggests four distinct types of impulse buying. The first is termed Pure Impulse Buying. This type of purchase is decided on the spot and its object is a novelty for the consumer which breaks the monotony of his usual buying pattern. As ingrained shopping habits are quite strong this sort of impulse purchase is rare.

The second type has been described as Reminder Impulse Buying. This is when the shopper is reminded in the store by the display of goods, or point-of-sale advertisements, of an item he habitually buys and of which he is running out of stock, or he may be reminded of a previous decision to buy a certain product.

Suggestion Impulse Buying denotes a purchase of items entirely new for the shopper of which he has no previous knowledge. His decision to buy is based on comparison and rational motives, as contrasted with the emotional and whimsical character of Pure Impulse Purchases.

Finally, there is the category with the seemingly contradictory name of Planned Impulse Buying. This type occurs when the consumer has some ideas about what he wants when he enters the store but is predetermined to buy certain bargains like special offers, free gift items, etc. A limited sample survey in America showed that over one-third of the housewives interviewed planned their menus whilst actually shopping in a supermarket. Self-service shopping appears to have encouraged the habit of making final purchasing decisions in the store, and a survey made by du Pont showed that the number of unplanned purchases in super-markets increased from about 38 per cent to nearly 51 per cent between 1949 and 1959.[4]

The Alfred Bird grocery survey found that impulse buying had been on the increase in Britain between 1960 and 1966. The 1966 investigation showed that 55 per cent of housewives used a shopping list when buying food. The people who had not planned to purchase but bought items because they saw them in the shop were 23 per cent. The comparable figure in 1960 was 12 per cent. The percentage of spontaneous purchases was higher in co-operatives and multiple shops (26 per cent and 31 per cent respectively) than in independent outlets (20 per cent), showing that the greater use of self-service technique increases impulse buying.[5]

Shopping goods

Shopping goods are those which are not bought frequently and the consumer's expertise and experience is considerably less than with convenience goods. Their unit value is high enough to justify a special trip to the town shopping centre where prices and qualities can be compared. The shopper may not know exactly what he wants when entering the shopping centre and his buying decision often depends on the information he receives – visually and ver-bally – from the shops and by scanning the shop windows. Fashion goods, shoes, furniture and jewellery are examples of typical shopping goods.

Speciality goods

Speciality goods are those for which the consumer has a strong preference, has usually a certain brand in mind and is not prepared to accept a substitute. They are bought without shopping around

---

[4] Hawkins Stern, 'The Significance of Impulse Buying Today', *Journal of Marketing*, April 1962, pp. 59–62.

[5] *Mrs. Housewife and Her Grocer, 1966*, published by Alfred Bird and Sons Ltd., London, 1967, Chart 9.

and the consumer visits the store stocking the required brand. Consumer durables, like washing machines, cars, watches and fancy groceries fall, among others, into this class.

It should be recognized that the important thing is the consumer's attitude towards the goods and that they do not inherently belong to one or other of the classifications. The same article may be a convenience good for one and a speciality good for another. Likewise, a certain article may be a shopping line for some consumers and a speciality for others. For certain consumers all goods are shopping goods, as the financially hard-pressed may shop around, even for convenience goods, to make a small saving. For others, shopping is a pastime and an enjoyment and they are prepared to spend a lot of time seeking out the best possibilities. Conversely, for some people shopping is a time-wasting nuisance and they will buy even substantial items in the first shop they come to. As incomes increase, more and more goods pass from the shopping goods into the convenience goods category.

The above examples of the goods belonging to the various categories are, therefore, not unalterable facts but illustrate only the attitude of the average shopper. What is important for the pricing executive is to know the proportion of consumers having certain attitudes to the goods he wants to market.

Other classifications

The classification of consumer goods does not always follow these lines. Sometimes the whole area is divided into two categories only: convenience goods and shopping goods. Other writers use the current goods (*marchandises courantes*) and occasional goods (*marchandises anomales*) distinction. This classification is roughly in line with the convenience goods – shopping goods categories.[6]

A different kind of classification distinguishes between staple and non-staple lines. Staples are everyday necessities, bought regularly, and about which the consumer has a fairly good idea of their prices. Sugar and bread, stockings and cigarettes, are staple lines. Non-staples are subdivided into 'reminder' and 'suggestion'

[6] Jane Aubert-Krier, 'Monopolistic and Imperfect Competition in Retail Trade', in Edward H. Chamberlin, *Monopoly and Competition and Their Regulation*, London, 1954, p. 285.

articles. Reminder articles are those which every household stocks and about which the consumer may appreciate a reminder, but his purchase will not increase his total consumption. Shoe polish and salt are reminder goods. Suggestion lines, on the other hand, are items that the shopper may not have intended to buy, but can be persuaded to because of their bargain or novelty value.[7]

Price awareness

Price awareness and price consciousness are two different consumer characteristics and, for anybody concerned with pricing policy, it is of interest to know the degree in which they play a part for the average consumer. The former is the ability of the consumer to remember prices, but price consciousness denotes the consumer's sensitivity towards price differentials. High price consciousness means that the consumer is not prepared to pay a higher price for a commodity and, if the price is above his expectation, he will switch his custom to a competitor. The price-conscious shopper will not appreciate features which distinguish the product if they are accompanied with a substantial price difference. Conversely, a consumer of low price sensitivity is not disturbed by paying more for an article in the shop of his liking, or for a good whose product features appeal to him. High price consciousness is usually based on high price awareness, while a low price consciousness may or may not be accompanied with high price awareness.

It is not easy to generalize whether the consumer remembers a lot of prices and is price conscious or not. Great variations may exist according to sex, income, age, type of product, etc. One can expect, however, that both price awareness and price consciousness is strongest concerning goods frequently bought. It has been stated that the average shopper cannot remember more than about a dozen prices correctly, but it may be that this view underrates the memory of the consumer.

The price awareness of women consumers has often been studied. As housewives control a large part of the family budget and, as convenience goods, especially, are often bought by them, their price awareness is of primary importance to the businessman. Though the extent to which women are responsible for

[7] W. G. McClelland, *Studies in Retailing*, Oxford, 1963, pp. 96–97.

buying decisions is a debatable question, it is clear that their role is important enough to concentrate research on them.

A Nottingham University research team investigated the price awareness of local housewives in 1958, with particular reference to frequently purchased foods and cleaning materials. Each respondent of the 425 successfully completed interviews was asked about the brand or type, the quantity and price of the commodities, if bought within the previous seven days. The first measure of price awareness was the percentage of prices remembered, irrespective of whether the prices given were correct or not. In 82 per cent of over 5,000 purchases the housewives named a price. A remarkable dispersion was found according to commodities. The highest recall percentages were linked with tea (95 per cent), eggs (93 per cent) and sausages (91 per cent). Bacon (84 per cent), butter (84 per cent) and jam and marmalade (82 per cent) occupied the middle of the scale, while the lowest percentages were elicited in respect of household soap (73 per cent), breakfast cereal (70 per cent) and flour (63 per cent).

The correctness of the remembered price could be checked only in respect of seven commodities, as the other articles were sold at such a variety of prices that a right one could not be established. Of nearly 1,900 purchases of the seven commodities 57 per cent were correctly priced. A further 25 per cent named prices incorrectly and the rest were 'don't knows'. Again, correctly remembered price figures showed a wide dispersion, the percentages for the seven commodities were: tea 79, coffee 68, sugar 67, jam and marmalade 95, margarine 46, flour 36 and breakfast cereal 35. The organizers of the survey remarked that the inquiry had revealed a much higher degree of price awareness than they expected.[8]

Another British survey tested housewives' memory about prices paid last time for six frequently bought grocery products. The following percentages of respondents did not remember the price paid last time at all: breakfast cereal 29, instant coffee 23, sugar 14, soap powder 14, tinned soup 23 and tea 11.[9]

The Colonial Study, a survey carried out by the American periodical *Progressive Grocer* in Colonial stores, also tested con-

[8] Andre Gabor and C. W. J. Granger, 'On the Price Consciousness of Consumers', *Applied Statistics*, November 1961, pp. 170–188.
[9] *Mrs. Housewife and Her Grocer, 1966*, published by Alfred Bird and Sons Ltd., 1967, p. 21.

sumers' price awareness, and the research method chosen was different from that of the Nottingham study. Fifty-nine frequently advertised items were selected, all of them characterized by highly competitive prices in the trade. They were displayed on tables in Colonial stores and several thousand customers, men and women, were asked to state the price of each item. The answers were classified under two headings: those naming the correct price and those guessing the price within plus or minus 5 per cent limits. Coca-Cola was the clear winner, 86 per cent of customers knew its exact price and 91 per cent were between the 5 per cent tolerance limits. Second on the list was Camel cigarettes, whose exact price was known by 39 per cent, with 54 per cent making an acceptable guess. The rest of the items elicited a lower recognition rate. It is interesting to note that the survey could not detect any substantial discrepancy in price awareness as between men and women and income levels and age seemed to make little difference. From these figures the study concluded that, though consumers found it difficult to name exact prices, they had a good general knowledge of the proper price range of fast-selling lines.[10]

Price consciousness

It has been asserted that the consumer's price consciousness has undergone a definite change in this century. This view holds that low personal incomes made the consumer very price conscious up to about the last war. Consequently, low-price policy was the most effective way of expanding turnover. The rapid rise of personal incomes after the war has dulled the price sensitivity of the public. In consequence, marketing policy has changed and there has been a transfer of emphasis from price to other selling efforts. Presentation of goods has improved, and expenditure on publicity and other non-price selling methods has increased. It is said that we are now on the threshold of a new development where quality will be the most important selling factor. According to this view, 'if every Englishman had an annual income of £50,000 there would be no price elasticity at all'.[11] Not everybody would agree with

[10] 'Colonial Study', a Report on Supermarket Operations and Customer Habits, *Progressive Grocer*, 1964, pp. 104–106.
[11] Max-Kjaer-Hansen, 'Marketing and its Importance in Pricing'. Lecture at a Symposium on New Developments in Pricing Strategy, Bradford University Management Centre, January 1967, Manual, pp. 58–60.

this opinion. It is true that shopping around comparing prices requires time and energy, and more and more people can afford the luxury of not being worried about small price differences. It is also true that the rapid growth of the variety of merchandise offered makes comparisons more difficult. But one should not stretch this line of thought too far. Today's well-stocked and well-equipped shops have made shopping a source of enjoyment for many, since people have substantially more spare time now than a few decades ago. People could perhaps afford to pay more for certain goods, but it is questionable whether they would want to. The post-war history of retailing shows that the remarkable expansion of large-scale retailers has been based mainly on price appeal. In America, the most prosperous country in the world, housewives recently picketed supermarkets and boycotted those whose prices were, in their view, exorbitant. The movement spread to at least a hundred cities all over the country and retailers reacted with price-cuts.[12]

The increasing mobility of the consumer does not support the view that price consciousness is on the decline either. A British study, based on the sample survey of 2,059 housewives, has shown a dramatic drop in the percentage of housewives who always go to the same grocery shop. While in 1957 52 per cent claimed to have a single family grocer, in 1960 the figure was 27 per cent and in 1966 only 24 per cent.[13] This change has taken place in face of the fact that grocers stock more and more household goods to encourage one-stop shopping and buying everything under the same roof. Another recent sample survey also concluded that the British housewife shops around more than before and loyalty to a regular retailer is declining. Three-quarters of those who changed shops did so because of prices and 58 per cent of respondents said they looked for the best bargains they could get, rather than continue to visit only their usual shop.[14] The price consciousness of housewives is also shown by the Alfred Bird survey. The majority of housewives put value for money in second place after cleanliness, when asserting the relative importance of buying motives.

[12] *Financial Times*, October 27, 1966.
[13] *Mrs. Housewife and Her Grocer, 1966*, published by Alfred Bird and Sons Ltd., London, 1967, Chart 8.
[14] *What Puts the Price up?*, published by J. Walter Thomson Co. Ltd., London, 1965, p. 6.

Other considerations, like freshness of stocks, quality, speed of service, honesty, friendliness, range of products, and length of opening hours, followed after the value-for-money criterion.[15]

The Colonial study found that consumers were not too much concerned with price when wanting to try a new item, but a lower price often induced them to switch to a competing brand. Half of the respondents bought a new item because of seeing it on special display, 17 per cent responded to advertising, 19 per cent to 'other people's' advice, 5 per cent 'just wanted a change', and only 3 per cent were impressed by cheaper prices. When they were asked about the reasons for switching to competing brands, one in four attributed it to special display, 21 per cent to lower prices, 19 per cent 'just wanted a change', 9 per cent followed 'other people's' recommendation, in 7 per cent of the cases the usual brand was out of stock, 6 per cent were influenced by non-price promotions like coupons, stamps and free samples, and 4 per cent by advertising.[16]

Price and quality

If quantity is plotted on the horizontal and price on the vertical axis, the regular shape of the demand curve is a line declining to the right, showing that a lower price elicits a higher demand. It has been observed, however, that the rule does not apply in respect of certain goods. Articles whose possession confers some social status or prestige on their owner, for example, may sell better at a higher than at a lower price. The presumption is that high-price articles are high-quality articles and high-quality articles belong to high-quality men.

According to certain opinions, as prosperity increases, more and more people consider quality as the primary buying motive and price as an indication of quality. This view points out that the range and complexity of goods is on the increase-making product evaluation more and more difficult. The consumer's bewilderment is added to by the technical terms of some advertisements, complicated names of chemical ingredients on labels, references to complicated research programmes, etc. More and more, objective

[15] *Mrs. Housewife and Her Grocer, 1966*, published by Alfred Bird and Sons Ltd., London, 1967, Chart 12.
[16] 'Colonial Study', op. cit., p. 118.

product evaluation, therefore, becomes impossible and the consumer must rely on certain indices of quality.[17] One of the important indices is price. Quality of products is also judged by the goodwill, size, age and financial success of the manufacturing firm. A well-known brand name is usually associated with the image of high quality. An exponent of this school of thought has gone as far as saying that

> If the present development continues, I think the younger generation may live to see the classical demand curve undergo a radical change. It will flatten out, or may perhaps be reversed, so that a rise in price results in an increase in demand. This latter extreme situation may arise if price in increasingly affluent societies comes to serve merely as an indicator of quality.[18]

Many would not subscribe to this view. As we have seen, there are ample signs that the consumer is still price conscious. The research reports published by the consumer associations have also undermined the credibility of the idea that the higher-priced goods are always higher-quality ones. Private brands of many large-scale retailers are lower-priced than the equivalent national brand. Still, the idea that price differentials express quality differences persists to a certain extent.

A number of investigations has shown that, when the consumer lacks information about the quality of various brands within a product class, he sometimes considers price as an indicator of quality. An experiment to this effect was made at Chicago University. Household goods, falling in the 50 cent to $1 price range, were selected for the experiment. Sixty respondents were asked to make a choice between a higher-priced and a lower-priced brand in four product categories. In order to hold constant all variables but price, the only differential information about the eight articles was their price. The assumption was that the brand regularly bought by the respondents was out of stock in a store, and A and B brands were offered instead – A brands being always lower-priced than B brands. The results of the experiment indicated that some people would sometimes choose the higher-priced of two alternative brands when acting purely on the information of

[17] Tibor Scitovsky, 'Some Consequence of the Habit of Judging Quality by Price', *Review of Economic Studies*, 1944–45, No. 32, p. 100.
[18] Max-Kjaer-Hansen, op. cit., pp. 58–60.

price. (30 per cent of respondents, for example, chose the more expensive razor blade.)[19] These findings were later reinforced by another similar experiment in America.[20]

At Nottingham University, consumer responses in respect of good-quality plain Wilton carpets were tested. The actual price per square yard was 72 shillings. Each respondent was shown a sample and asked whether she would buy it or not at various prices. Below 40 shillings the buying interest dropped considerably, prices in the 40 to 50 shilling range elicited about 60 per cent buying intention, and only about 30 per cent of the respondents wanted to buy the carpet in the 20 to 30 shilling range.[21]

We will see in Chapter 6 that various pricing practices in the retail trade are used which take into account not only the objective aspects of retail pricing, but also the somewhat irrational reactions of consumers. Such pricing methods include multiple pricing, the use of customary prices, odd prices, money-off promotions, and the so-called double pricing.

[19] Harold J. Lewitt, 'A Note on Some Experimental Findings About the Meanings of Price', *Journal of Business*, July 1954, pp. 205–210.

[20] D. S. Tull, R. A. Boring, M. H. Gonsior, 'A Note on the Relationship of Price and Imputed Quality', *Journal of Business*, April 1964, pp. 186–191.

[21] Andre Gabor and C. W. J. Granger, 'Price as an Indicator of Quality: Report on an Enquiry', *Economica*, February 1966, p. 51.

CHAPTER 5

The pricing of manufactures

When discussing the actual process of price-making in manufacturing industries, the first thing to realize is that the price is not looked at in isolation by the producer. The marketing success of any product depends on a variety of factors and price is only one of them.

The marketing mix

The factors influencing sales are described in American business literature under the name of 'marketing mix'.[1] The manufacturer's task is to design a marketing programme that would be conducive in achieving targets set in the light of the company's objectives. To achieve the set target the producer should take into account and co-ordinate the various elements of the marketing mix. Some of these factors are outside the control of the manufacturer, such as the general economic situation, changes in consumers' incomes and tastes, government regulations and competitors' activities. Other elements of the marketing mix *can* be manipulated by the producer, among which are: product design, packaging, branding, channels of distribution, personal selling, advertising and sales promotion, service, physical handling, fact-finding and analysis, and pricing. The price should harmonize with the other factors of the marketing mix. Lever Brothers' pricing policy was described by the Monopolies Commission as follows:

Pricing is brand-orientated and, in a sense, the 'price of a product is fixed in relation to what it is thought the market will bear', but this means taking into account a whole range of factors, such as the relative

---

[1] Neil H. Borden, 'The Concept of the Marketing Mix', in George Schwartz, *Science in Marketing*, New York, 1965, pp. 386–397.

consumer acceptance of the brand compared with other brands, costs of production and marketing, variations in the weight of expenditure on the different constituents of the 'marketing mix', the various aspects of competition, and increases in the standard of living. The 'marketing mix' of a brand is made up of a number of variables, including formulation and packaging, advertising and sales promotions, quantity in the pack and price, and the company is always trying to find the 'mix' which most appeals to the consumer.[2]

Multi-stage pricing

The often quoted Multi-stage Pricing method developed by A. R. Oxenfeldt of Columbia University takes account of the requirements of the marketing mix.[3] This approach arrives at the price in six successive steps, each of which is designed to exclude more and more elements of the various possibilities.

At the first stage the company selects the class of consumers to be the main target of the marketing operation. The choice may be the whole market, that is, all consumers regardless of their income levels, or just a smaller market segment, such as the high-income class or consumers of a certain age or with a certain hobby. Research into the demand of selected consumer groups will include observation about their price awareness and price sensitivity (see Chapter 4).

Secondly, the company chooses a brand image which is in harmony with the targets defined in the first step. The brand name, product design and package, the channels of distribution selected, the advertising media and copy, and the price itself puts the product into a certain category and this brand image should appeal to the particular requirements of the consumer group which has been selected as the main target.

The next step is the composition of the marketing mix. The main problem to be tackled when choosing the correct marketing mix is whether the promotion of the product should rest on price appeal or whether price should assume a subordinate role and preference be given to other considerations, like quality, service, advertising and special product features. The choice to a large extent is already determined by the previous selection of a certain

[2] 'Report on the Supply of Household Detergents', 1966, para. 54.
[3] A. R. Oxenfeldt, 'Multi-stage Approach to Pricing', *Harvard Business Review*, July–August 1960, pp. 125–133.

brand image. Decisions are taken at this juncture about the advertising budget, personal salesmanship, delivery, etc.

The next stage is the determination of the broad price policy to be adopted. Decisions are made in respect of the prices and whether they are to be set above, at, or below the competitive level. It may be decided to maintain stable prices in the face of fluctuating demand or follow a flexible pricing policy with frequent price changes. National versus regional price policy may be another question to decide at this stage (see Chapter 12).

The fifth step of Multi-stage Pricing is the selection of a price strategy. The distinction between price policy and strategy – according to Oxenfeldt – is that while the former is concerned with the normal situation, the latter takes into account unusual circumstances which are, by definition, short-period phenomena. The question of price strategy is, therefore, how to tackle a special market situation, such as the appearance of a new product on the market or how to stop declining sales.

After the completion of the five previous stages, a certain price bracket will emerge within which the actual price should be placed as the final step of price-setting. If sufficient information is available about demand and cost conditions, the marginal rule should be applied, otherwise the price should be set in the light of all relevant data. The multi-stage approach does not necessarily lead to a single price but narrows down the number of possible prices: '. . . one must beware of any pricing method that does lead to a single price, for such a method could not possibly take into account all the special circumstances which are relevant to a price decision and which vary so greatly from market to market and from time to time.'[4]

Product life-cycle

It is an undisputed fact that not many consumer goods available twenty years ago are on sale today in exactly the same form. Many have been discontinued altogether, others have undergone a change in design or composition and others are presented in an 'improved' package. A continuous stream of new products appears on the market year by year while many of the established ones disappear.

[4] A. R. Oxenfeldt, 'Multi-stage Approach to Pricing', *Harvard Business Review*, July–August 1960, p. 133.

It is often possible to detect various phases in the life of consumer goods. After an initial pioneering stage the product becomes established and carves out a market share for itself. A period of expansion follows up to a certain point, then stagnation sets in, which leads to the decline and fall of the product. Consequently, when formulating his pricing policy the entrepreneur should pay attention to the life-cycle phases of the products he markets.

Sometimes a new product represents a substantial departure from anything known before, or it may even open up a new market on its own. The inventor may have patent protection and often no one else is in possession of the know-how necessary to produce a similar article. This sort of perfect product differentiation confers a large degree of pricing freedom on the manufacturer. (When the distinctive features of a new product are not substantial, the producer has less latitude over price.) In this case he may decide to follow a high-price policy initially to recoup his research and capital expenditure before imitators enter the field. High prices may be coupled with heavy promotional expenditure. This pricing policy is sometimes referred to as 'skimming the market', as its aim is to separate the various market segments and skim the cream of the market that can afford the high price. At later stages price reductions can successively extend the market to lower and lower income groups. This pricing policy is a form of differential pricing (discussed in Chapter 11).

The second way open to the innovator is to use the so-called 'penetration price' or 'market expansion price' policy. In contrast with the high-price policy this method aims at immediate promotion of the product over the whole market, based on price appeal. Its obvious area is markets where the consumer's price sensitivity is high and where an immediate large turnover can lower production and distribution costs substantially. A high-price policy is always an incentive to potential competitors to enter the field. A low-price policy, on the other hand, often keeps competitors away.

After the take-off, successful products enlarge their market share and sooner or later competition stages a come-back. Competition takes place in technology, presentation, price and selling efforts. Later, the initially large upheavals of the market subside and a state of maturity is approached.

There are three different aspects of maturity which usually go hand in hand. The first is technical maturity, characterized by less and less product development in a given industry, accompanied by increasing standardization among brands. Manufacturing processes become well-established and widely-known. The second aspect of maturity refers to the market. Consumer acceptance of the products is widespread at this stage. Believing that most products in the field will give a satisfactory performance and, having experimented long enough with the available goods, the consumers are able to compare brands competently. The market approaches saturation point. Fewer and fewer new consumers are around and an increasing proportion of sales are repeat purchases and – in respect of consumer durables – replacement buyings. Thirdly, competitive maturity is indicated by increasing stability of market shares and price structures. The market has cooled down.[5]

It is also a sign of approaching maturity when retailers' private brands are put on the market. These are usually offered by retail stores at lower prices than the national brands, though often made by the same manufacturers to the same quality specifications. The producer of national brands often finds it profitable to utilize spare productive capacity by accepting private brand orders from large-scale retailers. He is often able to quote a substantially lower price as compared with the widely distributed and extensively publicized national brands. The appearance of numerous private brands within a product category may be an indication that manufacturers have over-priced their national brands beyond the acceptable limit.

Maturity brings about a certain harmonization of prices between competing brands. The consumer's knowledge of high-quality alternative brands weakens his brand loyalty and heightens his price sensitivity. Prices cannot be out of line with each other to any substantial extent as higher prices decrease sales and price-cutting may evoke retaliation by competitors. This does not mean complete price uniformity, but a traditional structure of prices reflecting historical factors and quality differences. The mature stage of a market may also be characterized by the spread of restrictive agreements among previous rivals (see Chapter 8) and by substituting various forms of non-price competition for price competition.

It would, however, be a mistake to picture the mature market

[5] Joel Dean, 'Pricing Policies for New Products', *Harvard Business Review*, November 1950, pp. 45–53.

as a static one. Established brands are constantly under review and gradual product improvements are introduced. New brands are also launched periodically, partly by established firms and partly by newcomers in the field. Though prices do not move much independently, indirect price-cuts are offered in the form of free gifts, coupons, and premium promotions. Therefore, brand shares do not entirely remain unchanged and the better marketing policy shows up. The extension of the product range of a firm may also be achieved by a merger with, or a take-over by, another company.

Backward cost pricing

New products are usually launched as the end-results of long business and technical research work. Ideas for new products may emanate from the marketing people or from engineers. Business research should investigate whether there is a chance of success for a new product, and what kind of product it should be, before embarking on costly technical experimentation. Such an investigation cannot fail to include prices. Researchers are perhaps likely to suggest a fairly narrow price range rather than a single price. The price range, combined with an estimate of possible sales, will indicate an approximate unit cost which may serve as a guide for technical research.

It is a widespread practice in certain industries to take, as the starting-point of pricing, the established price of a product or the established price structure of a product group. When a company wants to design a new product, first an acceptable price is located – perhaps with the help of consumer research – in relation to competing goods on the market. After the deduction of profit and distribution costs, the firm's new product development team is faced with the task of creating a line, with certain features, within the given cost range. This pricing approach is called 'backward cost pricing', 'demand backward pricing' or 'reverse cost-plus pricing'.

Such a pricing policy is practised, for example, in the motor industry where manufacturers concentrate on quality competition by attempting to build the best car within the predetermined price range. Straight price competition is very rare in the motor car industry.

The price is the starting-point for the manufacturer's strategic calculations. Having decided on the price, he proceeds to build the best car he can at that price. His selection of the price is determined by assessing the market in terms of the more successful models. The highly popular model often becomes a 'price leader' and sets the price round which other firms tend to cluster. Success comes to those firms whose models, selling at the conventional price for their class, make the greatest appeal to the public.[6]

Backward cost pricing is also practised in the domestic electrical appliances industry. As certain types are accepted by the public, a sort of general market price becomes established. A basic price exists for the standard product, and a spread of prices for the others depending on the various product features incorporated. Subsequent models tend to be designed to the accepted market price. A corollary of this price policy is that prices tend to be inflexible and hold stable for longer periods.[7] Other examples of backward cost pricing can be found in the footwear and ready-made clothing industry.

Market segmentation

The manufacturer often tries to increase his revenue by turning out variations of the original product for different groups of consumers. The advantage of such a market segmentation, in contrast to introducing a completely new line, is that the firm remains within its own field where it enjoys a good reputation, has expert knowledge, and well-functioning distributive channels. The market is studied in detail and certain segments are marked out as promising areas for product development. Variety in tastes and preferences is looked for among consumers and, if it does not exist, the producer endeavours to develop it, by offering variations of the product accompanied, perhaps, with large-scale advertising.

In some cases the new variation introduced may not differ physically from the original product, and is differentiated only by a new brand name and a different package. Still, in an economic sense, the new variation will count as a new product and may attract new consumers. In other instances the products are still

[6] Maxcy Silberston, *The Motor Industry*, London, 1959, p. 106.
[7] T. A. B. Corey, *Domestic Electrical Appliances*, London, 1966, p. 88.

essentially the same but contain certain modifications according to the requirements of a certain section of the market. Children and those on a slimming diet may be pinpointed as promising sub-markets, for example, and slight variations introduced on foods to attract them. In other fields a distinction may be made between standard and de-luxe models. These terms may describe genuine quality differences, but sometimes only the trimming, the design, or the colour may be different. The gold-plated version of a fountain-pen and the de-luxe versions of cars intend to widen the circle of prospective customers. An example of market segmentation is provided by the American home laundry products market (soap flakes, detergents, soaps, starch and bleach). In 1947–48 there were altogether 77 products on the market. By 1964 the consumer had a choice from among 355 products.[8]

The pricing problem of individual lines within a product group cannot be looked at separately, since the price of any one line influences not only its own demand but the sale of every other line as well. The task of the pricing executive is to take cross-elasticities into consideration and set up that price structure for the group of products which produces an optimum total return. (Cross-elasticity refers to the relationship between the change of price of a product and the change of demand in a possible substitute.) If, for example, the price of the de-luxe model is only marginally higher than that of the standard, many consumers will buy the de-luxe version. The consequence of this policy may be that less prestige value will be attached to the de-luxe model and the producer may lose those buyers who want to buy a distinctive product and are prepared to pay a high price for it. The manufacturer may achieve a better overall return by widening the price differential between the standard and the de-luxe model.

As in the case of individual product pricing, there are various ways to approach the question of pricing product variations. First of all, prices may be determined according to full costs. Total costs of producing the group of products are allocated among the different lines and augmented by the same percentage profit margin to give the selling price. The criticism of full-cost pricing is that it is a mechanical pricing method which disregards demand and the market completely and is, therefore, unsuitable as a means of arriving at the correct relative prices of a product group.

[8] *Nielsen Researcher*, Oxford Edition, July–August 1965, p. 6.

An improvement on the full-cost method pays attention to demand elasticities. Though production and distribution costs are allocated proportionately among the lines involved, various lines carry different profit margins. It is often thought that quality products can be sold at a disproportionately higher price than those of a mass market, since high-income people are not critical of prices when buying a quality article. Moreover, demand evaluation can be refined by keeping an eye on the various stages of the product life-cycle related to the individual lines and on the state of competition in the relevant market segments. Where relative prices are set in the light of demand and market requirements, and full costs are used only as an indicator of the price-floor below which actual prices cannot go, various lines will make unequal contributions to net profits. Knowing this, the obviously desirable policy of a firm will be to concentrate on replacing lines of low profitability with more successful ones.[9]

Pricing various product sizes

The manufacturer must also decide about price relations between various sizes of a certain product line. According to long-established practices in different trades, various sizes are either uniformly or differently priced and it may be advisable for the producer to comply with the existing practice, since consumers are conditioned to them. As a rule no price differentials exist, for example, in relation to various-sized leather shoes, adult outerwear, hats and stockings. Knitwear and underwear, on the other hand, are often sold at two or three prices according to measurements.

Where different prices can be applied, one idea may be to price the various sizes in exact proportion to the physical differences between them. This treatment suggests to buyers that all of them are treated on the same footing. The popular sizes of a line, however, may be produced at a disproportionately lower cost than the rest and competitors may not follow a proportional price scale. Therefore, demand and market conditions should not be disregarded.

In respect of many packaged consumer goods, a type of pricing policy is applied where the unit price of the product decreases as

[9] Joel Dean, *Managerial Economics*, Englewood Cliffs, N.J., 1961, pp. 471–485.

package size grows. Such pricing allows, in fact, a quantity discount for the buyer of the larger pack. The manufacturer does this partly because he can economize on the production and distribution costs of larger sizes as compared with the smaller ones. This policy may also be an effective way of sales promotion. If the consumer buys the equivalent of his monthly requirement instead of his weekly one, he will live in a state of compulsory brand loyalty for a month and will have no opportunity each week of choosing from competing brands.

Pricing replacement parts

Where products are differentiated the producer often has more pricing freedom in respect of replacement parts than in the original equipment itself. Once the consumer has bought a certain type of good he may not have a choice in buying replacement parts as the manufacturer of the original equipment is sometimes the only source of supply. Despite this monopoly situation, the manufacturer cannot fix replacement prices beyond a certain level. Exorbitant replacement prices may depress the sales of the original product itself, as consumers may inquire about spare-part prices before buying. In the case of a large demand for replacement parts, the buying firm may decide to manufacture them in its own workshop or get them manufactured on special orders elsewhere. The unit price of such alternatives is an obvious upper limit for pricing spare parts.

As in the case of other products, it may be advantageous not to have a neat relationship between sizes and prices of replacement parts. Demand considerations may override the benefit of giving equal treatment to consumers, and prices may be set according to the volume of demand, and the competition by alternative sources of supply, in different product sizes.

An illustration of replacement parts pricing can be found in the Monopolies Commission's report on electrical equipment for motor cars. Ignition coils, batteries, dynamos, windscreen-wiper motors, instruments, lamps and sparking plugs are generally bought from specialist firms and not made by the car manufacturer. The same electrical goods are also needed by the car-repair trade and the car-owning public. The Commission found that the major suppliers of these goods applied a substantial degree of price discrimination between the car manufacturers as buyers of the initial equipment on the one hand, and the distributive trade through which replacement parts reach the consumer on the other. The costs of supplying these two types of buyer are different, as components for initial equipment are normally delivered in bulk while replacement parts are individually packed and distributed to a large number of selling points. The price differentials established by the makers, however, went far beyond actual cost differentials and they earned a disproportionately higher profit on replacement parts than on initial equipment. The industry argued before the Commission that they were forced to quote very low prices to the powerful initial equipment buyers because otherwise they would have gone into the production of these components themselves. It was also argued that the consumer got the benefit of the low initial equipment price in the form of a lower price of the car itself.

The Commission rejected the industry's defence with the following words:

> We think that all of the monopoly suppliers in varying degrees have used price differentiation between initial equipment and replacements as a method of establishing and maintaining their own dominance and find the practice an effective and convenient way of minimizing the opportunities for competition to obtain a footing in the market ... the volume of future demand for replacements is largely affected, if not determined, by the volume of sales of initial equipment, so that replacement prices can to some extent be arbitrarily fixed. We believe ... that the practice is pursued for the purpose of maintaining market dominance and that the position of dominance so achieved can be used to secure an excessive rate of profit overall. We regard the practice, therefore, as objectionable in principle and against the public interest, in as much as it tends to perpetuate the dominance of individual component manufacturers in their particular fields, eliminating competition and providing opportunities for excessive profits.[10]

Renting

Manufacturers of certain durable goods, like business machines, conveyors, and special kinds of other machinery, sometimes follow a distribution and pricing policy where they do not sell the article

[10] 'Report on the Supply of Electrical Equipment for Mechanically Propelled Land Vehicles', 1963, paras. 990–996.

but rent it for shorter or longer periods. They may require either a rental payment fixed on a time basis, or they may quote a basic rent plus an additional charge in proportion to the actual use of the machine while in the possession of the client.

Xerox has made an impressive success with such a price policy in the United States. This company patented a new type of copying machine which could give legible dry copies quickly and did not require the use of any special paper. Deliveries started in 1960 and the machine (914 copier) has been described as probably the most profitable single product ever manufactured in America. The whole market expanded rapidly, from $200 million in 1960 to $700 million in 1966, and while Xerox commanded 38 per cent of the market in 1963, its share was 61 per cent in 1966 with 190,000 machines. Customers pay a fixed rental fee and a charge based on the number of copies they turn out. The cost of a copier is about $2,000 and, on an average, a machine brings in about $4,000 a year. The proportion of Xerox machines is not high, about one in five of the total number of copiers used, but they clearly dominate the high end of the market where most copies are made.[11]

Renting is a distribution practice adopted not only by manufacturers but also by retailers. Radio, television and car rentals are well-known examples in this field. When the period of renting is long this type of arrangement shows similarities with instalment selling.

The industrial buyer

A distinction is often made between the consumer as an amateur buyer – unable to make the best buying decision in respect of all the goods he needs – and the industrial buyer as an expert. The latter is described as being entirely objective while conducting business, in contrast with the consumer, who can also be influenced by emotional motives. Buying is a highly skilled job in industry, trade and agriculture and special experience is also required from the institutional buyer who purchases for schools, hospitals, central and local government, the armed forces, etc.

When selling products to the industrial and institutional buyer the manufacturer places special emphasis on quality, service and

[11] *Fortune*, November 1966, pp. 140–143.

price. Advertising will attempt to give information on these elements at the expense of pure persuasion. The industrial buyer investigates prices in detail, sometimes checking the pricing procedure of the supplier step by step. The price scrutiny of the industrial buyer has been described by an engineering company:

> Shortly before the production deliveries start, our own cost estimators and their counterparts from our customers get down to the question of price. Our customers' engineers are at least as knowledgeable as we are in these matters and from our detailed prints they prepare material costs and operation sheets with the appropriate costs of every part, and thus establish a target figure. In more than one case a customer has full access to our records, our methods, and our plant, and our own estimates are checked item by item and operation by operation with theirs. Sometimes our estimates are lower than theirs, in which case it is accepted and included in the final figure. In other cases theirs are lower than ours, in which case a discussion takes place to find out whether the methods and processes which they have suggested can, in fact, be achieved. Overhead charges are examined in the same way, and ultimately a total price is arrived at, which normally includes a profit of $2\frac{1}{2}$ per cent to 5 per cent. This price is not altered unless there is a major variation up or down in the costs of materials or labour, but costs are usually re-examined at least once a year during the continuance of the particular model.[12]

In spite of the predominance of quality, service and price, the industrial buyer also pays attention to such factors as the manufacturer's reliability in keeping delivery dates and maintaining uniform quality over a long period of time. The supplier with a good record in these respects may be able to command a higher price than his competitors.

[12] R. S. Edwards and H. Townsend, *Business Growth*, London, 1966, p. 266.

CHAPTER 6

Retail pricing

Retail markets

The nature of retail markets is a controversial issue in business literature. According to one opinion, retailing is an inherently imperfect sector of the economy where each retailer enjoys some monopoly power by virtue of the location of his shop, the selection of goods he carries, and the services he offers. It is pictured as a system of local oligopolies where a small number of retailers tacitly agree to share the market, apply customary margins, and are wary of upsetting the balance of power among themselves. The result of this is wide margins, high prices, and an excessive number of retail outlets operating below capacity level. This inefficiency is aided by the average consumer, whose knowledge about the variety of goods, qualities and prices is imperfect, and he is often not prepared to spend time seeking out the best buys. The nearest shop is patronized as a matter of convenience. Because of these factors, it has been stated that 'There is no doubt that the retail market is extremely imperfect: the sales of a retailer do not take place at prices determined by forces outside his control (except when they are fixed by the manufacturer), but are, within limits, determined by the price which he sets.'[1]

Various measures have been suggested to make this sector of the economy more efficient, ranging from the further extension of the co-operative movement into retailing to the restriction of the number of retail outlets by licensing, price control and the abolition of resale price maintenance.

Other commentators reject these views and emphasize the competitive nature of retail markets.[2] The history of modern retailing shows many examples where innovators used price appeal to take

[1] Henry Smith, *Retail Distribution*, London, 1937, p. 127.
[2] Julia Hood and B. S. Yamey, 'Imperfect Competition in Retail Trade', *Economica*, May 1951, pp. 119–137.

business away from traditional traders. Co-operative retailing in the second half of the last century was an attack on the traditional small shop charging high prices and giving credit to its customers. Consumers welcomed lower prices, cash payment and minimum service. Department stores and multiples also operated on the principle of high turnover and low prices, and by the turn of the century they were in the forefront of the changing retailing scene. Between the two wars the variety chain-stores emerged, applying large-scale retailing techniques over a wide range of low-priced goods. The cut-price grocery shop was a product of the 1930's. Finally, the rapid spread of self-service shops, supermarkets and discount houses after the last war was also the result of the successful application of the high turnover, minimum service, and competitive prices idea.

One cannot say, however, that the history of retailing consists only of a continuous flow of low-price retailers replacing high-price shops. Certain organizations have found that, after an initial breaking into the market by price appeal, it paid to offer more services and higher-quality goods, in other words 'to trade up'. Many examples of this can be found among department stores and multiples and a similar tendency can be detected among the discount stores in the United States. This process has been described as 'the wheel of retailing'. The hypothesis – though general validity is not claimed – states that new types of retailers usually enter the market as low-margin, low-price operators. Gradually they acquire better premises with higher investments and operating costs. Finally, they tend to become high-cost, high-price shops, vulnerable to new types of retailers who go through the same process. Department stores, for example, were vigorous competitors in the beginning and later became vulnerable to discount houses and supermarkets.[3]

The rapid advance of large-scale retailers proves that price appeal has been an effective competitive device because many consumers are prepared to compare prices and patronize low-price shops. The monopolistic position of favourably located retail shops has been considerably weakened in recent decades by the increased mobility of consumers. Improved public transport, the spread of car-ownership, and free Saturdays for a large proportion

[3] Stanley C. Hollander, 'The Wheel of Retailing', *Journal of Marketing*, July 1960, pp. 37–42.

of the population have facilitated shopping some distance away. New types of retailing methods, like mail-order, telephone buying and mobile shops, have extended the shopping alternatives available to the consumer. As average incomes have considerably increased, and many more families own cars and refrigerators, there is a trend towards less frequent shopping for food and household items. With the increase in the size of the average purchase it is more advantageous for the consumer to seek out the cheaper, though perhaps more distant, retail shop. Facing these developments, local corner-shops are forced to improve their efficiency, otherwise they cannot survive for long. They have already gone a long way by joining co-operative buying groups and wholesaler-sponsored voluntary chains.

The competitive pressure in retailing is also maintained by the constant flow of newcomers. Though many of these fail to succeed, and leave the field after a short time, the fact remains that entry into retailing is perhaps the easiest of all trades. Relatively small capital is necessary for a start, and no qualification is needed in this country. Therefore, if excessive profits are earned by retailers in a certain area, new competitors enter and profits are forced down.

Retail markets show signs of pronounced imperfections only in certain respects, where free competition cannot play its regulatory role. Resale price maintenance by manufacturers eliminates price competition among retailers. If it is widespread in a trade it results in high margins, and an excessive number of retail shops are kept in business. (Chapter 9 is devoted to the discussion of the main issues concerning this restrictive practice.) The other anti-competitive force in retailing may be government interference. Two examples of restricted competition, because of public regulations, are petrol-retailing and the off-licence trade.

Planning regulations have created small local groups of petrol stations competing with each other. Total sales in a local market are largely beyond the influence of retailers because they depend on the number of cars and the traffic flow in the area. In the circumstances price competition is a 'masochistic strategy'.[4] Price-cutting would benefit the group only if it increased sales, but as the volume sold remains virtually unchanged when prices are cut, all

[4] Harry Townsend, 'Competition in Petrol Retailing', *Three Banks Review*, March 1966, p. 23.

retailers suffer. In general, fairly stable prices and competition in service is typical of petrol-retailing. Still, competitive forces cannot be suppressed even under such conditions. When circumstances change price competition breaks out. This happened in the spring of 1967. As retail margins in the British petrol trade were the highest in Europe from the early 1960's, cut-price petrol companies began to operate. By 1967 they had about 10 per cent of the market and their continuous growth challenged the established position of the large companies. Esso, a subsidiary of the American Standard Oil Company of New Jersey, decided to counteract in March, 1967, and cut its prices by up to fourpence per gallon. Shell-Mex and British Petroleum countered Esso's challenge with a cut of up to threepence per gallon. Other companies followed suit.[5]

Another example where free competition in retailing is hampered by state interference is the off-licence trade. Licences for selling alcoholic drinks can be obtained from the licensing justices, who are usually local magistrates. The granting of a licence, in principle, depends on consumer need, the suitability of premises, and the proper administration of the business. Existing licence-holders nearly always register their objection to new applications, claiming that the area is already well served by off-licence shops and pubs. In the great majority of cases their opposition is successful. Under the present system, existing licencees, many of whom belong to the brewing industry, are protected from the competition of supermarkets. Only about 150 out of the 1,900 supermarkets held licences in 1966.[6] Licensed supermarkets immediately took the opportunity to reduce prices when the Distillers Company decided not to apply for exemption under the Resale Prices Act, 1964. Some of the 11,000 licensed grocers also followed the example.

Apart from these exceptional areas, competition is more or less active in retailing. As compared with other areas of business it is, in fact, one of the most competitive sectors of the economy.

Retail costs

It is an everyday experience of the consumer that the same article is offered at various prices in different shops. This cannot be attributed simply to the lack of effective price competition in

[5] *Financial Times*, March 2, 1967.   [6] *The Times*, April 21, 1966.

retailing. Prices may be out of line because of market imperfections, but the major factor behind the variety of retail prices for a certain good is the difference in the costs of running various shops. The price paid for an article in a shop is a payment, not only for the article, but for a certain amount of service linked with it. There is a considerable variation in the amount of service provided by various shops. One store, located in an exclusive street, is sumptuously furnished, stocks a large range of goods of all qualities and sizes, employs expert sales staff, and maintains a free delivery service. Another shop, situated in an 'ordinary' street, is without any luxurious fittings, the customer has to select from a few of the most popular lines without the advice of a sales assistant, queues to pay at the till, and takes care of delivery himself. It is obvious that the operation costs of the two shops will differ vastly. The former pays higher rent, needs more shelf space, more capital is tied up in stocks, and pays a higher wage bill than the other shop. The difference in costs is reflected in prices, and retail prices will vary even under extremely competitive conditions. Various shops cater for the needs of different classes of buyers who classify themselves, voluntarily, into one group or another and pay accordingly. Only an artificial restriction on competition, like resale price maintenance, can eliminate this natural retail price pattern. Otherwise retail prices vary because the various classes of shops are not in direct competition with each other. Effective competition is within their own ranks. Bond Street shops compete with each other and with Knightsbridge boutiques, but not with suburban back-street shops and market stalls. A top-class London fashion house competes for custom with his equivalent couturier in Paris, rather than with a low-price shop two streets away.

A further source of difference in the costs of various shops stems from their buying activity. In many trades skilful buying can increase turnover and reduce costs. A good selection of lines attracts customers, keeps down spoilage and prevents price-cuts to clear excessive stocks. The other aspect of buying is to find the cheapest source of supply. Large-scale retailers usually have a definite advantage in this respect. Because of their large orders they earn quantity rebates and, as a consequence of their bargaining power, they may also be able to negotiate special discounts with manufacturers. (More will be said about discounts and rebates in Chapter 11.)

Retail costs fall into two main categories: the cost of goods sold and the operating expenses. The former is obviously a variable cost, while operating expenses are partly variable and partly fixed costs. The characteristic feature of retailing is that a large proportion of operating costs are fixed in the short run; in other words, they do not change with turnover increases or decreases. Rent, managerial salaries, wages of sales staff, heating and electricity expenses, depreciation of fixtures, etc., do not change within fairly wide turnover limits. They may change, however, in the long run. Successful shops may employ additional staff above a certain level of sales or may extend their premises. Conversely, other retailers may follow declining sales by economizing on overheads. Variable operating costs, such as transport, packing materials, sales commissions to staff, etc., are usually of lesser importance among retail costs. The important consequence of this cost structure is that the operating cost per transaction declines sharply as sales expand, because the same amount of overhead costs are spread over a larger volume of turnover.

This preponderance of short-run overhead costs explains why the degree of success in retailing depends partly on how closely a shop can be operated to capacity, as only those which operate under optimum cost conditions are able to quote relatively low prices.

Pricing

When discussing manufacturers' pricing policies in the previous chapter, it was pointed out that price cannot be looked at in isolation, as it is only one of the factors of the marketing mix. The same applies to the retail trade. All aspects of the retail marketing mix must be harmonized – including prices – according to the principles of a general business policy. Every retailer must decide, first of all, which class of consumers he wants to attract, whether he will run a high-class store with an emphasis on service, or a shop with a mass appeal, or a compromise between the two types.

This primary decision will influence his choice of shop location to a large extent. The impact of competition varies with location and this, in turn, has a bearing on the pricing policy of the retailer. Some exceptional retail outlets enjoy the custom of a virtually captive public, like shops operating at sports matches, theatres, the catering services of trains, and those in far-away isolated places. In spite of increased consumer mobility, it is perhaps true to say that the private shop in convenient locations, usually selling convenience goods, still has more pricing freedom than high street operators. High street shops are forced to quote keener prices because their competitors are only a few steps away, and customers are able to compare prices without much effort once they have taken the trouble to go to the high street area.

Every retailer has to make a decision about the various other aspects of business policy as well. He must decide whether counter service, self-service or self-selection is to be adopted, about the quality and range of merchandise to be stocked, about the number and quality of sales staff, whether sales on credit should be made, about delivery service, advertising policy, pricing, etc. The particular combination of all these elements will bring about a certain level of fixed costs, which should be allocated among the turnover of various lines. The total overhead costs, plus the variable part of operating costs, plus the minimum net profit considered necessary to stay in business, will set the minimum gross profit target the retailer should aim at.

Relative prices

Almost invariably, retail firms are multi-product firms. They sell more than one line and often, as in supermarkets, 4,000–5,000 lines. Under such circumstances the pricing problem of individual lines is interrelated; retail pricing is essentially *joint pricing*. The retailer's main interest is the profit he earns on his total turnover, not the profitability of individual lines.

The distinction between fixed and variable operating costs is often only of theoretical importance. In practice it may be held that it is not worthwhile to separate them, to cost each line as accurately as possible. To spare administrative expense, total operating costs are often considered for pricing purposes.

The allocation of operating costs among the various goods carried always contains some arbitrary elements. The crudest way is to use a uniform percentage mark-up for the pricing of all lines. This is, essentially, the application of the average-cost method, also used in manufacturing industries, according to which every article must carry a share of overheads proportional to its value.

The merit of this method is its simplicity, but its mechanical application could be self-defeating for the retailer. It disregards actual costs of selling various lines and does not pay any attention to the demand side of pricing.

A more refined approach to retail pricing takes into account the turnover of various lines, the slow-moving and fast-moving items, competitors' prices and other relevant factors, and applies a range of mark-ups rather than one general mark-up. These margins are often widely used across the whole trade and are referred to, therefore, as 'customary mark-ups'. They usually demonstrate the fact that price competition tends to concentrate on fast-moving lines since the consumer buys them frequently and often remembers the price.

Supermarket mark-ups, for example, range from 6 per cent to 35 per cent. At the lower end of the scale there is tea with about 6 per cent and sugar with a 7 per cent margin. Butter and cigarettes average 10 per cent. This margin is not the same for the varieties of a particular product group. Coffee, for example, commands a 13 per cent average margin, but, within the average, the fast-moving items earn a lower and the slow ones a higher figure. Similarly, bread averages 18 per cent but with a spread between varieties. Among the high-margin lines are frozen foods with 25 per cent, fresh fish with 30 per cent, and meat pies with 26 per cent. The special equipment required for frozen foods and the substantial wastage of fresh fish and meat pies are partly responsible for their high margins. Non-food items like china, glass and kitchen ware take higher margins. Slower-moving items outnumber fast lines, but account for a smaller proportion of turnover. Supermarkets expect to make their profits on the slower-moving items, since competition has forced down prices on the other items. There are also profit possibilities in fresh meats, cheeses and perishables where comparison of prices is more difficult for the customer than with branded goods.[7]

Another method of distributing operating costs is the use of square foot or foot-run of shelving, or the counter space, occupied by the various products as an allocation basis. This approach is no less arbitrary than the previous one. Shelf and counter space across the shop varies in sales promotional value. Detailed studies show that customers do not pay equal attention to every part of a large

[7] *The Economist*, May 6, 1967, p. 584.

store and there is often a definite difference in sales when the same product is stocked on the top, medium or bottom shelf. Furthermore, the sale of a line is also dependent on the articles displayed on the neighbouring shelves, since *they* may be the goods which attract the shopper to the particular part of the shop. The other difficulty is the false logic involved here. Allocation of space takes into account the margins of various lines, and those earning higher profits are given more shelf or floor space than the others. Thus space allocation itself is based on assumed prices when the aim of the exercise is, in fact, to *set* prices.[8]

The danger of these arbitrary cost allocations is that the retailer does not know the actual costs of handling a certain line and the actual net profit earned on it. To conduct a purposeful pricing policy he should know the actual contribution of various lines to his profit. There have been experiments to analyse retailing costs in depth. The McKinsey and Colonial studies in America are well known in this respect.

Under the sponsorship of General Foods Corporation, the McKinsey management consultant company prepared a study on pricing in American food retailing. The report states that in food distribution no function has been more neglected by management than pricing. It was found that, instead of hard thinking, the prices of competitors were often blindly followed. In other cases, the same prices were rigidly applied over vast territories by chain-stores, regardless of local competition. Historical margins were frequently used and management often did not know whether certain prices just covered costs, or were making a profit or a loss, as they had no information on the break-down of operating costs.

An experiment to find out whether there was a significant difference in the product-handling costs of various items was made. Sixteen dry grocery products were traced and studied, from their receipt at the warehouse, through storage to store delivery, and through all in-store functions like price-marking and shelving. Accordingly, handling costs were subdivided into three groups: warehouse costs, delivery costs and store costs, and within each group direct and indirect costs were distinguished. Time studies and statistics helped the inquiry. Substantial differences were found in the magnitude of direct costs among various products.

[8] W. G. McClelland, *Studies in Retailing*, Oxford, 1963, p. 93.

The report concluded that knowledge of cost elements would help retailers in pricing, in improving delivery methods and space management, and would be a starting-point for cost reduction. To make this practical, the report suggested that the 5,000 lines stocked by a supermarket could be divided into 100 groups with similar handling characteristics.[9]

Retailing costs were also analysed by the Colonial study which has already been mentioned in Chapter 4. This report broke down the total turnover of a sample of supermarkets into seven departments. Gross margins, operating costs, and net profits were studied and analysed. All expenses were allocated as far as possible on a direct use basis. Two service departments were set up for reasons of cost allocation: the 'front-end' department for the checkout operation and a 'general' department for all other functions. Costs incurred in these two departments were treated as indirect expenses and reallocated among the selling departments, on the basis of each selling department's share of units handled by the checkout or according to percentage of sales. The study showed that gross margins were not in line with costs throughout the whole store. Margins in the various departments varied according to competition, tradition, season, etc. Departments with relatively small turnover, such as produce, frozen foods, health and beauty aids, and other non-foods, contributed to net profits to a larger extent than their share in total turnover. Health and beauty aids, for instance, accounted for 3 per cent of total turnover and for 13 per cent of total profits. Other non-foods, equally, had a 3 per cent share of turnover and earned 10 per cent of profits. On the other hand, strong competition forced down margins in the meats, dairy, grocery and bakery products departments. Meats commanded a 24 per cent share of turnover but only 8 per cent of total net profit. Ten per cent of the turnover was made on dairy products but only 6 per cent of profits were generated by this department. Groceries had a 45 per cent turnover, and with about a 46 per cent share they were the main contributors to net profits. Finally, bakery products contributed by 4 per cent to both the turnover and the profit of the stores.[10]

[9] 'The Economics of Food Distribution', *McKinsey – General Foods Study*, October 1963.

[10] 'Colonial Study', A Report on Supermarket Operations and Customer Habits, *Progressive Grocer*, 1964, pp. 73–80.

Selective price-cutting

Whenever a retailer wants to give a boost to his sales by price-cutting he is confronted with the choice of a general low-price policy – spread over the whole range of stock – or selective price-cutting. Most students of retailing would agree that a few dramatic price-cuts on a limited number of items will be more conducive to increasing turnover than a small reduction on all goods. It has already been mentioned that it is a generally accepted view that the consumer remembers only a small sample of prices. Therefore, a marginal reduction on all prices may remain unnoticed.

In respect of frequently purchased items, the consumer is likely to notice the reduction but, if it is very small, he will not be impressed. There are opinions that below a certain level price-cuts are an ineffective promotional device. But selective price-cutting should not, necessarily, be confined to a few lines; a group of items or a whole department may be chosen. The Great Atlantic and Pacific Tea Company, for example, sometimes fought against local competition by selecting a department, like meat, where all prices were kept at an especially low level.[11]

All goods stocked in a shop compete for the attention of the consumer. Still, from the point of view of selective price-cutting, goods fall into two categories: competitive and complementary goods. Competitive goods are substitutes for each other and, therefore, a price-cut in one of them will increase its own demand at the expense of demand for its substitutes. Sale of complementary goods, on the other hand, will react favourably to the price-cut and, if the article and the degree of price reduction is correctly selected, it will result in a higher overall net return. A price reduction on a line which will attract more customers should result in an increased volume in sales of complementary goods, which will more than compensate for the loss on the line that has been cut in price. A special category of selective price-cutting is the so-called loss-leader tactic.

Loss-leaders

Loss-leader tactics have been the centre of much controversy in business and political circles. The term 'loss-leader' usually denotes

[11] A. D. H. Kaplan, Joel B. Dirlam, Robert F. Lanzillotti, *Pricing in Big Business*, Washington, D.C., 1958, p. 182.

an extreme form of selective price-cutting, where a certain brand is offered to the public at less than its wholesale price, or at less than the wholesale price plus a certain proportion of overheads.

It is alleged that loss-leader selling is an unethical business practice which works against the interest of the consumer, the manufacturer and other retailers. Antagonists of loss-leader selling claim that it misleads consumers. They are lured into the shop by the attractiveness of a bargain which gives the impression that the shop follows an all-round low price policy. Once they are in the shop, however, other articles are sold to them at normal or even above normal price to make good the price-cut on the loss-leader. If other prices are not raised, the retailer may make additional charges for credit, or delivery, or cut out certain services. It may also happen that the weak points of a product, which has been advertised at a sensationally low price, are pointed out to the customer once *in* the shop, and he is persuaded to buy another article on which a higher margin is earned. This variety of loss-leader tactics is called 'bait-selling' or 'switch-selling'.

The manufacturer's interest is alleged to be prejudiced in more than one way if his brand is selected for loss-leader tactics. Dramatic price-cuts may destroy the high-quality image of a product built up by him, shoppers lose confidence in it and sales decrease. Furthermore, where a certain brand is singled out as a loss-leader by a shop, other retailers may also cut its price to meet competition. Price-cutting of the brand may spread further, lowering retail margins so much that the shopkeepers lose interest in it and will recommend other makes to their customers, or they may stop stocking it altogether and substitute it with alternative goods offering a higher profit.

Retailers making deep price-cuts are also accused of spoiling the market for certain goods and unsettling the orderly process of distribution. Such a pricing policy, it is argued, may lead to price wars, to the detriment of both the retail trade and the manufacturers.

The problems arising out of loss-leader selling are often exaggerated. It is not easy, in the first place, to define loss-leader tactics precisely. There is no definition of the practice which could give guidance in every conceivable case. One solution could be to stipulate the wholesale price as the floor below which retail prices are labelled as loss-leaders. This would be a less controversial definition, but even this could not be applied to every situation. Some retailers of fashion goods, for instance, follow a pricing policy of quoting prices well above the invoice price at the beginning of the season, later they drop it to a lower level and, at the end of the season, they sell out the remaining stock below the wholesale price to clear the shelves for new goods. They think in terms of making a reasonable profit on certain lines over the whole season, averaging high and normal profits with losses. It would be unreasonable to call the last stage of this pricing policy loss-leader selling. The difficulty of definition is even greater when one tries to define the floor as invoice cost plus expenses incurred to sell the article in question. Overhead costs are usually distributed according to an arbitrary formula and may not have a direct relationship with actual costs. This definition would require retailers to allocate their costs in such a way that all goods stocked carry a proportionate part of overheads, and this is not always the practice.

Apart from the problem of definition, the case against loss-leader selling can be refuted on many grounds. The argument of consumer gullibility does not hold much water. It is contradictory to allege that the consumer is price conscious enough to discover the low price of the loss-leader, but unable to see that other prices in the shop are high, or that the purpose of the bargain-offer was to persuade him to buy later another product instead of the loss-leader. Retailers do not need, necessarily, to raise prices of other goods when making deep cuts on certain lines, since they may achieve higher profit from selling a larger volume of other goods at the old price. Extra charges for credit, or delivery, or the absence of certain expected service may also be noticed and taken into account by consumers. It is also arguable whether price-cutting destroys confidence in a product. In certain exceptional cases, such as when high-class luxury goods are involved, this may be so, but this is not the general pattern. Well-established leading brands, which, as a rule, are selected for loss-leader purposes, are unlikely to lose the consumer's trust as the brand name itself guarantees the expected quality.

It is also debatable whether the interest of the manufacturer is harmed if his product is selected for loss-leader tactics. Price-cutting of a certain brand often boosts its sales and is welcomed by the manufacturer. Loss-leaders enjoy, usually, a prominent position on the market and retailers would find it difficult to discontinue stocking these brands, or to divert demand to other higher-priced brands. Price wars are rare – and short-lived – phenomena in retailing. It is, however, in the nature of things, that the more efficient retailers are ready to enlarge their sales by undercutting the others. Whether it is done by a general reduction of prices or by selective price-cutting does not make much difference. The dividing line between selective price-cutting and loss-leader selling is blurred. In practice loss-leader tactics usually just turn out to be cases of competitive pricing. Cases of selling below cost are few and far between. After the abolition of resale price maintenance in Canada in 1951, a survey was conducted into the effects of loss-leader selling by the Restrictive Trade Practices Commission. The report stated that

> in the opinion of the Commission this very considerable amount of evidence, which is derived from the many sources indicated, supports the conclusion that the practice of selling articles at prices below net purchase cost is not prevalent in any of the lines of trade for which information was obtained in the inquiry. In fact it appears that sales on such a basis are made infrequently and the evidence does not suggest in any way that selling of this sort is a practice in any line of trade, even among a minority of the dealers.[12]

Multiple pricing

Retail prices usually refer to one unit. It has been observed, however, that sales can be boosted by offering two, three or more, units for a price. This pricing technique is called multiple pricing.

There is an old story that a retailer was not able to clear his stock of a certain article at sixpence each. He offered them at 1s. 6d. for three, and sales soared. This may not be a true story, but it is not an impossible one. The Colonial study shows that multiple pricing can be an effective sales promotional device. Changes to multiple pricing in Colonial shops, as a rule, resulted in increased sales and, conversely, sales dropped when multiple pricing was discontinued.

There are certain rules that should be observed when embarking on multiple pricing. The first is that a multiple price-offer has to appear to be a saving for the consumer, otherwise he will not buy.

[12] 'Restrictive Trade Practices Commission', Report on an Inquiry into Loss-leader Selling, Ottawa, 1955, p. 244.

This saving may be an imaginary or a real one but the consumer must *think* that he is getting a reduction. During the Colonial experiment two articles were offered at multiple prices without offering any saving. One of them was a branded tomato juice. Its regular price was 33 cents a bottle and, during the test, three of them were offered at 99 cents. Sales increased by 70 per cent. The other article was a well-known canned meat and the experiment was designed to test the consumers' reaction when 'customary multiple pricing' was changed to larger offers. The customary price for the canned meat in question was two for 25 cents. During the experiment six units were on sale for 75 cents. Sales remained virtually at the old level; consumers did not respond to the new offer!

In all other cases in the test, multiple prices were set slightly below individual unit prices, e.g. a 23 cent product was offered for 45 cents for two, thus offering a genuine but small saving to the consumer. Similarly, when multiple prices were reverted to unit prices during the experiment, the single unit was priced slightly higher, e.g. a three for 25 cents cocktail juice was priced at 9 cents per unit. Almost invariably, sales increased when multiple prices were introduced and decreased when discontinued.

It is held that multiple pricing is aided if the arithmetic involved is fairly simple, as consumers dislike difficult mental exercises while shopping. The articles selected for multiple pricing should be those frequently bought by households, because consumers do not want to keep a large stock at home over a longer period. The effectiveness of the multiple price offer also depends on the availability, size and price of competing brands, and the alternative sizes and prices of the same brand. Larger sizes at lower prices compete with multiple-price offers of smaller sizes. If larger sizes offer a good saving, multiple pricing is less likely to be successful. The experience of Colonial stores was that the most effective area of multiple pricing was within the one dollar limit. Above this level consumers tended to think twice before buying a larger quantity to obtain a small saving.[13]

Customary prices

Certain retail prices have become traditions, the consumer is used to them and looks upon them as the 'right price' for the good

[13] 'Colonial Study', op. cit., pp. 128–132.

concerned. Such prices are sometimes termed 'customary prices'. The variations on the customary price theme are: price-lining, price-zoning, price-points, and below round figure prices.

Price-lining

Price-lining takes place both in respect of convenience goods and shopping goods. The public is used to the idea, for example, that a bar of chocolate is either 6d. or 1s. Manufacturers, consequently, believe that in the case of changing costs it is better to alter the quantity and leave the price of chocolate bars untouched. Some ice-cream manufacturers similarly believe that it is desirable to sell in units for which a single coin exists, like 6d. and 1s.[14]

In respect of articles of higher unit prices, price-lining does not necessarily take the form of a definite price but sometimes of a price-range (price-zoning). It is believed that the consumer can become confused with too many prices and, therefore, it is useful to channel prices into categories. The shopper often has a price or price-range in mind that he is prepared to pay for an article when entering a shop, and he may even indicate it to the sales staff. According to certain opinions, a minimum of three basic price-lines are necessary for each type of merchandise to cater for the low, medium and high-price demand.

Price-lining often involves standardization and is, therefore, advantageous to the retailer. The simplification of the price structure makes buying less complicated, a more complete range of sizes and colours can be stocked within the price-lines, prices may be decreased and a larger turnover achieved. It has also been claimed that self-selection of merchandise is facilitated by price-lining, so leading to further economies. However, price-lining introduces inflexibility into pricing. In an inflationary economy, established price-lines come under pressure sooner or later. Existing prices can only be maintained under such conditions if there is a deterioration in quality, or if the article, redesigned and given some extra feature, can be promoted to a higher price range. Whether a policy to this effect is advisable or not will depend on individual circumstances. Problems also arise in respect of certain goods when prices are falling. To maintain existing price-lines,

[14] Ronald S. Edwards and Harry Townsend, *Business Growth*, London, 1966, p. 186.

quality improvements may be introduced but it could still be competitively disadvantageous and it may be wiser to drop the price.[15]

A variation of the application of customary prices is the pricing policy of a certain price fixed for all goods sold by a department or by a shop. Alternatively, an upper limit may be introduced for all merchandise stocked, rather than a fixed price. Marks and Spencer Ltd., for example, has grown out of a penny bazaar. Michael Marks opened his first penny stall in Leeds market in 1884, where a wide variety of goods were on sale priced at a penny. This pricing policy could not survive the inflation during the First World War. In the inter-war years the company, impressed by American examples offering a wide range of goods within the dollar price limit, operated a five shilling price ceiling in its shops.[16] Woolworth made its initial success with a policy of not selling any article over the sixpenny price-point.

Odd prices

It is a widely held opinion in certain trades that the consumer shows a particularly strong price sensitivity at certain critical points. Many retailers think that a penny below the next shilling, or a sixpence below the next pound, increases sales because these prices seem to be lower than they are, and raising the price to the next shilling or pound would decrease sales disproportionately. Conversely, high-class retailers often assume that consumers are not much concerned with the odd additional shillings when the prices are quoted in guineas, and not in pounds, or even prefer paying guineas to pounds. A director of a cutlery manufacturing firm put it this way: 'How do we fix our prices? You know what a price is, don't you? 19s. 11d. is a price. At least it is for a hardware dealer. It would be 21s. in a jeweller's.'[17]

According to a British study, housewives favour the penny below round figure price in respect of some articles but not of others. Two markets were investigated; one was nylon stockings,

---

[15] Q. Forrest Walker, 'Some Principles of Department Store Pricing', *Journal of Marketing*, January 1950, pp. 529-537.

[16] *The Times*, May 18, 1966.

[17] Harry Townsend, 'Economic Theory and the Cutlery Trade', *Economica*, August 1954, p. 238.

where practically every brand under ten shillings is priced in this way, the other was an undisclosed market where this pricing practice was not customary. The outcome of the inquiry was that consumers' attitudes were conditioned by the long-standing practices of various markets.[18]

> We have concluded that the attitude depends largely on the price structure prevailing in a particular market. If sellers in the market are obsessed with the idea that 4/11 is a 'good' price, while 4/10 and 5/– are 'bad' prices, a certain proportion of the public will be induced to look upon 4/11 as a 'real' price and 5/– as a 'phoney', simply because no known brand happens to be available at this price. But where prices are fixed without attention to the 'penny-below' doctrine, no such idea will take root in the consumer's mind.[19]

The corresponding pricing practice in America often takes the form of quoting 49 instead of 50 cents, 79 instead of 80 cents, and 98 or 99 cents instead of a dollar. In the 1930's a large American mail order store experimented with these customary prices. The intention was to eliminate them if they proved to be of no special significance to sales, and thereby to economize on accounting expenses. They selected a group of items and priced them with rounded figures in several regional catalogues, while in the remainder of the edition the same commodities figured at customary prices. Detailed past and current figures about sales allowed the company to eliminate other variables to a reasonable degree. The result was perplexing. The change from customary to rounded prices halved the sales of some lines, left others unchanged and increased some considerably. On the whole, losses were balanced by gains and the experiment did not produce any conclusion.[20]

Money-off pricing

Manufacturers sometimes try to promote the sale of their brands by selling a certain quantity at a lower price to the retailer and by putting money-off labels on the packs. This pricing method is

[18] Andre Gabor and C. W. J. Granger, 'Price as an Indicator of Quality: Report on an Enquiry', *Economica*, February 1966, p. 61.

[19] Andre Gabor and C. W. J. Granger, 'Price Sensitivity of the Consumer', *Journal of Advertising Research*, December 1964, p. 43.

[20] Eli Ginzberg, 'Customary Prices', *American Economic Review*, June 1936, p. 296.

usually applied to food and toiletry products. Characteristically, the original price is not printed on the pack and the consumer is supposed to know the regular price of the article. Research has been carried out on sixty-five brands carrying money-off labels, marketed both in Britain and America. The investigation found that, below a reduction of 10 to 12 per cent, money-off promotion had little effect on the competitive position of a brand.[21] It is, therefore, more advisable for the manufacturer to offer a larger reduction on a smaller quantity of merchandise than to spread a smaller discount over a large volume. Pence-off promotions can give a temporary fillip to sales, but have no lasting effect on the long-term trend. It is a simple and flexible marketing device, it can be launched speedily and at low cost and, therefore, can be used to fight localized price competition.

Double pricing

Finally, mention should be made of double or dual pricing, a pricing method where two prices are shown on the price tag or on the pack of the article: the original higher price crossed out and substituted with a new low price. As we will see in Chapter 10, this pricing practice may raise issues of public policy.

[21] *Nielsen Researcher*, Oxford Edition, July–August 1964.

CHAPTER 7

Monopolies and restrictive practices: The institutional background

Before the Second World War common law regulated the area of monopolies and restrictive trade practices in Britain. As far back as 1299, for example, an English court decided that an agreement among candlemakers that none of them should sell a pound of candles at a lower price than the other was illegal.[1] Up to the seventeenth century legal practice was against restraints of trade. A more lenient line was gradually adopted later, leading to a complete reversal of the legal attitude. By the end of the last century, courts considered restrictive agreements as justifiable business tactics. In spite of this, in the decades before the First World War, restrictive practices were not an important feature of the British economy.

The First World War, the post-war slump and the world depression of the 1930's brought a substantial contraction in business competition. In 1931 the country abandoned the Gold Standard, and industry received substantial protection by the imposition of import duties in the following year. To secure satisfactory prices and eliminate surplus capacity, all sorts of restrictive agreements, like price-fixing, quota schemes, resale price maintenance, exclusive dealing arrangements, etc., became widespread in British industry. Large numbers of trade associations sprang up which regarded their chief task as the enforcement of these agreements by persuasion, fines, stop-lists and boycotts. Under pressure from interested parties, the government sometimes even provided legal sanctions for anti-competitive arrangements. Price-fixing and restriction on output were features of the Coal Mines Act of 1930, for example. The Cotton Industry Reorganization Act provided for minimum prices for yarn in 1939. Control over the marketing

[1] Fritz Machlup, *The Basing-point System*, Philadelphia, 1949, p. 1.

of agricultural products was introduced by the Agricultural Marketing Acts of 1931–33.

In the first half of this century there was a trend towards larger business units; industrial concentration was on the increase. Public opinion was often hostile, but changeable, about monopolies. The Committee on Trusts, in 1919, went so far as to recommend a tribunal to investigate abuses by dominant firms. Though a Monopolies Bill was actually drafted in the following year, no legislation was passed in this field in the inter-war years.

The Monopolies and Restrictive Practices Act, 1948

After the last war special committees investigated a number of industries with restrictive practices, such as the radio valves, cotton textile machinery, cement, building materials, etc., industries. These reports were reminders that restrictive practices can operate against the public good. In the climate of full employment and inflation there was a hardening of public opinion in respect of market domination and restrictive practices. In 1948 the Monopolies and Restrictive Practices (Inquiry and Control) Act was placed on the statute book.

The guiding principle of the Act was that monopolies and restrictive practices were not *per se* against the public interest; they required individual investigation. Accordingly, a case-by-case approach was adopted. An independent consultative body, the Monopolies and Restrictive Practices Commission, was set up and charged with the task of investigating and reporting on individual industries.

The Board of Trade was given power to select and refer cases for investigation to the Commission and was made responsible for the publication of yearly reports on the Commission's work. Membership of the Commission was limited to not less than four and not more than ten members, each to be appointed by the Board of Trade, for a period of three to seven years. The Board was also authorized to select one member as chairman. Until 1953, with the exception of the chairman and one other commissioner, members were engaged on a part-time basis. Among the appointed ten commissioners there were civil servants, academic economists, barristers, industrialists, an accountant and a trade union official.

The Act applied to conditions where at least one-third of the goods in question were supplied or processed in the United Kingdom, or in any substantial part of it, and where any one person or group of persons prevented or restricted competition, and where, as a result of an agreement or arrangement, goods were not supplied at all. It also applied to exports of commodities, the production of which took place under conditions of restricted competition. Prevention or restriction of competition could be the result of an agreement between firms, or of simply conducting their affairs in a way leading to restriction or the elimination of competition. Thus legislation covered the supply, processing and export of goods by monopolies and oligopolies. Practices relating to employment and wages were excluded. The supply of services came under the Act only when it was linked with the supply, processing or export of goods. Accordingly, the Act referred to wholesaling, retailing and other distributive activities, but not to pure services like insurance, banking, etc. Nationalized industries also remained outside the scope of the legislation.

The definition of what constitutes a commodity and what area can be considered as a substantial part of the United Kingdom remained questions open to interpretation by the Board of Trade and the Monopolies Commission. In actual fact the interpretation of these terms was not stringent. Commodities were classified in reasonably broad categories, and the Greater London Area and Central Scotland were considered as substantial parts of the country in two investigations.[2]

The idea of public interest was defined in a rather vague way in the Act. Section 14 stated that to determine whether a condition is against the public interest

... all matters which appear in the particular circumstances to be relevant shall be taken into account and, among other things, regard shall be had to the need, consistent with the general economic position of the United Kingdom, to achieve:

a the production, treatment and distribution by the most efficient and economical means of goods of such types and qualities, in such volume and at such price as will best meet the requirements of home and overseas markets;

b the organization of industry and trade in such a way that their

---

[2] 'Report on the Supply of Building in the Greater London Area', 1954, and the 'Report on the Supply of Sand and Gravel in Central Scotland', 1956.

efficiency is progressively increased and new enterprise is encouraged;

c the fullest use and best distribution of men, materials and industrial capacity in the United Kingdom; and

d the development of technical improvements and the expansion of existing markets and the opening up of new markets.

Where the Monopolies Commission finds that certain practices operate against the public interest, it may, being an advisory body, recommend appropriate action to remedy the situation prevailing in an industry. The Government is, however, not obliged to act on the recommendations of the Commission. The reports of the Commission are laid before Parliament by the Board of Trade and published. Issues of the publication which would damage business or public interest are not made public.

There are two ways open to the Government to bring about a change in the industries investigated by the Commission. The industry may voluntarily undertake to stop certain undesirable practices. If, at a later stage, the Board of Trade has reasons to believe that the industry has not honoured its voluntary undertaking, a follow-up reference may be made to the Monopolies Commission under section 12 of the Act. Such a reference was made, for example, in respect of the imported timber industry in 1957. Alternatively, the relevant Government department may issue a statutory order declaring certain arrangements unlawful. Contravention of such a statutory order is a civil offence. Orders were issued concerning dental goods in 1951, and imported timber after the follow-up report under section 12 of the Act in 1960. In the great majority of cases, however, the Government negotiated voluntary undertakings with the industries under reference. The implementation of the Monopolies Commission recommendations has often been subject to long delay in the past. In the case of electric cables, the Government acted more than two years after the publication of the report. Between the publication of the follow-up report into imported timber and the issue of a statutory order, two years also passed.

The general report

Section 15 of the Act empowered the Board of Trade to require the Commission to submit reports on the general effect on the public interest of various business practices adopted, which might come under the heading of monopolies and restrictive practices. Only one report of such general nature has been produced, on Collective Discrimination, published in 1955.[3] The report covered the following areas:

1 Collective discrimination by sellers, without any corresponding obligation on buyers
2 Collective discrimination by sellers in return for exclusive buying
3 Collective adoption by sellers of a policy of maintaining resale prices or imposing other collateral obligations on buyers
4 Collective discrimination by sellers to enforce resale prices or other contract terms
5 Collective discrimination by buyers, without any corresponding obligation on sellers
6 Aggregated rebates

The majority of the Commission concluded that these types of agreement were widespread in British industry and, in general, adversely affected the public interest, though in special circumstances the use of some of them might be justified. Accordingly, it was recommended that the practices in question should be prohibited by law, and provision be made for exemption on grounds which would be set out in the legislation. The minority of the Commission was against these findings. Instead, they recommended that all agreements and arrangements should be registered and subjected to detailed examination, to decide whether they were operating against the public interest and should or should not be prohibited.

An important omission of the general report was that its reference did not cover the most widespread restrictive practice, namely common and minimum price agreements. To amend this, a second general reference was made to the Commission during 1955. It was requested to report on common and minimum price agreements and level tendering. This reference was, however, withdrawn because of the measures to introduce new legislation, resulting in the Restrictive Trade Practices Act, 1956.

[3] 'Collective Discrimination': A Report on Exclusive Dealing, Collective Boycotts, Aggregated Rebates and other Discriminatory Trade Practices, Cmnd. 9504, 1955.

The Monopolies and Restrictive Practices Commission Act, 1953

The fact that the Commission was composed mainly of part-time members had the advantage that they remained in contact with practical business life, but it slowed down the pace of their work. Their first report, on dental goods, was published in 1950. In the following year two reports were made final (cast-iron rain-water goods, and electric lamps) and two more reports were published in 1952 (insulated electric wires and cables, and insulin). The Government was anxious to improve the Commission's work and, accordingly, the 1948 Act was amended five years later by the Monopolies and Restrictive Practices Commission Act, 1953.

The new Act was intended to strengthen the Commission. It increased the maximum membership from ten to twenty-five and permitted its division into working groups, each containing not less than five commissioners. In the following years the membership of the Commission was increased to sixteen, conducting their inquiries in two groups simultaneously. The new legislation helped to speed up the Commission's work to a certain extent. Between 1950 and 1956, that is before the second reorganization of the Commission as a result of the 1956 legislation, twenty reports were published on special industries, apart from the general report on Collective Discrimination. Of these twenty reports there were only three in which the main restrictive practice investigated was judged to be in the public interest. Thus the Commission underlined its appreciation of the virtues of competition.

The Restrictive Trade Practices Act, 1956

The Monopolies Commission's general report on Collective Discrimination paved the way towards new legislation in the field of monopolies and restrictive practices. The Restrictive Trade Practices Act was passed in 1956, and in this an important change was introduced in the fundamental approach towards restrictive practices. The 1948 Act followed the neutral approach. It was not presumed that restrictive practices, as such, were either in favour of or against the public interest. This issue had to be decided by the Monopolies Commission after having investigated specific industries. The 1956 Act, on the other hand, declares that restrictive practices are against the public interest unless their detrimental effects are outweighed by certain 'specific and substantial' benefits to the public.

The Act provides for the establishment of a new high court, the Restrictive Practices Court, and for the appointment of a Registrar of Restrictive Trading Agreements. The Court is composed of five judges and up to ten lay members, knowledgeable or experienced in industry, commerce or public affairs. Following the recommendation of the minority of the Commission in the general report on Collective Discrimination, the compulsory registration of all restrictive agreements was ordered and the new Court was called upon to judge whether or not the restrictions on competition were against the public interest. Whether it was an appropriate arrangement on the part of the Government, which bears the sole responsibility for economic policy, to pass on the power of investigating restrictive practices to the judiciary was questioned.[4]

The definition of an agreement is fairly wide in the 1956 legislation. The Act covers any understanding, whether oral or in writing, where restrictions are accepted by two or more parties in respect of prices, conditions of supply, quantities and qualities of goods, processes of manufacture applied, and classes of buyers and sellers. Firms which are members of trade associations are assumed to be parties to any agreement made by the association. The Act refers only to goods. Services and agreements with employees are outside the scope of the legislation and export agreements are also exempted. The term 'public' in the Act not only covers the consumer but also business firms as intermediate buyers and users of goods. No guidance is given, however, concerning the definition of public interest.

The criteria guiding the Court in its judgements are laid down in section 21 (1) of the Act. The Court is called upon to perform a double task when scrutinizing an agreement. First, it should judge whether the agreement confers some benefit on the public by virtue of one or more of the seven possible ways, usually referred to as 'gateways', enumerated in this section. In the second balancing act the Court is required to compare the benefits of the agreement with any detriment to the public arising from its operation. The onus of proof, that the beneficial effects of an agreement are

[4] C. Grunfeld and B. S. Yamey, 'Restrictive Trade Practices Act, 1956', *Public Law*, Winter 1956, pp. 316–317.

greater than the harm done to the public, rests with the defendant. Only those agreements can be approved of which the benefits outweigh the detriment. An agreement may, therefore, be beneficial in some respects but can still be declared to operate against the public interest under the scrutiny of the balancing act. The part of this section which deals with the balancing act is commonly known as the 'tailpiece'.

Section 21 (1) states that a restriction shall be held to be contrary to the public interest unless the Court is satisfied:

(a) that the restriction is reasonably necessary, having regard to the character of the goods to which it applies, to protect the public against injury (whether to persons or to premises) in connection with the consumption, installation or use of those goods;

(b) that the removal of the restriction would deny to the public as purchasers, consumers or users of any goods other specific and substantial benefits or advantages enjoyed or likely to be enjoyed by them as such, whether by virtue of the restriction itself or of any arrangements or operations resulting therefrom;

(c) that the restriction is reasonably necessary to counteract measures taken by any one person not party to the agreement with a view to preventing or restricting competition in or in relation to the trade or business in which the persons party thereto are engaged;

(d) that the restriction is reasonably necessary to enable the persons party to the agreement to negotiate fair terms for the supply of goods to, or the acquisition of goods from, any one person not party thereto who controls a preponderant part of the trade or business of acquiring or supplying such goods, or for the supply of goods to any person not party to the agreement and not carrying on such a trade or business who, either alone or in combination with any other such person, controls a preponderant part of the market for such goods;

(e) that, having regard to the conditions actually obtaining or reasonably foreseen at the time of the application, the removal of the restriction would be likely to have a serious and persistent adverse effect on the general level of unemployment in an area, or in areas taken together, in which a substantial proportion of the trade or industry to which the agreement relates is situated;

(f) that, having regard to the conditions actually obtaining or reasonably foreseen at the time of the application, the removal of the restriction would be likely to cause a reduction in the volume or earnings of the export business which is substantial either in relation to the whole export business of the United Kingdom or in relation to the whole business (including export business) of the said trade or industry; or

(g) that the restriction is reasonably required for purposes connected with the maintenance of any other restriction accepted by the parties, whether under the same agreement or under any other agreement between them, being a restriction which is found by the Court not to be contrary to the public interest upon grounds other than those specified in this paragraph, or has been so found in previous proceedings before the Court,

and is further satisfied (in any such case) that the restriction is not unreasonable having regard to the balance between those circumstances and any detriment to the public or to persons not parties to the agreement (being purchasers, consumers or users of goods produced or sold by such parties, or persons engaged or seeking to become engaged in the trade or business of selling such goods or of producing or selling similar goods) resulting or likely to result from the operation of the restriction.

The Registrar is responsible for keeping records of restrictive agreements. The register is open to public inspection. All agreements remain on the register, even if they have been terminated, with the exception of those removed by the Board of Trade according to section 12 of the Act as having no substantial economic significance. It is also the duty of the Registrar to prepare and select cases for the Court.

No special sanction was created by the Act to enforce the decisions of the Court. Any restriction found by the Court to be against the public interest is declared to be void. Upon the application of the Registrar under section 20 the Court can 'make such order as appears to the Court to be proper' to enforce the judgement or prevent the defendant making any other agreement to the like effect.

Section 22 provides for variations of Orders of the Court. Application can be made by the Registrar, or by a party to the agreement, upon evidence that there has been a material change in the circumstances in an industry. Upon the application of a party to an agreement, the Court's decision condemning an agreement can be reversed. Equally, the Registrar may apply to change a favourable decision to the contrary if there is sufficient evidence that circumstances have significantly changed.

The registration procedure revealed that restrictive agreements were not evenly spread in the economy. Some major industries, like cement, carpets, farming and paint, registered only a few agreements. Others, such as food, building, iron and steel, textiles and road-making, reported more than 150 agreements each.[5] In June 1966 the register contained 2,550 restrictive agreements. 2,110 of these agreements had previously been partly brought to an end by the parties and had been partly varied so as to remove all restrictions from them; others expired and were not renewed.[6]

A number of weaknesses of the 1956 Act have been pointed out by the Registrar. First of all, there is no penalty for failure to submit an agreement for registration. If the Registrar has reasonable cause to believe that a firm or a trade association may be a party to an agreement subject to registration, a notice may be sent out requiring information. Failure to comply with such a notice, or making a false statement, does constitute an offence, but cases undetected by the Registrar remain unpunished. In his first report the Registrar stated that about 10 per cent of registrations had resulted from enforcement procedures.[7] The proportion of new registrations due to enforcement procedures later increased steadily, and in the period covered by the fourth report (July 1, 1963, to June 30, 1966) it amounted to three-quarters of the new registrations. The Registrar remarked: '. . . I believe that this failure to comply with the law is too often due to the wider realization that no ill befalls parties who do not register, and that once registered their agreements' chances of survival are slim.'[8]

Another loophole of the Act is that information agreements can be operated without registration and achieve the same effects as common price agreements. (This problem will be discussed in the next chapter.)

The Registrar was also troubled by the obligation placed upon him by a House of Lords decision in 1963, according to which all registered agreements, whether subsisting or determined, should be referred to the Restrictive Practices Court. This, he found, was unnecessary and wasteful, as it was more important to refer live

---

[5] 'Registrar of Restrictive Trading Agreements', Report for the Period 7th August 1956 to 31st December 1959, Cmnd. 1273, January 1961, para. 37.
[6] 'Restrictive Trading Agreements', Report of the Registrar, 1st July 1963 to 30th June 1966, Cmnd. 3188, pp. 7–8.
[7] Cmnd. 1273, op. cit., para. 26.   [8] Cmnd. 3188, op. cit., pp. 2–5.

agreements to the Court than dead ones. To deal with this problem a radical change in the law was suggested. The Registrar proposed to make it unlawful to enter into an agreement which should be subject to registration, or to amend an existing agreement without the leave of the Court. The Court would give leave if it appeared that the agreement was not contrary to the public interest. When making this suggestion, the line of reasoning adopted by the Registrar was that, as previously less than 1 per cent of all registered agreements had been found to be consistent with the public interest, the present freedom of making and operating agreements until the law catches up with them can serve the public good only in very few cases.

Finally, it was pointed out by the Registrar that the order made by the Court concerning an agreement which has been found to be contrary to the public interest may be too narrow to prevent the parties making another agreement which may achieve the same purpose as the terminated one.

The new status of the Monopolies Commission

After the enactment of the 1956 Act the Monopolies and Restrictive Practices Commission ceased to investigate restrictive trade practices relating to the home market and was renamed the Monopolies Commission. The maximum number of commissioners was reduced from twenty-five back to ten and the provision of the 1953 amending Act, allowing the setting up of working groups, was repealed. After the 1956 Act the Monopolies Commission concerned itself with the following conditions:

First, single firm monopolies where the firm or group of related concerns supplies, processes or, in cases of exports, produces one-third of the goods in the United Kingdom.

Secondly, where two or more firms together are responsible for at least one-third of the supply of a good, prevent or restrict competition in a way which renders it an agreement not subject to registration under the same Act.

Thirdly, restrictive practices concerning exports if they cover at least one-third of all the goods in question produced in the United Kingdom.[9]

References may be made by the Board of Trade concerning the

[9] Alex Hunter, *Competition and the Law*, London, 1966, p. 13.

general effects of certain practices in the future too, and the range of the general matters which can be investigated by the Commission was even extended. The 1948 Act restricted the area of general references to practices already examined by the Commission. This restriction was removed by the 1956 legislation.

After the 1956 Act the Monopolies Commission is not called upon to comment on restrictive trading agreements as such, but may evaluate the consequences on the public interest of the participation of a dominant firm in an agreement.

The Monopolies and Mergers Act, 1965

The Monopolies and Restrictive Practices (Inquiry and Control) Act, 1948, was amended once more by the Monopolies and Mergers Act, 1965.

The principal Act was changed to cover not only goods but also the supply of services of any description, ranging from laundries and garages to banking and professional charges. A further important new measure, introduced by the amendment, empowered the Board of Trade to exercise price control, if necessary, where a monopoly was found to be against the public interest. The Board may declare price discrimination unlawful, and it may require suppliers to publish price lists, and prohibit them from charging prices different from those in the published lists or notifications, and may regulate prices.

Moreover, the Board of Trade may now prohibit or restrict the acquisition of the whole or part of a company by another firm and may divide and dissolve monopolies. Extensive powers have also been conferred on the Board of Trade concerning mergers which can be referred to the Commission for investigation.

The new Act further broadened the scope of general inquiries that may be required from the Monopolies Commission. In the future the Board of Trade can require the Commission to submit a report on the general effect on the public interest of specified practices in the field of monopolies and restrictive practices, and on the desirability of action of any specified description as a means of remedying or preventing undesirable practices. In the first reference under the law, the Commission was asked to look at the practice of some baby food manufacturers selling only through chemists or to a few selected grocers. The Commission reported in February, 1967, condemning the restricted distribution system.[10]

To cope with the new tasks, the Monopolies Commission was once more strengthened by the Act. Its maximum membership was raised to twenty-five and it was permitted to work in groups simultaneously, as was the case between 1953 and 1956.

In February, 1967, the President of the Board of Trade announced in Parliament that the Government intended to introduce legislation to strengthen and extend the Restrictive Trade Practices Act. Information agreements (see Chapter 8) would be brought within the scope of the Act, and temporary exemption from registration would be possible in cases where agreements are positively beneficial to the national economy. The Government's legislative programme for the 1967–68 Parliamentary session did not contain, however, any amendment of the Restrictive Trade Practices Act.

American legislation

In the United States the Sherman Act of 1890 was the first piece of anti-trust legislation. Two principles were established by this Act. First, that every contract or combination in the form of trust or otherwise, or conspiracy in restraint of trade is illegal; and secondly, that it is punishable for any person to monopolize, or attempt to monopolize, or combine or conspire with other persons to monopolize, trade. Thus the Act made the creation of monopoly and restraints of trade illegal and punishable, by dissolution of the companies involved, prohibition of certain practices, fines and imprisonment and by paying for damages caused to competitors.

The language of the Act was vague. Terms like 'combination', 'restraint', 'monopolize' were not precisely defined. Therefore, the interpretation of the Act caused many problems to Courts in the ensuing years. The Federal Government's willingness to apply the law was also inconsistent. In 1895 the Supreme Court did not break up the American Sugar Refining Company, who controlled 98 per cent of the market, on the ground that it was a manufacturing business, while the Sherman Act covered only commercial enterprises! The two most famous cases in the following decades were the compulsory liquidation of John D. Rockefeller's Standard Oil Company of New Jersey and the American Tobacco Company

[10] *The Economist,* February 11, 1967, p. 538.

in 1911, because they exerted 'an unreasonable restraint of trade'. After these decisions, monopoly, as such, was considered illegal in America only if it restrained trade to an unreasonable degree.

The interpretation problems of the Sherman Act necessitated new legislation to make its intentions more explicit. In 1914 a new anti-trust Act, the Clayton Act, was enacted which outlawed specific undesirable business practices. The most interesting part of the Act, from the point of view of this book, was section 2, which prohibited price discrimination between buyers when it was not justified by cost differences. This measure was directed against large companies who tried to break small competitors by quoting extremely low prices in their local markets and higher prices else-where. Other sections of the Act were directed against exclusive selling, the acquisition of shares of competing companies, and the so-called 'interlocking directorates', where one person is a director of more than one competing company. Only the prohibition of interlocking directorates was absolute under the Act, the other practices being forbidden only in cases where the effect could possibly lessen competition substantially or tended to create monopoly. This qualification made the policing of the Act difficult.

The Federal Trade Commission was set up by the Federal Trade Commission Act in the same year to investigate undesirable business practices. Section 5 of the Act declared 'unfair methods of competition' unlawful. The Act did not specify the meaning of unfair methods and so it was up to the Commission to interpret the law.

Until the 1930's the interpretation of the three anti-trust Acts was not stringent. Monopoly was still tolerated, unless found guilty of abusive practices or of controlling an overwhelming part of the market. The United States Steel Company, for example, was exempted of monopoly charges in 1920 since it did not abuse its monopoly power. The International Harvester Company's dominant position (almost two-thirds of the market) and price leadership was also condoned by the Supreme Court on similar grounds in 1927.

The change came in the early 1930's, when a harder line was taken against monopolies by the Department of Justice. In 1945 and 1946 the Aluminum Company of America and the 'Big Three' tobacco companies were found by the Supreme Court to be monopolies, though they did not abuse their power. The 'unreasonable restraint of trade' principle was, however, reinstated in 1948 in the Columbia Steel case.

The Clayton Act was once more amended by the so-called Celler Anti-mergers Act in 1950. It prohibited the merger of competing firms by the acquisition of assets. (The acquisition of shares was already outlawed by the original Act.) In 1957 a Supreme Court decision extended the ban to vertical combinations. Du Pont was not permitted, for instance, to hold shares of General Motors, since it was one of its suppliers.

Ironically, some American legislation at the same time seemed to work against competition. The Robinson-Patman Act, later popularly called the 'Chain Store Law', amended section 2 of the Clayton Act in 1936. Wanting to defend independent retailers against competition from chain-stores, the Act prohibited quantity discounts to large buyers in excess of actual cost reduction on substantial orders. In addition, unreasonably low retail prices were also prohibited when they aimed to stifle competition. Discriminatory pricing was permitted by the Act, however, to meet a low price charged by a competitor.

All these federal anti-trust laws apply only to inter-state commerce and trade and to the export trade. Most of the individual American states have their own anti-trust laws dealing with local markets.

The federal anti-trust laws are enforced by two bodies: the Anti-trust Division of the Department of Justice and the Federal Trade Commission. The former acts on complaints and institutes criminal or civil proceedings against companies in the name of the Government. The Court may issue an injunction to bar the firm from certain practices, or may require a certain change in the company's policy, or may order the breaking up of a monopoly. An out-of-court settlement in the form of a 'consent-decree' has often been found a remedy against undesirable practices. A long legal battle in court can thus be avoided by an undertaking by the company to refrain from certain policies. The Federal Trade Commission also acts on complaints, but can investigate on its own initiative, and considers its task to be, not so much the punishment of companies, but the prevention and correction of restrictive practices. It conducts hearings and may issue 'cease and desist' orders which, in case of violation, can be supported by a court injunction. The Commission's decisions can be challenged in court.

Seven top executives of leading heavy electrical equipment manufacturing companies received thirty-day gaol sentences early in 1961 for the violation of the Sherman Act. Twenty-four other gaol sentences were suspended and the defendants were fined a sum of nearly $2 million. The conspirators of General Electric had to resign, but those of Westinghouse were soon back in their jobs. The complaint against the electrical industry was made by the Tennessee Valley Authority that it was receiving identical and highly priced bids for work put out to tender. The industry is highly concentrated, four-fifths of heavy electrical equipment is made by Westinghouse and General Electric companies. Collusion was proved beyond doubt in court. A dramatic fall in the prices of heavy electrical equipment followed the court case. Bids for steam turbines and power transformers were 30 per cent less than a year before and prices of some other items fell by up to 50 per cent.[11]

At the time of writing the Department of Justice is conducting an anti-trust investigation into the motor car industry which has continued for many years, but no decision has been made as to whether any action should be taken.[12]

[11] *Financial Times*, February 8, 1967.
[12] *The Economist*, November 11, 1967, p. 625.

CHAPTER 8

Price agreements

Since price is usually the most effective competitive weapon, the majority of restrictive agreements are concerned with prices. Statistical evidence of this came to light during the registration procedure under the Restrictive Trade Practices Act of 1956. The first report of the Registrar stated that of the 2,240 agreements registered up to the end of 1959, about two-thirds were connected, in one way or another, with selling prices. Price agreements were even more predominant among the 970 agreements classified as important by the Registrar, as 790 of these, that is over four-fifths of them, contained some form of price restriction. Of these 790 price agreements, 730 were entered into by manufacturers mainly among themselves, and not with their buyers.[1] The proportion of price agreements within all restrictive agreements, naturally, varied from industry to industry. A private investigation revealed, for instance, that in the food industry 200 agreements were registered by June 1959 and, of these, 133 were related, directly or indirectly, to prices.[2]

Since the passing of the 1956 Act, a large number of price agreements have become ineffective for various reasons. Some have been abandoned by the parties concerned, others expired by lapse of time, yet others have been removed from the register as being unimportant and, finally, some have been terminated by court action.

In its fourth report the Registrar stated that a considerable advance had been made in this field:

The comparatively small number of agreements which have been defended has, I think, tended to leave an impression that not much

---

[1] 'Registrar of Restrictive Trading Agreements', Report for the Period 7th August 1956 to 31st December 1959, Cmnd. 1273, January 1961, paras. 40–43.

[2] N. Cuthbert and W. Black, Restrictive Practices in the Food Trades, *Journal of Industrial Economics*, October 1959, pp. 35–38.

progress has been made and that many registered agreements continue in operation and remain to be dealt with; further, that a new generation of registrable agreements made after and in the light of the Act remains virtually untouched. The position now is that a mass of price-fixing agreements has been dismantled and there is no backlog of important new agreements awaiting their turn to be referred to the Court; any important new agreement can be referred to the Court as soon as registration is accomplished. Further, of the agreements at present on the register and not yet disposed of by the Court, I think it is unlikely that more than a handful will be defended by the parties before the Court.[3]

Price agreements fall into three categories: common or fixed, minimum, and maximum price agreements.

The essential feature of common price agreements is that they fix specific prices for precisely defined goods produced or traded in by the participants. The purpose of minimum price agreements, on the other hand, is to establish a floor price for the market. The signatories of such an agreement do not lose their pricing freedom completely. They remain free to choose any price, but cannot quote a price below the stipulated minimum. Maximum price agreements are designed to provide an upper limit to prices charged in a certain industry. In practice most of the price agreements are concerned with common or minimum prices. Maximum prices are rarely subject to agreements in industry and trade.

It is important to realize that the economic effects of price agreements are to be judged on their actual performance, rather than on the name of the category into which they fall. If, for example, a maximum price agreement operates in such a way that practically all prices quoted are on the maximum level, the effect of the agreement is identical with that of a common price agreement. This was the conclusion of the Restrictive Practices Court when passing judgement in the case of the Federation of Wholesale and Multiple Bakers' price agreement. Prior to April 1958 the Federation made a recommendation to its members, the plant bakers, concerning the retail prices and distributor margins of bread. After April 1958 the Federation decided to recommend maximum retail prices. The Court found that virtually no bread was sold at less than the recommended retail price and, therefore, maximum prices

[3] 'Restrictive Trading Agreements', Report of the Registrar, 1st July 1963 to 30th June 1966, Cmnd. 3188, January 1967, p. 1.

were in actual fact fixed prices.[4] Another illustration of this point is provided by the yarn-spinners' case before the Restrictive Practices Court. The Court found that in the depressed spinning industry the minimum price stipulated in the price agreement had become 'very nearly' the fixed price.[5]

The smooth operation of price agreements is sometimes fraught with difficulties. It is inevitable that the loyalty of some of the parties to an agreement is stronger than that of others. Efficient firms, for example, may be penalized by a price agreement designed in such a way as to accommodate the high-cost competitors also, and this may weaken their loyalty. The policing of an agreement is particularly difficult if a large number of geographically scattered firms belong to a trade association. The coherence of a price agreement usually weakens when business conditions are depressed and firms are tempted to increase turnover by quoting lower prices. A Sheffield cutlery manufacturer explained why he did not attend trade association meetings: 'I don't go because the fellows there are too insincere. A manufacturer gets up and makes a speech condemning the prices we are getting. We all ought to agree to charge, say, 19s. a dozen. There are cries of Hear! Hear! all round. The speaker finishes, walks into the next room and takes up the telephone – Get out a new price list! we are charging 18s. 6d.'[6]

A variety of arguments have been advanced both before the Monopolies Commission and the Restrictive Practices Court in defence of common and minimum price agreements.[7] These investigations showed that it is not possible to generalize about the economic effects of price agreements and that each case has to be judged in the context of its individual circumstances.

Price stabilization

One of the arguments advanced in favour of price agreements is that they are necessary to even out price fluctuations in response

---

[4] Federation of Wholesale and Multiple Bakers (Great Britain and Northern Ireland) Agreement, 1959, L.R.1 R.P.387.

[5] Yarn Spinners' Agreement, 1959, L.R.1 R.P.118.

[6] Harry Townsend, 'Economic Theory and the Cutlery Trade', *Economica*, August 1954, p. 234.

[7] For a detailed analysis see Charles K. Rowley, *The British Monopolies Commission*, London, 1966, pp. 109–148, and R. B. Stevens and B. S. Yamey, *The Restrictive Practices Court*, London, 1965, pp. 51–88.

to changing demand conditions. The usual contention is that unhampered price competition drives out some firms from the industry during a slack period of business, and lost capacity cannot be replaced at once when conditions improve. Additional capacity will come forward only as a consequence of a high price, and the public loses more on higher prices than it gains on the temporary price reductions in the depressed phase. It may be questioned whether or not price fluctuations are desirable and that price agreements are the right means to mitigate their effects. Demand changes may reflect changes in consumer attitudes and it may, therefore, not be desirable to counteract them. Where the demand fluctuation is a reflection of the change in the general economic situation, a price scheme may operate in a way that intensifies rather than mitigates output fluctuations. In a depression, the higher price secured by the price agreement depresses demand while, in a boom, output is higher as a result of the lower price.

The price stability argument was used, for example, when phenol producers sought to justify their fixed price agreement under paragraph (b) of section 21(1) before the Restrictive Practices Court. The association submitted that, at that time, there was a surplus in phenol which was expected to persist for five years, followed by a shortage in supply. It was alleged that, without the restriction, the price of phenol would fall by 25 per cent, and tar would be directed from distillation for use as a fuel, with a consequent loss of many valuable chemicals derived from tar distillation. As, in that event, some distillers would close down, phenol would be in short supply. The Court found that the price fixed by the agreement was substantially higher than the competitive level and contended that a lower price might generate new uses and new demands at home and abroad. The agreement was declared to operate against the public interest.[8]

The British Electrical and Allied Manufacturers' Association also used the price stabilization argument in defence of its minimum price agreement before the Monopolies Commission. The agreement was designed to prevent price-cutting in depressed periods in an industry of few manufacturers and high fixed costs. The Association failed to convince the Commission that manufacturing capacity would be eliminated in depression, and booms

[8] Phenol Producers' Agreement, 1960, L.R.2 R.P.1.

would be linked with high prices in the absence of the agreement.[9]

Another possible use of the price stabilization argument may concern declining industries, where a price agreement is designed to retard the contraction process by keeping prices above the free market level. Especially in industries with heavy capital investment, the danger of cut-price competition often arises when unused capacity exists. It is not easy, however, to judge whether a temporary depression is the beginning of a long-term decline or not. Apart from the question of diagnosis, the cure is also problematical. No sweeping generalization is helpful in this respect. Free price competition does not necessarily lead to the best results. It cannot be automatically assumed that the least efficient firms leave a declining industry first. Sometimes the most dynamic firms switch to a new field in search of higher returns. It can be argued, on the other hand, that the moving out of factors of production from a declining industry should not be hampered. In the interests of the whole economy such adjustments should take place, in spite of some eventual hardship in the declining sector.

The calico-printing industry has tried to defend its minimum price scheme before the Monopolies Commission on the ground that it prevented cut-throat competition in a declining industry. As unit production costs increased rapidly when output was lagging in the industry, it was contended that price-cutting would result in substantial losses which, in turn, would tempt companies to reduce quality standards and spend less on research and development. The Commission did not find that the calico-printing market was in a state of long-term decline or that substantial excess capacity existed, and concluded that the industry misjudged fluctuations of demand for permanent decline.[10]

The price stabilization argument was also used by the cotton industry before the Restrictive Practices Court. The minimum price scheme in the contracting cotton industry was designed to guard against the outbreak of cut-throat competition and to preserve capacity. The industry claimed that though the public benefited from price-cutting temporarily, prices would rise steeply in the case of a revival of demand if capacity had been eliminated.

[9] Report on the Supply and Export of Electrical and Allied Machinery and Plant, 1957.
[10] Report on the Process of Calico Printing, 1954.

The Court found that spinning was a contracting industry and high-cost producers were destined to go out of business. The high prices secured by the scheme did not altogether prevent this process but retarded it considerably. There was a substantial amount of excess capacity in the industry, much more than the reserve capacity necessary to meet any sudden increase in demand. As the agreement hindered the reorganization of the industry the Court declared it to be against the public interest.[11]

A third variation of the price stabilization theme states that uniform prices save the buyer the trouble of seeking out the cheapest source of supply. It is usually contended that, as a result of a price agreement, administrative costs will be saved and the risk of carrying stocks would be materially decreased. It should, however, be pointed out that a uniform price for all customers denies the benefit of skilful buying to firms who are superior in this respect to their competitors. Some consuming firms may want to buy when the market is weak and may prefer to undertake the risk of carrying stock to paying a uniform price fixed by a price agreement among producers.

The linoleum-makers claimed before the Monopolies Commission that their minimum price agreement promoted price stability and created confidence in stocks, in an industry where raw material prices fluctuated considerably. When fixing minimum prices, the Linoleum Manufacturers' Association took a view of future costs so that prices could remain unaltered for some time. The Commission was, on the whole, impressed by the argument, though it remarked that users might have been better served if prices had fluctuated with the costs of materials: when prices were low, users would have clearly benefited and, in periods of high prices, only those who were ready to pay for them would have bought stocks.[12]

The Black Bolt and Nut Association successfully defended its common price agreement before the Restrictive Practices Court by arguing that purchases of bolts and nuts avoided the necessity to 'go shopping' by making a great many inquiries before placing orders. It was claimed that fixed prices saved administrative expenses for buyers in an industry where there were over 3,000 varieties of standard-sized bolts and nuts and numerous more

[11] Yarn Spinners' Agreement, 1959, L.R.1 R.P.118.
[12] Report on the Supply of Linoleum, 1956, para. 191.

specialized sizes. The Court decided that because of the great variety of goods produced by the industry, the administrative savings to stockholders and large and medium-sized buyers were a substantial and specific benefit under paragraph (b) of section 21 (1) of the Act.[13]

The glazed and floor tiles industry, on the other hand, could not justify before the Court that its fixed delivered pricing agreement on standard tiles and fittings benefited the public (merchants, fitters and builders) by the avoidance of having to go shopping. The Court held the view that, though some costs were involved in negotiating prices, the benefit of the price agreement could not be substantial, particularly in view of the small number of producers in the industry.[14]

Investments

A further argument in favour of price agreements runs that stable prices enable management to take a better long-term view and formulate investment policy with more confidence. It is also alleged that an agreement may lead to a higher level of investment. Furthermore, it is sometimes claimed that a price agreement enables the industry to pool information and, by planning investments on an industry level, to eliminate wrong decisions. Price agreements do not necessarily raise the level of investment in an industry. By securing a more sheltered life for firms who are parties to an agreement, and by retaining high-cost firms in business, they may even discourage investment in more modern machinery. Efficient firms are able to raise sufficient capital under competitive conditions. It may also be argued that investment planning by trade associations is too rigid and an investment allocation scheme limits the expansion of efficient firms.

The cement industry claimed under gateway (b) of section 21 (1) before the Restrictive Practices Court that, apart from lower prices, its common price agreement benefited the public by a planned expansion of capacity, resulting in the efficient use and the avoidance of excess capacity. The minimum return which would attract investment in new works was said to be higher under

[13] Black Bolt and Nut Association's Agreement, 1960, L.R.2 R.P.50.
[14] Glazed and Floor Tiles Home Trade Association's Agreement, 1964, L.R.4 R.P.239.

free competition than under the price agreement because of the greater risk. The Court was satisfied that cement prices were, in fact, fixed at a level lower than would be required to attract new investment to the industry under competitive conditions and upheld the agreement.[15]

Among other arguments, the Black Bolt and Nut Association also claimed before the Restrictive Practices Court that the rate of capital investment would decline in the industry in the absence of its price agreement. The Registrar argued in Court that the scheme did not promote, but hindered, investment because the more efficient producers could not expand, being unable to attract new custom by price-cutting. In a free market there is an incentive to invest in modern machinery to reduce production costs and to extend turnover by price reduction. The Court rejected the argument that the removal of the price restriction would reduce the overall rate of capital investment in the industry.[16]

Quality

Price agreements are often defended on the ground that they safeguard and improve product quality. The argument states that, in the case of free price competition, price-cutting develops which puts pressure on profits and margins, and manufacturers are tempted to recoup their losses by lowering quality standards. The weakness of this argument is that price agreements may secure a more comfortable margin but they do not guarantee the maintenance or improvement of quality standards. Price agreements definitely safeguard quality only in cases when they are supported with additional agreements on quality standards. Even so, it can be argued that the exclusion of a low-quality product is not always desirable. If low quality is reflected in price, the product may meet the need of some consumers who prefer to buy a cheap low-quality article to a high-quality expensive product. It is desirable that quality choice should not be restricted.

The carpet industry tried to justify its fixed price scheme under paragraph (b) of section 21 (1) of the Act, by referring to the possible debasement of quality in the absence of the price agreement. It was argued that, without the agreement, qualities would not be

---

[15] Cement Makers' Federation Agreement, 1961, L.R.2 R.P.241.
[16] Black Bolt and Nut Association's Agreement, 1960, L.R.2 R.P.50.

maintained, and the public would lose confidence in quality and price. The industry also claimed that carpet prices would be unstable and, therefore, distributors would not hold adequate stocks, with a resultant lack of choice for the public. The Court took the view that manufacturers would guard their reputation and quality would not be affected by the termination of the scheme. Accordingly, the agreement was declared to be against the public interest.[17]

In support of its minimum price agreement, the Hard Fibre Cordage Federation prescribed the sizes and runnages of cordage produced and their breaking strains. The Monopolies Commission admitted that production economies might spring from the standardization of sizes and would not have objected to the recommendation of a quality code. The Federation's arrangement was, however, obligatory. The Commission declared it to be against the public interest for the reason that the buyer should be able to obtain the kind of cordage he wants if he is willing to pay for it. The Federation's supporting agreement restricted consumer's choice in another direction. Manufacturers were prohibited from selling any manila trawl twine better than the pre-war second quality twine, and cords and twines made from waste fibre. The Commission held the view that individual manufacturers should not be prevented from meeting the demand for these very high- and very low-quality cordages. Accordingly, this arrangement was also pronounced to be contrary to the public interest.[18] But the Commission was not consistent in its line about the quality argument. It usually approved of quality agreements in cases when it did not object to the price-fixing agreement itself, as in the Linoleum case. The Commission found it difficult to assess the effect of the common price system on the quality of the linoleum produced, but concluded that there was a tendency to maintain a high quality, though guaranteeing no higher quality than would exist under price competition.[19]

[17] Federation of British Carpet Manufacturers' Agreement, 1959, L.R.1 R.P.472.
[18] Report on the Supply of Hard Fibre Cordage, 1956, paras, 302 and 305.
[19] Report on the Supply of Linoleum, 1956, paras. 188 and 190.

Research and co-operation

A further defence of price agreements alleges that free price competition leads to narrow profit margins and a consequent reduced expenditure on research. It is also claimed that price agreements promote co-operative research and the exchange of technical and commercial information. In opposition to this view one may point out that competition may well be an incentive to research efforts, and technological progress may be better served by keenly competitive conditions. Co-operative research is not definitely superior to individual research either. A co-operative arrangement may, in fact, weaken research efforts within an industry.

The Associated Transformer Manufacturers operated a minimum price agreement. The Association claimed under gateway (b) before the Restrictive Practices Court that the abrogation of the agreement would reduce prices and profits, which in turn would lead to a decrease in expenditure on research adversely affecting product quality, collaboration, and exchange of information among members. The Court agreed that in the absence of the price agreement some reduction of prices was likely, but was not satisfied that there would be a curtailment of research and development and a reduction of quality. In the Court's opinion buyers were well qualified to scrutinize quality and its preservation was particularly essential in a competitive situation.[20]

The Permanent Magnet Association successfully defended its minimum price agreement before the Restrictive Practices Court. The Association established a technical committee, a patent pool, and a central research laboratory. There was a constant exchange of know-how between the members. The technical co-operation enabled members to compete in research with large international companies and to be in the forefront of magnet technology. The agreement also prevented an inventor (a firm) from exploiting its monopoly position by charging high prices. The Court accepted the Association's assertion that the co-operative research arrangement was beneficial to the public interest.[21]

The Monopolies Commission reported on the supply of insulin in 1952. The three concerns who manufactured insulin in this

[20] Associated Transformer Manufacturers' Agreement, 1961, L.R.2 R.P.295.
[21] Permanent Magnet Association's Agreement, 1962, L.R.3 R.P.119.

country collaborated fully in technical matters, in the buying of the principal raw material (ox-pancreas), and agreed to charge common prices. The Commission found that the prices were based on the costs of the most efficient producer, the quality of insulin was unsurpassed and prices were practically the lowest in the world. The agreement was found not to be operating against the public interest; the only qualification was that the chief buyer, the Ministry of Health, should exercise some supervision on prices and profits in the future.[22]

Standardization

It is sometimes argued that excessive product differentiation is economically undesirable and that standardization leads to production economies and lower prices. Price agreements are claimed to be the prerequisites of, or incentives to, standardization. Price agreements may further the cause of standardization in certain cases, but many industries have introduced it without imposing a restriction on the pricing freedom of individual companies.

The Restrictive Practices Court approved the glazed and floor tiles industry's price agreement as it promoted standardization of its products. This was accepted as a specific and substantial benefit under paragraph (b) of section 21 (1) of the Act. The thirteen members of the Association agreed to sell standard tiles, fittings, and certain related goods at fixed delivered prices. For non-standard sizes members were obliged to charge 25 per cent more or the actual cost of manufacture, whichever was the greater. The Registrar argued that free competition would regulate prices and the extent of standardization in a more satisfactory way. The Court was, however, satisfied that the substantial degree of standardization could not have been maintained without the agreement, that standardization had brought costs down, and that cost economies had largely been passed on to the customer.[23]

Powerful buyers

Price agreements are sometimes designed to protect manufacturers from the extensive market power of large buyers. Powerful

[22] The Supply of Insulin, 1952.
[23] Glazed and Floor Tile Home Trade Association's Agreement, 1963, L.R.4 R.P.239.

buyers may be able to extract an unduly low price from suppliers. It is usually claimed that such a situation can lead to some detriment, like deterioration of product quality or less expenditure on research, and that, therefore, a price agreement is necessary to secure reasonable prices. The justification of this argument does not turn on the fact that a substantial concentration exists on the buying side but on the actual behaviour of these large organizations.

The Mining Rope Association claimed, under paragraph (d) of section 21 (1) of the Act, that its common price agreement was necessary to negotiate fair terms with the National Coal Board as the preponderant buyer. Using a certain classification, the NCB was alleged to be responsible for 82 per cent of the demand for a certain type of rope. The Court applied a wider product definition and considered the NCB as buyer of only 38 per cent of home sales. It concluded that the NCB could not be held to control a preponderant part of the trade and declared the agreement to be against the public interest.[24]

The Water-tube Boilermakers' Association claimed that the Central Electricity Generating Board, between 1952 and 1958, placed 83 per cent of the total home orders for water-tube boilers. Its price agreement was alleged to be necessary to avoid a situation where members quote unremuneratively low prices in order to get one of the Board's contracts. The Court rejected the case because it found that the restriction was unnecessarily wide, applying not only to the preponderant buyer but to all buyers, home and abroad.[25]

Unemployment

A further argument in defence of price agreements is that the long-run effect of price competition in a depressed industry leads to the elimination of some of the producing firms, followed by a decrease in output and rising unemployment. Unemployment is always a controversial economic phenomenon because of its social consequences. On pure economic grounds, however, declining industries should not be kept artificially alive because of fear of

[24] Agreements of the Mining Rope Association, the Wire Rope Manufacturers' Association, and the Locked Coil Manufacturers' Association, 1964, L.R.5 R.P.146.
[25] Water-tube Boilermakers' Agreement, 1959, L.R.1 R.P.285.

unemployment. Labour set free by one industry may be better used elsewhere in the economy. Individual industries are not likely to judge these wider implications on an objective basis, being interested parties. Alternatively, a case may be made out that, as price agreements increase capital investment, they also increase employment of labour in an industry. Once again, this point cannot claim general validity. Investment in labour-saving machinery, for example, may not cause a rise but a drop in employment.

Under paragraph (e) of section 21 (1) of the Act, the Yarn Spinners' Association attempted to justify its minimum price scheme. It claimed that if the agreement was terminated, within a year over 20 per cent of the workers in the cotton-spinning industry would become unemployed, with a serious effect on the level of general unemployment in certain areas. Though the Court rejected the price agreement itself, it accepted the fact that, on balance, the abrogation of the scheme would lead to local unemployment.[26]

The jute goods manufacturers also tried to justify their seven minimum price agreements before the Restrictive Practices Court by claiming that the removal of the agreements would have caused serious and persistent unemployment in Dundee and its environs. It was contended by the manufacturers that the agreements were necessary for the operation of the Jute Control, run by the Board of Trade, to protect the industry against low-cost Indian and Pakistani competition. The Court concluded that the Jute Control could secure the same level of protection in the absence of price agreements, and therefore rejected the case.[27]

Exports

It is sometimes maintained that a price agreement is necessary to keep up the existing level of exports or to increase it. A healthy domestic market is said to be the pre-condition of good export performance. Intense price competition may jeopardize research and development expenditure and may lead to quality deterioration, with an adverse effect on exports. We have already argued that research activity is not necessarily curtailed under free price competition, and quality is not necessarily debased either. In addition,

[26] Yarn Spinners' Agreement, 1959, L.R.1 R.P.118.
[27] British Jute Trade Federal Council's Agreements, 1963, L.R.4 R.P.399.

the opponent of the argument may point out that, if a price agreement increases the domestic prices of an industry, the home market will be smaller than otherwise, economies of scale may not be fully exploited, and export prices may, therefore, be higher than otherwise and result in lowering the volume of exports. Intensive domestic price competition is likely to be a more powerful stimulus to exports than the more secure climate of a price agreement.

The water-tube boilermaker industry succeeded in satisfying the Court that its price agreement was instrumental in obtaining foreign orders. The value of export contracts was substantial in relation to the whole trade and was obtained in the face of keen international competition. Exports were helped by intensive research and development and by the fact that companies were able to recover a high percentage of their overhead costs from their sales to the home market. The industry claimed that if the arrangement had been abrogated, home market prices would have been reduced, with a consequent decrease in research and loss of export orders, as higher prices would have been quoted for foreign orders. The Court decided that the abrogation of the agreement would be detrimental to the industry's export performance and that the agreement, therefore, conferred a specific and substantial benefit on the public under gateway (f) of section 21 (1) of the Act.[28]

Under paragraph (f) of section 21(1) the Associated Transformer Manufacturers also claimed before the Restrictive Practices Court that the discontinuation of their minimum price agreement, a consequent fall in prices which would result in a reduction in expenditure on research and development and a quality deterioration, would prejudice exports. They submitted that their export agreement – another agreement among transformer manufacturers not subject to registration under the 1956 Act – which resulted in collaboration and level tendering (a pricing practice where identical prices are quoted by different companies in response to a tender), would not survive. The Court was not impressed by these arguments and even remarked that the export agreement may have adverse effect on exports as level tendering is a practice disliked by buyers.[29]

[28] Water-tube Boilermakers' Agreement, 1959, L.R.1 R.P.285.
[29] Associated Transformer Manufacturers' Agreement, 1961, L.R.2 R.P.295.

Concentration

A further effect of price agreements is that, in certain cases, they prevent concentration in an industry, since small firms cannot be driven out of business by large rivals by quoting lower prices. Whether the prevention of concentration is in the public interest or not varies from industry to industry. The retention of the small firm is sometimes equivalent to the retention of the inefficient.

Suppliers of copper semi-manufactures argued before the Monopolies Commission that their common price agreement is necessary – among other reasons – to make it more difficult for any single company to obtain a virtual monopoly of the trade. 'Uncontrolled competition in price would . . . lead to the development of highly specialized concerns, each with a virtual monopoly of its own range of products, with consequent strategic as well as economic disadvantages.' The Commission found that minimum prices were unnecessarily high in the industry and declared the agreement to be against the public interest.[30]

Ancillary restrictions

The mere stipulation of price is not always sufficient to ensure the smooth working of a price agreement, as the parties may attempt to gain advantage over their competitors by following the agreed price but offering other benefits to their customers. To eliminate possibilities of easy infringement, price agreements are often supported by detailed rules concerning not only quality requirements but also trade terms, like discounts, quantity rebates, trade-ins, services attached to sales, etc.

Ancillary restrictions claim to be necessary to support the main price-fixing restriction by the cement industry – under paragraph (g) of section 21 (1) – were: common margins to approved merchants, standard terms and conditions of sale, a deferred rebate scheme to large users and merchants related to their aggregated purchasers, and rebates to cement and asbestos manufacturers. With the exception of the deferred rebate scheme to large users and merchants, and one minor exception relating to length of contracts, the Court found that these restrictions were necessary in

[30] 'Report on the Supply and Export of Certain Semi-manufactures of Copper and Copper-based Alloys', 1955, paras. 290 and 310.

support of the price agreement, and were found to be not against the public interest.[31]

The level of prices

The economic effects of any price agreement largely depends on the agreed level of prices and the resultant profits in comparison with prices and profits under free competition. A change in the agreed price may alter the effect of an agreement entirely. When scrutinizing an agreement both the Restrictive Practices Court and the Monopolies Commission have paid attention to these factors. Prices have generally been expected to be lower, or at least not higher, than otherwise. This condition has become practically a prerequisite for an agreement to be found not contrary to the public interest by the Court.[32] As we have seen in the previous chapter, a safety valve for undesirable changes in agreements passed by the Court is provided by section 22 of the 1956 Act, under which provision the Registrar can apply to the Court to review its earlier decision.

When approving the common price agreement of the Black Bolt and Nuts Association, for example, the Court was satisfied that the industry was efficient, as compared with similar industries abroad, and that the profits made were not excessive as the prices fixed by the agreement were found to be reasonable. There were no provisions in the agreement specifying the basis on which prices were to be fixed in the future. Though the Association gave assurances to operate the agreement on the same basis as in the past, the Court noted that if prices were fixed at an unreasonable level at any time, it would be a material change in the relevant circumstances and the Registrar could apply to the Court under section 22 of the Act.[33]

Though the Monopolies Commission did not always think that price agreements were operating against the public interest, it usually expressed the opinion that they could do so in the future. When giving approval to agreements, the Commission often recommended some safeguards to protect the public interest

[31] Cement Makers' Federation Agreement, 1961, L.R.2 R.P.241.
[32] James P. Cairns, 'The Restrictive Practices Court and Reasonable Prices', *Journal of Industrial Economics*, March 1964, pp. 133–141.
[33] Black Bolt and Nut Association's Agreement, 1960, L.R.2 R.P.50.

against potential abuses. As a rule, price supervision by uninterested parties and improvements to secure efficiency were recommended.

When judging the level of prices, both the Restrictive Practices Court and the Monopolies Commission focused their attention on costs. In most cases the 'just price' was conceived by them as the cost-determined reasonable price.

The possible harmful effects and eventual merits of price agreements were summarized by the Monopolies Commission as follows:

> Any common price agreement is suspect on the grounds: (i) that there is a risk of exploitation of the market by the associated suppliers, even if at any particular time it can be shown that prices bear a reasonable relationship to costs; (ii) that it hinders the normal process by which low-cost producers expand their business at the expense of high-cost producers, and (iii) that it removes an important incentive to reduce costs. On the other hand, a common price system, by spreading the business among the associated suppliers, makes it harder for any single concern to obtain a virtual monopoly of the trade. For example, a company of large financial resources, which is party to a common price agreement, is thereby debarred from using those resources to drive financially weaker parties to the agreement out of business, by continually underselling them at prices which do not cover its costs. Further, since common prices will tend to be more slowly adjusted to changes in market conditions than competitive prices, they may restrain the rise in prices in times of excessive demand, and will almost certainly steady their fall when demand is slack. In a severe slump, they may alleviate the worse consequences, both for capital and labour.[34]

Selective price-cutting agreements

The rigidity of price agreements is sometimes lessened by selective price-cutting arrangements. This may constitute an aggressive marketing policy to defeat outside competition by means of price-cutting on certain products, in certain geographical areas, or in respect of a selected group of buyers.

The Metal Windows Association used selective price-cutting to obtain tenders for its members in competition with outside

[34] 'Report on the Supply and Export of Certain Semi-manufactures of Copper and Copper-based Alloys', 1955, para. 287.

manufacturers. Selected members reduced their prices by an average of 6 per cent, but in some cases by over 20 per cent. The Association considered these cuts as defensive action against outside competitors who undercut the Association's list prices. The Monopolies Commission took a sombre view of this practice. It concluded that its aim was to ruin outside competition. Agreement prices were fixed on a level to compensate members for the loss of profit on price-cuts, and so the rest of the buyers had to foot the bill for this policy. Competition should have been met by a general lowering of prices. Accordingly, the termination of the practice was suggested by the Commission.[35]

Information agreements

Before the 1956 Act, information agreements were virtually unknown in this country. After the implementation of the Act many abandoned price agreements had been replaced by agreements on the exchange of information on prices. They have been known in the United States for fifty years under the name of 'open-price agreements'. These agreements are not subject to registration under the Restrictive Trade Practices Act, if the sole obligation accepted by the parties is the sending of information to a central agency. In practice, information is usually exchanged through a trade association. Members send information on orders, prices, trade-terms, export consignments, etc., to the trade association, which brings it to the notice of all other members. They may also periodically meet to discuss the trade situation and matters of mutual interest.

The exchange of information among firms belonging to the same industry cannot be deplored. Well-informed buyers and sellers improve the functioning of the market. More information spread among sellers leads to a narrowing of the range of prices, to greater price stability, and facilitates cost comparisons for productivity analysis purposes.[36]

The problem of information agreements is that members may develop an attitude which amounts to an understanding of prices and thus avoid price competition altogether. Such an arrangement

[35] 'Report on the Supply of Standard Metal Windows and Doors', 1948, paras. 236-238.
[36] Alex Hunter, *Competition and the Law*, London, 1966, pp. 169-180.

is equivalent to a common price agreement and comes within the purview of the 1956 Act. The dividing line between the circulation of information and a tacit understanding to act in a certain way is very narrow. Experience in the United States has shown that there is a strong tendency for information agreements to become anti-competitive forces. The Monopolies Commission also arrived at a similar conclusion in respect of the car battery industry. Leading car battery manufacturers, belonging to the British Starter Battery Association, dropped their common price agreement in 1957 and, three years later, entered into an information agreement which was not subject to registration as it did not impose any restriction on its parties. The Monopolies Commission found a stability and a consequent continuing uniformity of prices after 1957 in the top-price battery trade. The Commission held the view that the information agreement encouraged the quoting of similar prices and terms and discouraged competition among manufacturers, and therefore operated against the public interest.[37]

The price agreement made by the galvanized tank manufacturers was declared to be against the public interest in an undefended case by the Restrictive Practices Court in 1959. All members gave an undertaking not to make any similar arrangement without notifying the Registrar. In spite of that, the industry made an information agreement and, consequently, six years after the ending of the price agreement the members still quoted identical prices. Eight companies admitted that on two occasions they made informal arrangements as to the prices they would charge. The companies were found to be guilty of contempt of court and were fined in excess of £100,000. The Court gave warning that if such cases were repeated the punishment would not necessarily be only financial.[38] The tyre manufacturers were also fined for contempt of court for introducing a 'rate notification scheme' in replacement of an agreement condemned by the Court.[39]

It is the task of the Registrar of Restrictive Practices to separate restrictive and non-restrictive information agreements and to

[37] The Monopolies Commission, 'Report on the Supply of Electrical Equipment for Mechanically Propelled Land Vehicles', 1963, paras. 1034–1037.

[38] Galvanized Tank Manufacturers' Association Agreement, 1965, L.R.5 R.P.315.

[39] Agreement of the Mileage Conference Group of the Tyre Manufacturers' Conference Limited, 1966.

secure the registration of the former. To prove collusion among members of a trade association is, however, a very delicate matter. Identical prices are not necessarily a sign of collusion and particularly not so in cases of standardized products. Where product differentiation is absent, competition tends to concentrate on price and price differentials tend to disappear. Thus greater price uniformity may well be only a sign of keener competition. There is no law against price leadership and price followership and against discussions on conditions of trade and of prices among competitors.

The difficulties experienced with information agreements were already pointed out in the Registrar's first[40] and second reports.[41] In his third report the Registrar stated that information agreements do provide a framework within which, consciously or unconsciously, there may arise undertakings about prices, and suggested that all such agreements should be made subject to registration.[42]

The Government responded to the suggestion of the Registrar in the White Paper on Monopolies, Mergers and Restrictive Practices in 1964:

> ... the Government are not prepared to see the intention of the 1956 Act undermined by agreements or arrangements for the exchange of information the purpose and effect of which is to limit competition. They therefore propose to bring information agreements within the scope of the 1956 Act and thus to make them registrable and subject ultimately to consideration by the Court. ... It is not, however, intended to make all information agreements registrable forthwith. The Board of Trade would be empowered to call them up for registration by Order which would be subject to negative resolution of Parliament. The Board would, however, use this power to call up only such classes as appeared to be serving as a device for circumventing the Act. They would see that the use of this power would not involve the frustration of beneficial exchanges of information. ... [43]

---

[40] 'Report for the period 7th August 1956 to 31st December 1959', Cmnd. 1273, January 1961, para. 25.

[41] 'Report for the period 1st January 1960 to 30th June 1961', Cmnd. 1603, January 1962, paras. 10–14.

[42] 'Report for the period 1st July 1961 to 30th June 1963', Cmnd. 2246, January 1964, para. 18.

[43] 'Monopolies, Mergers and Restrictive Practices', Cmnd. 2299, March 1964, paras. 30–34 and 40.

The Government also recognized in the White Paper that grounds enumerated in section 21 of the 1956 Act were not suitable for the defence of information agreements in Court. Such agreements may not limit competition but they do not confer any specific benefit on the public. Therefore, the Government envisaged introducing a new ground of justification as an alternative to section 21. This new ground would enable respondents to plead that an agreement was not against the public interest because it did not restrict or deter competition. The use of this new ground would not be limited to information agreements.

As related in the previous chapter, the Government announced in the House of Commons in February 1967 that it would seek legislation to amend the Restrictive Trade Practices Act and to bring information agreements within its scope.

CHAPTER 9

Resale price maintenance

Resale price maintenance is usually described as an agreement between the supplier and his distributors, where the former imposes the condition that his product should be re-sold at a fixed price, or for not less than a minimum price. Less frequently, the term also covers similar price agreements in respect of maximum prices.

Resale price maintenance can be introduced either by the manufacturer, or the wholesaler, or the importer. Where the manufacturer imposes the condition of resale price maintenance, and this is the most usual case, the parties undertaking the restriction are either the wholesaler, or the retailer, or both of them. The same applies where the importer is the supplier of the price-maintained article. Sometimes, however, only the wholesaler and the retailer are the contracting parties. The wholesaler may introduce resale price maintenance, for example, concerning the sale of his private label brands.

Resale price maintenance can be introduced either independently by a supplier, or a group of suppliers may agree to maintain their resale prices. This collective resale price maintenance may be supported by a further horizontal agreement among suppliers to act collectively against price-cutting distributors. There are two main methods of collective enforcement. Suppliers may agree not to supply distributors whose names appear on a published stop list because they failed to obey stipulated resale prices. The other enforcement method is based on an approved list of buyers who undertake to maintain retail prices. Where supplies are confined to approved buyers, the failure to obey maintained prices is a breach of agreement, the penalty for which is the removal from the list and the stopping of supplies. Naturally, the supplier can also attempt to enforce resale price maintenance by withholding supply from individual price-cutters. However, he may find this move self-defeating as, unless he is one of the market leaders, distributors can easily switch over to competing brands and he would lose trade. Moreover, if he wants to penalize a particular retailer he cannot do it without the support of all his wholesalers. For these reasons collective enforcement is a more effective way of securing obedience.

Trade associations went to considerable lengths to prevent price-cutting in certain cases in the past. Before the last war, for example, there was a strong price maintenance in the tobacco trade. Every retailer was required to enter into an agreement with the Tobacco Trade Association, the representative body of manufacturers, before he could obtain supplies. The main problem of policing price-fixing was the detection of the source from which the price-cutter received his supply. The Tobacco Trade Association set up an elaborate machinery of control, the main weapon of which was the use of codes on the packages. Some small mark, or a misprint, or an extra comma, or an inscription in invisible ink – which could be detected only after chemical treatment – was put on the label or carton of goods sold to traders who were believed to supply price-cutting retailers. As a second step, test purchases were made in price-cutting shops and goods were examined for code signs on them to locate the supplier. However, price-cutters tried to defend their practice. They scrutinized packages before buying them. Some had staff to remove marked packaging and even repacked goods or cut off mutilated labels, and one or two used ultra-violet rays to discover hidden code marks.[1]

Economic effects

As has been discussed in Chapter 6, the same article may be sold at various prices in different shops under unhampered price competition in retailing. Resale price maintenance, however, eliminates price competition at the retail level and sets a uniform or minimum price. It disregards the fact that the cost of doing business varies from shop to shop and therefore retail prices should vary. A certain article subject to resale price maintenance is sold for the same price everywhere, regardless of the various amounts of service attached to its sale and the turnover of the shop.

When setting the uniform or minimum retail price, the supplier

[1] Herman Levy, *Retail Trade Associations*, London, 1942, pp. 85 and 151.

must allow a reasonable margin to all distributors, including the least efficient ones, otherwise they would not stock the brand. Under these conditions the level of resale prices will be governed by the costs of shops whose operating expenses are the highest. As low-cost retailers are prevented from quoting lower prices, the average level of prices will be higher in trades where resale price maintenance is entrenched than it would be under retail price competition.

A further reason why prices are higher under price-fixing than under competition lies in the fact that resale price maintenance diverts competition from price to services. Not being able to cut prices, shops will try to attract more patronage by offering more elaborate services. At a later stage the cost of extensive services will eat into the initially comfortable margins, and pressure will be exerted on the manufacturer to increase retail prices. Moreover, pressure on margins also develops because high guaranteed margins attract a large number of newcomers into retailing. The same amount of trade will be done by more retailers than before, thus increasing the cost of distribution. Surveys in countries which have legally banned resale price maintenance show that prices have decreased after the abolition.

Where a considerable proportion of goods in a certain field are covered by resale price maintenance, uniform or minimum high prices will affect the structure and efficiency of the retail trade. As price competition is eliminated among retailers, efficient operators are unable to expand at the expense of their competitors as much as they could otherwise. Resale price maintenance keeps high-cost retailers in business who cannot stand up to the pressures of price competition. Innovators who wish to introduce new retailing methods, relying on large turnover and narrow margins, are unable to enter the field. Discount shops, for instance, have not been able to develop in this country for a long time because of the strict resale price maintenance policy of many consumer durable and household goods manufacturers. Resale price maintenance stands, therefore, in the way of necessary changes in distribution. The long-term effects of higher prices are the retention of in-efficient shops, and, consequently, the employment of an unnecessarily large amount of economic resources in the retail trade.

Though traditional retailers are usually anxious to get under the protective umbrella of resale price maintenance, the manufacturer also may have good reasons to introduce it.[2] One reason for introducing price maintenance on the initiative of the producer may be to eliminate or restrict competition among the producers themselves. By eliminating price competition among distributors the manufacturer aims at avoiding pressure by retailers to lower his trade price. This sort of pressure may develop when, as a result of severe price competition, retail margins have narrowed beyond a certain limit. The lowering of the trade price on the part of a certain manufacturer upsets the existing balance of power in the industry, and other producers may retaliate. Such effects of price competition among retailers can be mitigated by price agreement among manufacturers, accompanied by quotas or resale price maintenance. In other cases only collective resale price maintenance may be applied, or producers may maintain their resale prices individually even if there is no demand for it by the distributors.

A further reason for the introduction of price maintenance by the manufacturer may be that he intends to win the retailers' support to promote his brand. The assured high margin on a price-maintained line is an incentive to the retailer to display, advertise and recommend the product. In other instances the motive for the adoption of price maintenance may be the desire to feature a uniform price in the manufacturer's advertisements. It may also be held by the producer that the maintenance of the existing structure of retail trade is in his interests, since free price competition may lead to the emergence of large-scale retailers with strong bargaining power. Concerning articles bought on impulse, the manufacturer may want to introduce resale price maintenance to keep the numerous small retailers in business as his turnover may depend on the number of selling points. Some manufacturers claim that resale price maintenance is necessary to ensure the provision of satisfactory before- and after-sales service by the trade. This opinion is usually held in respect of technical goods. Finally, some manufacturers may look upon resale price maintenance as a means of protecting themselves from the presumed ill-effects of loss-leader selling.

The manufacturer will not always achieve these desired objectives by the introduction of resale price maintenance. As we have

[2] For a detailed analysis see B. S. Yamey, *The Economics of Resale Price Maintenance*, London, 1954, pp. 3–72.

seen, the elimination of price competition at retail level does not necessarily relieve the manufacturer of pressures from distributors to widen margins. The protective effect of price maintenance may only be temporary. Pressure for higher margins for the retail trade may also develop under resale price maintenance after a while, in consequence of the larger number of shops and more elaborate services. The effects of initial dealer co-operation after the introduction of price maintenance may also be offset by the competitive adoption of resale price maintenance by other producers. Furthermore, it is not really necessary for the manufacturer to introduce price maintenance for the sake of his advertising, since recommended prices can also be featured in advertisements (see Chapter 10). Again, in spite of their stronger bargaining power, large-scale retailers are not always against the interests of the producer, as by quoting lower prices they may enlarge the market for his product. When one evaluates the effects of numerous small retail outlets on the demand of goods bought on impulse, the sales-increasing effect of more selling points ought to be balanced against the opposite effect of higher prices under resale price maintenance. The weakness of the argument that fixed prices are necessary in the interests of providing satisfactory service is that higher margins only make it possible to give more service but do not ensure it. This is so in respect of both before- and after-sales services. The fallacy concerning the ill-effects of loss-leaders has already been exposed in Chapter 6 on Retail Pricing.

It is also contended that not only traditional retailers and manufacturers but also consumers may benefit from maintained resale prices. Price maintenance is claimed to protect consumers from high prices charged by retailers, especially in locations where competition is restricted. It is also said that the public is saved the trouble of shopping around to find the best buys and enjoys the convenience of being able to buy at the nearest shop. The larger number of shops operating under resale price maintenance is also alleged to add to the convenience of the public. Further benefits are derived by the consumer from the wider selection of goods carried by stores and the more elaborate services supplied. According to this argument the position of the specialist shop may be jeopardized under free price competition, since general shops may concentrate on selling fast-moving lines at a low price and leave the specialist shops with the unprofitable part of the trade. Finally, resale price maintenance is claimed to safeguard product quality for the benefit of the consumer, as free retail price competition leads to pressure for higher margins which, in turn, may lead to the deterioration of quality.

In defence of unrestricted retail price competition a few points should be made. First, resale price maintenance stipulating a minimum price does not necessarily protect the consumer against being overcharged. The retailer is only under contractual obligation to charge not less than the minimum price, but he is free to charge more. Admittedly, this will happen only in exceptional cases, as the maintained price is already inflated to some extent and the widespread knowledge of the price among customers will act as a barrier to raising the price easily. It is perfectly true that the elimination of the need to go shopping around, the existence of a larger number of shops, a wider selection of goods and more services, do benefit the consumer. But this is only one side of the coin. These benefits should be contrasted with the higher prices under resale price maintenance. Many consumers would prefer to dispense with these benefits and pay less for the goods, or pay extra for services like delivery and after-sales maintenance. Under price maintenance the consumer is denied the choice. It would be difficult to prove the general validity of the argument that specialist shops are driven out of business under price competition to the detriment of the consumer. If their number is decreasing in a certain trade, it only proves that many consumers prefer to buy low-priced popular lines in general shops, and that there is no need for so many specialist outlets carrying a wide range of stocks. The quality deterioration argument also stands on shaky ground. Quality deterioration is not a necessary consequence of price competition in retailing.

Public policy

The practice of resale price maintenance in this country goes back to the end of the last century. These were the years when large-scale retailers were increasingly competing in price and traditional retailers began to feel the effects of price competition. Resale price maintenance was looked upon by them as a kind of protection against the expansionist large stores. During the following decades, one of the main preoccupations of many trade associations was to persuade manufacturers to introduce price maintenance and, once introduced, to secure its effective operation.

Though price maintenance proved to be a controversial issue and, according to some critics, an economic evil, it was not made the subject of any official inquiry until 1920. In that year a Sub-Committee of the Standing Committee on Trusts investigated 'the extent to which the principle of fixing a minimum retail price by manufacturers or associations prevails; what are its results, and whether the system is, in the interest of the public, desirable or otherwise'. The majority of the Sub-Committee concluded that if the price charged by the manufacturer to the retailer is a fair and reasonable one, resale price maintenance is to the advantage of the public. At the same time, they recommended the setting up of a tribunal to deal with specific complaints of excessive charges on the part of monopolies, trusts, or combinations.

Ten years later, the Committee on Restraint of Trade reported that it did not regard the price maintenance system as free from disadvantages from the public point of view, but it was not satisfied that, if a change in the law had been made, there was any reason to think that the interests of the public would have been better served.

The Lloyd Jacob's Committee on Resale Price Maintenance submitted its report in 1949. Its recommendation was to outlaw collective price maintenance schemes but to leave the manufacturer's right to maintain the resale prices of its products untouched. The Committee's blessing on individual resale price maintenance was, however, not without qualification. It added that provision should be made 'for such price reductions as are justified by low-cost distribution, or by a regular policy of distributing surplus profit to the customer'. To achieve this purpose it recommended that the Government should invite consultations with the principal national organizations in trade and industry to consider means of ensuring that this policy was made effective. One member of the Committee, Henry Smith, the economist, took a different view on individual resale price maintenance. He stated that the acceptance of the right of the manufacturer to determine retail prices is also the denial of the usefulness of competition in the distributive trade.

Following up the Committee's recommendation, the Government asked a number of trade organizations for suggestions, but did not receive any constructive response. Therefore, it was announced in a White Paper in 1951 that the Government's intention was to outlaw not only collective but individual resale price maintenance as well. This decision was based on the view that the economic objections to resale price maintenances were no less great when the practice was carried on by individuals than when it was done collectively. The Labour Government did not have time, however, to implement legislation on this subject.

The Monopolies Commission surveyed collective agreements to adopt and enforce resale price maintenance when, at the request of the Government under section 15 of the Monopolies and Restrictive Practices (Inquiry and Control) Act, 1948, it reported on the question of Collective Discrimination in 1955. In respect of agreements on the adoption of resale price maintenance the majority of the Commission concluded:

> Whatever its advantages . . . resale price maintenance by individual manufacturers acting independently of one another restricts the ability of distributors to compete with one another in price. It therefore also to some extent restricts the freedom of the consumer to choose between different methods of distribution. Both these restrictive effects are intensified by agreements between manufacturers which oblige the parties to them to fix the resale prices of their goods; and they will usually have the further restrictive effect of compelling manufacturers who might otherwise prefer not to sell their goods in this way to fall in line with the majority. They thus make it more difficult for both manufacturers and distributors to try different methods of marketing their goods, and for the consumer to choose freely between them. We see considerable disadvantages in these additional restrictions of freedom of choice, and we do not think that the protection afforded to distributors by such agreements does in general promote economies in distribution or that it is justified as a means of preserving standards of service. We conclude, therefore, that such agreements generally operate against the public interest.[3]

The majority of the Commission concluded that agreements on enforcement of resale price maintenance also operated against the public interest on the grounds that such agreements place excessive power in the hands of trade associations, who can use it against individual members, or even against outside traders. Further, they make the system of price maintenance more rigid and more wide-

---

[3] 'Collective Discrimination', Cmnd. 9504, 1955, para. 146.

spread, eliminate price competition between retailers and are likely to lead to a waste of economic resources.[4] The majority view was that, similar to other restrictive practices investigated, collective resale price maintenance and enforcement agreements should be prohibited by law and exemptions granted only in exceptional cases. The minority of the Commission disagreed, and recommended that such agreements should be registered and investigated individually. The Commission did not pronounce on individual resale price maintenance as it was outside the scope of its reference.

The reports of the Monopolies Commission about various industries between its inception and 1956, also contributed to mould public opinion in respect of resale price maintenance. The Commission always condemned collective enforcement of retail prices, such as in the reports on dental goods, electric lamps, copper semi-manufactures and tyres. The attitude of the Commission was different towards individual enforcement of resale price maintenance. Though not invariably, the Commission generally approved of individual price maintenance, such as in the case of rubber footwear and standard metal windows.

The Restrictive Trade Practices Act, 1956

Following these preliminaries, legal restriction on resale price maintenance was imposed by the Restrictive Trade Practices Act, 1956. Part II of the Act declared the collective enforcement of resale price agreements illegal. Collective price maintenance was not outlawed but required to be registered as any other restrictive agreement, and the Restrictive Practices Court was called upon to decide whether it was contrary to the public interest.

At the same time, section 25 of the Act greatly facilitated the enforcement of individual resale price maintenance. The supplier was empowered to take price-cutting dealers to court, regardless of whether they were in direct contractual relationship with him or whether they had acquired the goods from a third person. Based on this provision, a number of manufacturers obtained injunctions against price-cutting retailers after the implementation of the Act. These cases meant adverse publicity for the issue of individual resale price maintenance, since traders often claimed in

[4] Ibid., para. 175.

court that substantially smaller margins were sufficient to cover their costs of doing business than those they were forced to charge.

After the 1956 Act, the grocery trade was the first where resale price maintenance started to disappear. The development of self-service techniques resulted in lower operating costs and multiples were anxious to expand by means of price-cutting. Early in 1957, aggressive retailers began to cut grocery prices. Initial cuts concentrated mainly of Nescafé and fruit squashes. Nestlé tried to prevent price-cutting for a while, but it spread fast and soon reached such proportions that effective action was not possible any more. The introduction of Maxwell House coffee without resale price maintenance also contributed to Nestlé's decision not to enforce resale prices. High profit margins encouraged price-cutting of fruit squashes. Between the middle of 1957 and 1959 price-fixing ended on most branded grocery items. Many manufacturers found that they had benefited from the change.[5]

In the late fifties, resale price maintenance was still a deeply entrenched practice in many branches of British industry, such as in the cigarettes, confectionery, motor car, books, chemists' goods, radio and electrical goods, etc., trades. In 1960 Professor B. S. Yamey estimated that about one-quarter of personal consumer expenditure on goods and services was spent on price-maintained goods.[6]

After the breakdown of resale price maintenance in the grocery trade, price-cutting became more frequent in other trades too. Notably there was a bout of price-reduction of electrical goods in 1961 as a consequence of falling consumer expenditure. Price-cutting received various reactions from manufacturers. Some turned a blind eye to cut prices, others took action under section 25 of the 1956 Act and sued retailers. By 1964, although resale price maintenance had been removed from toiletries, household goods and tyres as well as groceries, it was still a widespread practice in many retail sectors.

The Council on Prices, Productivity and Incomes, in its first report in 1958, suggested that the Government reconsider the

---

[5] J. F. Pickering, *Resale Price Maintenance in Practice*, London, pp. 117–125 and 157.

[6] B. S. Yamey, *Resale Price Maintenance and Shoppers' Choice*, Hobart Paper, London, 1960, p. 8.

individual enforcement of resale price maintenance incorporated in the 1956 Act.

The Government's endeavour to keep prices stable led to an internal Board of Trade inquiry into the economic effects of resale price maintenance early in 1960. Its report was not published but was believed to have come down against price-fixing.

In 1962, the Molony Committee on Consumer Protection stated that the repeal of section 25, the provision of the 1956 Act which permitted individual enforcement of resale prices, might greatly benefit the consumer.[7] The Consumer Council, which was set up following the recommendation of the Molony Committee, also came down on the side of the abolition of resale price maintenance at the end of 1963.

In the meantime judgements passed by the Restrictive Practices Court and the reports published by the Monopolies Commission also kept the issue of resale price maintenance alive, and prepared the way for further legislative development.

Resale price maintenance agreements as ancillary restrictions to common price agreements were considered in the cement[8] and standard metal window[9] cases under paragraph (g) of section 21 (1) by the Restrictive Practices Court. In both cases resale price maintenance was concurred with by the Court because the main agreements were found not to be operating against the public interest. The Monopolies Commission also investigated the supply of standard metal windows before the Restrictive Practices Court, and arrived at a similar conclusion both in respect of the price agreement and the supporting resale price maintenance arrangement.[10]

The 'acquittal' of the Net Book Agreement by the Restrictive Practices Court was an important event in the history of resale price maintenance, as this was the first case when the Court adjudicated on collective resale price maintenance as a main restriction of an agreement.[11] The Publishers Association based its case on gateway (b), claiming that the ending of price maintenance would deny the public specific and substantial benefits, and on

---

[7] 'Final Report of the Committee on Consumer Protection', Cmnd. 1781, 1962, para. 902.
[8] Cement Makers' Federation Agreement, 1961, L.R.2 R.P.241.
[9] Standard Metal Window Groups' Agreement, 1962, L.R.3 R.P.196.
[10] Standard Metal Windows and Doors, 1957.
[11] Net Book Agreement (1957), 1963, L.R.3 R.P.246.

gateway (f), claiming that a substantial reduction of export earnings would take place. Of the 12,000 or so retail outlets selling books, about 750 were stockholding booksellers carrying a wide range of stock. The preservation of the stockholding booksellers was considered of primary importance by the publishers. A number of important changes in the trade were foreseen by the Association if resale price maintenance was discontinued. It was envisaged that the number of stockholding booksellers would decrease, because price-cutting of best-sellers by multiples would divert trade from them and they would be left with the less profitable part of the trade. They would also lose trade because public libraries would switch their custom to specialist library suppliers. It was argued in Court that the decrease in the number of stockholding retailers would lead to higher book prices for the public. Surviving stockholding booksellers would reduce their pre-publication orders and would buy fewer books for stock. This would have the effect of publishers reducing the size of editions and, therefore, retail prices would go up. Total book sales would decline because of higher prices and booksellers would put pressure on publishers for higher margins, raising retail prices further. An additional consequence of the discontinuation of the Net Book Agreement was claimed to be fewer published titles and the exclusion of the publication of some works of literary and scholastic value. The Association also submitted that the higher home prices of books would cause a reduction in exports and that the higher level of exports was essential, not only for commercial reasons, but also to propagate British culture abroad. (Of the £79 million book turnover, £32 million was exported in 1961.) Though the Registrar argued against price maintenance in the book trade, the Court upheld the agreement based on gateway (b) of section 21 (1). The Association's case based on gateway (f), was, however, rejected. The decision was partly based on a precedent of price-cutting of books in the Montreal area of Canada after the abolition of resale price maintenance. The correctness of the decision was questioned by commentators.

Following the 1956 Restrictive Trade Practices Act, the Monopolies Commission continued to pronounce on resale price maintenance by dominant firms. Its controversial report on the cigarette and tobacco industry was published in 1961. Before the 1956 Act, the industry enforced resale prices collectively. Later

there was no collective agreement among manufacturers to maintain prices and they practised enforcement of stipulated prices
individually. The Commission found that individual resale price
maintenance in this industry did not operate against the public
interest. It argued that if there were abolition of resale price maintenance '. . . if a sufficient number of smokers took their custom
to the cut-price shop, there might be a substantial reduction in the
number of retail outlets. It might be held that the advantages
gained by some smokers through reduced prices were counter-
balanced by the inconvenience caused to others by a reduction in
the number of sources of supply and by the possible damage to
those engaged in the trade generally.' Professor Allen, a member
of the Commission, disagreed on the following grounds: 'I can see
no reason why consumers in general should be prevented by the
arbitrary decision of the manufacturers from choosing how they
shall distribute their custom – as between buying their cigarettes
at high-cost and high-price shops which may afford them some
convenience of location and service, or at low-cost shops which are
ready to pass on their economies to the purchasers. If resale price
maintenance were abolished, the number of retail outlets and the
structure of the distributive trade in cigarettes would come to
depend on the preference of consumers as expressed in the way
they choose to spend their money, and not, as at present, on the
manufacturers' dictate which frustrates their freedom of choice in
one important respect. If the number of outlets are reduced, this
would be because an insufficient number of customers was prepared to pay a price high enough to cover the costs of supplying
them at certain high-cost points of sale – in other words, because
of the effective competition of the low-price shops.' The majority's
decision was widely criticized in various quarters. In two subsequent reports, on motor accessories and wallpapers, the Commission came down against resale price maintenance. All these
events prepared public opinion for further legislation against price
maintenance.

The Resale Prices Act, 1964

Individual resale price maintenance was outlawed by the Resale
Prices Act, 1964. The Act declared void the imposition of resale
price maintenance by the supplier and prohibited the withholding

of supplies from a dealer on the ground that he had sold or was likely to sell the supplier's goods at less than the stipulated resale price. From this general ban exemptions can be obtained in special cases. The Registrar of Restrictive Trading Agreements and the Restrictive Practices Court were chosen as the machinery for granting exemptions.

Exemptions can be obtained in three ways. First, the Act prescribed a three months' period, ended on November 15, 1964, during which suppliers and their trade associations could give notice to the Registrar claiming registration. This action in itself exempted the applicants from the provisions of the Act until the Court's decision. The Court examines the registered price agreements and may order that particular classes of goods be exempted. Secondly, the supplier who did not claim registration during the prescribed three-month period in 1964 can apply directly to the Court for exemption at any time under section 7 of the Act. This provision takes care of suppliers who missed the initial registration period, of new products entering the market, and of the needs of newly formed companies. Thirdly, under section 7 the Court can review any previous decision under the Act on application either by the Registrar or a supplier. Both types of application under section 7 can be made only with the prior leave of the Court and no provisional exemption is granted to the applicants. Leave of the Court is granted only if *prima facie* evidence of facts is produced in the case of a late application, upon which an exemption order could be made. In the case of an application for review, evidence of a material change in the circumstances should be proved. Thus the 1964 Act represents a stricter line of public policy. While under the 1956 Act new registration of agreements can be made without limitation, prior permission is required in respect of individual resale price maintenance under the 1964 Act.

The basic assumption of the Act is that resale price maintenance is contrary to public interest. If a supplier wants to convince the Court that in a particular industry this is not so, he is required to prove that the detriment to the public interest of maintained resale prices is outweighed by other advantages. These possible advantages are grouped under five headings in section 5 (2) of the Act. Resale price maintenance may be approved by the Court if, in the absence of maintained prices: '(a) the quality of the goods available for sale, or the varieties of the goods so available, would be substantially reduced to the detriment of the public as consumers or users of those goods; or (b) the number of establishments in which the goods are sold by retail would be substantially reduced to the detriment of the public as such consumers or users; or (c) the prices at which the goods are sold by retail would in general and in the long run be increased to the detriment of the public as such consumers or users; or (d) the goods would be sold by retail under conditions likely to cause danger to health in consequence of their misuse by the public as such consumers or users; or (e) any necessary services actually provided in connection with or after the sale of the goods by retail would cease to be so provided or would be substantially reduced to the detriment of the public as such consumers or users.'

If it appears that the retention of resale price maintenance in a certain industry is in the public interest under one or more of the five gateways, the Court is called upon to balance these advantages against the detriment to the public caused by price-fixing. This balancing act decides finally whether price maintenance is held to be in the public interest in the trade concerned.

Section 2 of the Act makes it illegal for any supplier to withhold supplies from a distributor on the grounds that he has sold or is likely to sell the goods at a cut price. Loss-leader selling is, however, exempted from the general ban. Section 3 of the Act permits the withholding of supplies from a dealer who has used the article as a loss-leader. Loss-leading is defined as the resale of goods '. . . not for the purpose of making a profit on the sale of those goods, but for the purpose of attracting to the establishment at which the goods are sold customers likely to purchase other goods or otherwise for the purpose of advertising the business of the dealer.' Two exceptions are permitted to this provision: when the goods are sold by the dealer at a genuine seasonal or clearance sale and when the goods are resold as loss-leaders with the consent of the manufacturer. Section 4 of the Act allows any supplier to persuade others to stop supplying retailers using loss-leader tactics.

This provision of the Act is broadly in line with the corresponding 1960 Canadian legislation. Canada prohibited resale price maintenance unconditionally in 1951. An amendment of the Act eased the general ban in respect of loss-leader tactics in 1960. The Canadian legislation went further than the 1964 Act in that it also permitted the withholding of supplies from the retailer if he did not provide the services that customers might reasonably expect from him.

After the enactment of the Act, about 700 notices were given to the Registrar, within the specified period, claiming exemption. About 650 of them were submitted by individual suppliers and about 50 by trade associations representing their members. There was considerable overlapping among the notices, some of which claimed exemption for more than 200 different products. As a result of some withdrawals and rejections, the total number of notices finally dropped to 654. The Registrar was required to publish lists of the classes of goods registered. Following the Brussels Nomenclature, on which Customs tariffs are based, the Registrar identified and published almost 500 classes of goods temporarily exempted from the Act.[12] A few important trades, such as motor vehicles and accessories, wallpaper, paints and most sports goods, in which it had been a standing practice previously, decided to discontinue resale price maintenance and did not apply for exemption.

It is the Registrar's duty to refer cases to the Court. After deciding on the scope of reference, and on the parties interested, the Registrar serves the notice of reference on all those entitled to take part in the proceedings. Those who have entered an appearance are required to submit a statement, within three months, describing the provisions of the Act on which they intend to rely and the facts and matters which they allege entitle them to rely on those provisions. If the Registrar receives these statements from the interested parties, formal Court proceedings will be instituted where they will have the opportunity to defend the case. If, however, no appearance is entered in response to a notice of reference, or no statement of case is submitted, on the Registrar's application the Court issues Orders declaring that the classes in question are no longer exempted from the prohibition of resale price maintenance. The list of classes of goods in respect of which the Court has made such orders is published from time to time by the Registrar.

Having applied for exemption, the supplier can attempt to substantiate his claim in three distinct ways. First, reference can be made to factual experience in the past in his own trade or in

[12] 'Restrictive Trading Agreements', Report of the Registrar, 1st July 1963 to 30th June 1966, Cmnd. 3188, pp. 42–44.

another branch of industry. Events may be quoted from the time before the introduction of resale price maintenance. This sort of evidence cannot reach back, however, too far into the past – as the Court may reject it as being irrelevant under today's conditions. Alternatively, it is possible to quote the example of a trade where the practice of resale price maintenance has been abandoned voluntarily, or has been terminated by the Court. A further possibility of using past experience or evidence may arise for industries whose case will come up in Court not as an outcome of registration in the initial period. As these cases may be heard any time in the future, these industries will have the opportunity of drawing on events experienced after the passing of the 1964 Act. It is conceivable, for instance, that an industry did not apply for exemption within the specified period in 1964. After a lapse of time, however, changes may occur in the field which raise the hope of making out a successful case for exemption. The industry may attempt to prove, for example, that the quality of goods or the number of retail outlets or the provision of 'necessary services' were 'substantially' reduced as a consequence of the abandonment of resale price maintenance after the passing of the 1964 Act. In possession of this evidence, the industry may institute a case for exemption and refer in Court to factual past experiences.

Secondly, industries may claim exemption based on hypothetical future events. The upholding of the Net Book Agreement by the Court under the 1956 Act was largely based on this sort of argument – on the hypothetical case of what would have happened if resale price maintenance had not been continued in the book trade (fewer titles published, higher prices, fewer stockholding bookshops). The Court rightly emphasized in its judgement that any such assessment of the effects of the removal of price maintenance is bound to be speculative. In the first case judged under the 1964 Act, the chocolate and sugar confectionery trade also based its unsuccessful defence on hypothetical future events in the absence of resale price maintenance (small turnover, less selling points, higher prices, smaller selection of goods).

The third possibility open to the supplier is to refer to foreign examples in support of his case. The difficulties of comparison between different countries are obvious and it is up to the Court to accept or to reject such evidence. In general, the Court has been reluctant to consider arguments based on foreign experiences.

Still, as we have seen, when the Net Book Agreement was approved by the Court, the judgement was partly based on Canadian experiences in the book trade.

The first individual price maintenance case under the 1964 Act before the Restrictive Practices Court was contested by the chocolate and sugar confectionery trade. The hearing lasted for forty-three days, the longest in the history of the Court, between April and July 1967. The five major manufacturers – Cadburys, Rowntrees, Frys, Mars and Mackintosh – argued that if resale price maintenance was abolished there would be fewer shops serving the public, the variety of confectionery available would be more limited and higher prices would prevail. They based their argument on the fact that confectionery turnover is dependent on the number of selling points, as consumers buy two-thirds of their sweets and chocolate on impulse. It was stated that the total number of retail shops selling confectionery was about 250,000 and about 60,000 of them were specialist sweet shops commanding roughly half of the total value of sales. The respondents estimated that as a consequence of price-cutting, mainly by supermarkets, about one-third of sweet shops would go out of business by 1972 if resale price maintenance was discontinued. This would reduce the £324 million confectionery consumption by 11 per cent during the next five years. Lower turnover was envisaged to lead to higher retail margins, higher prices and a smaller variety of confectionery offered for sale.

The Court was not impressed by the arguments advanced and refused to grant an exemption to the chocolate and confectionery trade. It found that the industry's forecast about the future course of the trade was too pessimistic. In the Court's view the supermarkets would not be able to divert such a substantial trade from sweet shops as was submitted by the industry. They were responsible for only $3\frac{1}{2}$ per cent of total sales. It was envisaged by the Court that in the early days of free price competition there would be price-cutting but the position would stabilize later. As supermarkets and self-service grocers stocked only leading lines of chocolate and confectionery, price competition would develop only in respect of these lines. The Court held the view that it was unlikely that supermarkets would promote confectionery for more than 14 weeks in a year, apart from the special promotion of seasonal lines at Christmas and Easter. Except in these special periods, supermarkets would not be likely to promote more than one line of confectionery at a time. Thus, even those high street confectioners whose shops were near to supermarkets would not be exposed to price competition in respect of all leading lines at any one time. As far as the cheaper range of confectionery is concerned, sweet shops would be virtually immune to price competition. The Court also held the view that the diversion of trade to supermarkets would be relatively small. The number of specialist sweet shops forced to close down would be, perhaps, between 600 and 700 out of 60,000 by 1972. The reduction in the number of existing confectionery outlets would not appreciably affect the convenience of the public at all.

The Court did not agree with the assumption that a fall in the total consumption of confectionery would follow as a result of the abolition of resale price maintenance. If anything, a small increase in consumption could be expected. The argument of higher prices was also discounted by the Court: 'We find ourselves unable to hold on the evidence before us that the abolition of resale price maintenance is likely to make any appreciable difference one way or the other to the prices at which confectionery would be sold by retail in general and in the long run.' The Court also rejected the view that price competition would result in a substantial reduction in the varieties of confectionery available for the public.

The judgement made it clear that the Court did not take it into account that the abolition of resale price maintenance would drive some retailers out of business and cause financial loss to others. The Court considered these effects only in so far as they affected the consumer.[13]

Resale price maintenance in the U.S.A.

Resale price maintenance is generally referred to as 'fair trade' in America, a name invented by the proponents of this practice. Before the 1930's both collective and individual resale price maintenance was prohibited by the Sherman Act, 1890, and the anti-trust laws of individual states. Certain forms of individual price maintenance were, however, accepted by the Courts.

With the arrival of the 1930's the general economic depression hit American retailing and, at the same time, large-scale retailers

[13] *Financial Times*, July 26, 1967.

were increasingly competing by means of cut prices. Trade associations representing independent retailers and wholesalers campaigned for fair trade legislation to protect traditional operators.

California was the first state to enact a fair trade law in 1931. In intra-state commerce a contract between the seller and the buyer, specifying resale prices, became binding with the exception of closing-down sales, damaged and deteriorated goods, and sale of goods by order of a court. The law proved to be ineffective, since traders who did not sign contracts were free to cut prices. An amendment of the law was passed, therefore, in 1933, adopting the so-called 'non-signers' clause'. This amendment made it obligatory for every trader in the state to obey stipulated resale prices, even if not a signatory to an agreement, provided at least one dealer had signed an agreement with the manufacturer. Under the pressure of organized retailers, other states also gradually adopted fair trade laws along similar lines. Since 1931, with the exception of Alaska, Missouri, Texas, Vermont and the District of Columbia, all states have passed fair trade laws. These laws are not criminal statutes; the injured person must sue the offender for injunction and damages:

> The statutes legalizing resale price maintenance were whipped through the legislatures at breakneck speed. There is no record of hearings available in any state. The California law was supposed to contain a provision authorizing a producer to require 'any dealer' to maintain a stipulated price. The text enacted, however, was garbled. Instead of 'any dealer', it read 'in delivery', so the authorization made no sense. The care with which the laws were considered is indicated by the fact that this version was passed by the House and the Senate and signed by the governor, not only in California, but also in Arizona, Iowa, Louisiana, New Jersey, New York, Pennsylvania, and Tennessee.[14]

Under further pressure from the distributive trade, Congress enacted the Miller-Tydings Act in 1937 that legalized fair trade among states which passed fair trade laws permitting the practice. A Supreme Court case against an offending firm in 1951 disclosed that the non-signer provision was not in the 1937 Act, and therefore non-signers were not under the obligation to obey maintained prices in inter-state trade. The decision had a dramatic effect and

---

[14] Clair Wilcox, *Public Policy Toward Business*, Homewood, Ill., 1966, p. 709.

price-cutting spread all over the country within a few days and the fight for new legislation began.

In 1952 Congress enacted the McGuire Act, which legalized the use of the non-signers' clause in inter-state trade. One of the supporters of the fair trade cause was Senator Humphrey, who summed up his conviction this way: 'I am for fair trade. As a senator, I am for fair trade because it serves the public interest. As a former druggist, I am for fair trade because it enables efficient small business to survive by promoting fair competition in the market-place. As a consumer, I am for fair trade because it keeps prices down.'[15]

Opponents of fair trade contested the existing law in the state courts. Since 1953 the position of fair trade laws has considerably weakened in America. By 1964 about half of the forty-six states that had legalized resale price maintenance either ruled out their fair trade law entirely, or nullified their non-signers' clause. A further setback to fair traders was a court decision in 1957, which rules that a re-seller located in a non-fair-trade state can sell in a fair-trade state at any price he chooses (the Masters Mail Order decision). Under the new circumstances many manufacturers abandoned resale price maintenance.

In 1964, a new unsuccessful attempt was made to legalize fair trade on a nation-wide scale – regardless of state laws – by the so-called 'Quality Stabilization Bill'.

[15] Senator Hubert H. Humphrey, Jr., 'The Case of Fair Trade', *Tide*, June 13, 1952. Reprinted in J. Howard Westing and Gerald Albaum, *Modern Marketing Thought*, New York, 1964, p. 133.

CHAPTER 10

Recommended prices

As the retail price is one of the most important factors in determining the volume of sales, no manufacturer is indifferent to the retail prices of his products. This is an issue of primary importance within the framework of his general price policy. Based on different assumptions, he may assume different attitudes in this respect.

First, the producer of manufactured branded goods may leave the price determination of his products at the retail level to the play of free market forces; that is, retailers are free to sell the products at whatever prices they like. This policy does not mean passivity on the part of the manufacturer. He is likely to keep a constant watch on the prices of his own and competing brands, and if, in his judgement, the retail prices of his products are comparatively too high or too low, he is able to influence them to a certain extent by altering the trade price. This may be a policy designed to last for an indefinite period, or may be intended just to give a temporary fillip to a brand in such cases as the financing of a 'money-off' promotion, or a multi-unit offer in the retail shops lasting for a short period. Similarly, when launching a new product, manufacturers sometimes offer a special introductory price to retailers if they order above a certain quantity and within a specified period.

The opposite course open to the manufacturer is to achieve complete control over retail prices by imposing resale price maintenance. This policy is based on the assumption that a uniform retail price confers certain benefits on his business. Though the Resale Prices Act, 1964, outlaws resale price maintenance, the manufacturer can still retain or introduce it with the consent of the Restrictive Practices Court (see Chapter 9).

The third way to influence retail prices is the application of recommended or suggested retail prices by the manufacturer. In this case the producer specifies a retail price for the product but does not insist on its enforcement. Such a pricing method incorporates elements of both the other two policies. Specification of a certain retail price for a product by its manufacturer is characteristic of resale price maintenance. On the other hand, to leave the task of actual price-setting to the retailer is a feature typical of free retail price competition.

What effect has price recommendation on the setting of actual retail prices?

Recommended price as maximum price

It is important to note that retailers will overstep recommended prices only in exceptional circumstances. The retailer might charge a higher price than the recommended one in exceptional locations and in special cases where competition is not effective, or the cost of distribution is exceptionally high, for example, in out-of-the-way villages, mountain resorts, theatres, etc. As a rule, however, the recommended price tends to be the maximum price in practice. The reason for this is not that the retailer looks upon recommended prices as sacrosanct, but because he cannot charge more than the consumers are willing to pay. The consumer is reluctant to pay a higher price for a product than that which is printed on the pack, published in the price list, or featured in advertisements inserted by the producer. The average consumer considers this price as the maximum price and he is likely to transfer his custom to another shop if he finds that a shop, working under competitive conditions, charges more than the recommended price.

Sometimes the recommended price is not widely known by the consumer, it does not appear on the pack, and has not been advertised. The retailer is unlikely to charge more than the recommended price even in this case. The shopper may ask the retailer about the list price and he may find it difficult to refuse this information. Furthermore, the retailer may also reasonably suppose that his competitors will not overstep the recommended price and he therefore feels that he should act likewise.

Actual price-setting

When calculating his selling price of goods without a recommended or maintained retail price, the retailer has to base his calculation on one fixed factor only: on the trade price, that is, the price at which he has bought the article from the producer or wholesaler. As recommended prices tend to function as maximum prices, in the case of price recommendation the retailer has one additional fixed factor to reckon with; the trade price and the recommended price are the limits within which he ought to place his actual selling price. In other words, he knows his maximum gross margin before embarking on actual price-setting. The next step for the retailer would be to compare the maximum gross margin with his standard margin, that is the margin he usually charges on similar lines. Three distinct situations can be distinguished here. First, the long-term pricing policy of the retailer is not affected by the recommended price if the maximum margin coincides with his usual margin, the margin generally applied by him. This coincidence means that the retailer would be charging the same price for the price-recommended product as he would in its absence. On the other hand, products with recommended prices may be selected for temporary price reduction. These articles possess a special virtue that makes them especially appropriate to be used for selective price-cutting. Consumers are often doubtful about the extent of price-cutting by retailers when only the retailer's corrected price-tag (a practice known as double pricing) shows the difference between the original and the cut-price, but they are prepared to give more credit to price-cutting if a published list price, or a printed price on the pack, has been subjected to reduction. Moreover, the recommended price might have been featured in advertisements and made familiar to the public.

While resale price maintenance was a standing practice in this country, price-maintained brands were equally apt to be selected for price-cutting. The essential difference was, however, that price-maintained brands could not be singled out for price reduction without the risk of retaliation by the manufacturer.

A recent study on the actual pricing practices of large-scale grocers shows that recommended prices are welcomed for price-cutting purposes: 'On the whole, large buyers like the recommended retail price on the individual pack, simply so that it may be crossed off and their own price substituted, the extent of the price-cut thereby being perfectly clear to the customers.'[1]

---

[1] *Study of Top Grocery Buyers*, published by Pritchard, Wood and Partners Ltd., London, 1962.

The second type of situation arises when the maximum gross margin is smaller than the usual one, that is, when the recommended price is set at a relatively low level. Price recommendation in this case will act as a definite disincentive for the retailer to stock the product, since he cannot earn even his normal profit on it. His natural endeavour will be to back those competitive brands on which he can make a higher return.

Knowing this, manufacturers are likely to set recommended prices at a level high enough to accommodate all retailers, including the inefficient ones, working under normal conditions. Consequently, the level of recommended prices is likely to be higher than the competitive price level, which constitutes another similarity with resale price maintenance.

If the manufacturer intends to follow a low price policy by setting his recommended prices at a relatively low level, he is likely to achieve wide distribution only if he is able to create a strong consumer insistence for his product. By advertising it widely he may exert some pressure on the retail trade to stock the article in spite of the comparatively low margin.

In the third case, the maximum margin permitted by the suggested price is higher than that generally applied by retailers. To this kind of price policy they may react in two different ways.

Some retailers are likely to look upon high recommended prices as a good opportunity for more effective price-cutting. We have already considered the merits of recommended prices from the point of view of temporary price-cutting when the maximum margin coincided with the usual margin. A larger maximum margin extends these merits. A higher recommended price gives an opportunity for the retailer to offer a greater price reduction to his customers if he wishes to do so. In many cases higher price-cutting will impress customers and sales will be stimulated.

On the face of it, this seems to be a heaven-sent promotional method for the manufacturer. What he ought to do is simply to have a higher suggested price printed on the pack and his sales will soar; he will gain extra sales without any promotional expenditure. Unfortunately this is not so, for limiting factors are at work. Whatever the extent of price reduction may be, the most important selling factor is the actual retail price. Substantial fictitious price reductions, linked with high retail prices, are unlikely to be a successful sales policy. Actual retail prices are largely dependent on the trade price, at which the retailer buys. Furthermore, customers may suspect quality in certain cases if the price reduction is above a certain rate. With electrical goods, for example, the usual practice is that outdated models are sold at substantially reduced prices. A price reduction on a current model might convey the impression that it is a discontinued line, a faulty product or a 'shop-soiled' unit. Finally, it would be self-defeating for the manufacturer to stretch the level of recommended prices upwards beyond a certain point. As we will see below, a number of retailers do set actual retail prices on the level of the recommended price, and if this price is too high the manufacturer's sales suffer in these shops.

The second category of retailers look upon recommended prices more as an opportunity to earn a higher margin than as an opportunity for more efficient price-cutting. This type of retailer adheres to the recommended price, that is, he tries to sell the product at the maximum price. Naturally, competition may force him to make price concessions, but his basic attitude is to try to exploit the advantages of higher margins.

Empirical studies

To illustrate the two attitudes one can refer to Canadian and Swedish experiences.

A public inquiry was carried out in Canada into the effects of the abolition of resale price maintenance in 1954. The statistical material incorporated in the published report also contains some reference to the question of recommended prices. Of 70 retail shops selling household electrical appliances in a certain district, 51 reported that they did not observe the manufacturers' recommended resale prices on one or more items, while 19 reported that they did follow them. Among the 70 shops the number of chain-stores and individual shops was roughly equal, and this proportion was retained among the two groups who cut prices and applied the recommended prices; but the chain-stores generally sold more items below suggested prices than the individual shops.[2]

An inquiry concerning the effects of the 1954 abolition of

[2] 'Restrictive Trade Practices Commission', Material Collected by Director of Investigations and Research in Connection with an Inquiry into 'Loss-leader' Selling, Ottawa, 1954, pp. 146–159.

resale price maintenance was also carried out in Sweden in 1955. According to this inquiry, 75 per cent of shops observed suggested prices in relation to 65 commodities, and more than 90 per cent of retailers selling gramophone records kept to suggested prices.[3]

The Swedish Price and Cartel Office published a report on recommended prices in the branded household cleaning materials and toilet articles field in 1956. Recommended prices of these goods allowed a 25–30 per cent retail margin and, including the wholesale trade, a total distributive margin of 33–44 per cent. The inquiry had found that prices of toilet soap and toothpaste were 8 per cent below the recommended price, cosmetics and other toilet articles about 1 per cent, and cleaning materials other than detergent powder about 3 per cent below. Another Swedish survey, in the same year, investigated prices in the electrical household goods trade where more than 95 per cent of goods had recommended prices. Actual prices were about 8 per cent below the recommended level.[4]

After the breakdown of resale price maintenance in the British grocery trade, a private sample survey probed into recommended prices. It was found that on a certain day 50 per cent of grocers offered one or more cuts on the manufacturer's recommended price in three product groups: coffees, soft drinks and toilet soaps. One should bear in mind, however, that these product classes are particularly prone to be selected for price competition in the grocery trade.[5]

When investigating prices of soaps and detergents, the Prices and Incomes Board (see Chapter 15) looked at price increases in 1964 and 1965:

> The increases immediately experienced by consumers may not always have been in line with the rises in manufacturers' recommended prices. Although recommended prices and any changes in them are nation-wide, manufacturers have been in the habit of making special offers involving more or less local and temporary price reductions in connection with sales-promotion drives. These have continued during the period in which recommended prices were being increased. Secondly, in the general absence of r.p.m., soap and

---

[3] Soren Gammelgaard, *Resale Price Maintenance*, OEEC, Paris, 1958, pp. 103–104.

[4] *Cartel*, April 1959, p. 47.

[5] *Nielsen Researcher*, Oxford, September 1961.

synthetic detergent products have been offered by competing retailers with a wide range of reduction, extending sometimes to as much as 10 per cent. Without an extensive inquiry it is not possible to be specific, but it has been suggested to us that on average soap and synthetic detergent products are retailed currently at something like 3 per cent below the recommended price.[6]

The Monopolies Commission also reported on the extent of adherence to recommended prices in the field of detergents.

> The extent to which retailers followed the retail prices . . . recommended by the manufacturers varied. Unilever believes that price-cutting was widespread, amounting to a national average of 3 per cent below recommended prices, while P & G (Procter and Gamble) says that 25 per cent of the retail trade has been selling continuously at prices substantially below its recommended prices while a further 10 per cent has done so from time to time. This is generally confirmed by the evidence which we have received from distributors. . . .[7]

The degree of observance of recommended prices is dependent on the temporary business climate. When trade is brisk more retailers are likely to adhere to recommended prices than in a slack period. When the post-Korean war boom in electrical appliances collapsed in the United States, for example, price-cutting below recommended price was widespread among retailers. Manufacturers and retailers had large stocks on hand. According to an estimate, 'not more than 10 per cent and probably a good deal less' of radios, T.V. sets, and home appliances were sold at suggested list price in the New York area in this period.[8]

All these illustrations refer to a limited section of the retailing scene, but they still show that there is a tendency among a certain proportion of retailers to insist on suggested prices. A more detailed empirical study would be likely to reveal that a relatively large number of low-cost retailers disregard recommended prices, while the less efficient high-price retailers are more inclined to observe prices suggested by the manufacturer. Progressive retailers are likely to appreciate recommended prices for giving them an opportunity for more effective price-cutting, but otherwise they

[6] Report No. 4, 'Prices of Household and Toilet Soaps, Soap Powders and Soap Flakes, and Soapless Detergents', Cmnd. 2791, October 1965, p. 4.

[7] 'A Report on the Supply of Household Detergents', 1966, p. 13.

[8] 'Who Pays List Price?', *Fortune*, June 1952, p. 104.

are not strongly influenced by them. The real strongholds of recommended prices are likely to be those retailers who follow traditional trading methods, who do not engage in competition unless they are forced to, and who rely on high margins.

The different attitudes of retailers impose on the manufacturer the delicate task of finding the appropriate level of recommended prices. He must balance his interest between those shops which look upon suggested prices as an opportunity for a more effective cut-price policy and those which base their actual prices on the recommended ones. The two tendencies must be reconciled in the common recommended price.

The producer's motives

In some cases price recommendation may be used by the producer to set a maximum level to retail prices. A study of the women's outerwear industry has pointed out, for example, that recommended prices were applied with a double purpose. They were partly used for advertising purposes, sometimes prefixed with the words 'approximately' or 'about', because manufacturers believed that the exclusion of such prices might discourage sales, since some customers might have thought that the garment was too expensive. The other reason for the use of advertised recommended price was to ensure that the retailer would not place the garment in a higher price range than that intended by the manufacturer.[9]

Suggested retail prices may have a bearing not only on the pricing policy of retailers but on the publicity of both the manufacturers and retailers. Indeed, in certain cases this may be the main motivating force which induces the producer to apply recommended prices. Advertising policy can be affected by the application of recommended prices in three distinct ways.

First, consumer advertising by the manufacturer may be affected. He may hold the view that the sales effectiveness of an advertisement is enhanced if the copy includes the retail price of the product. In the absence of resale price maintenance the recommended price can be featured in advertisements.

Secondly, in trade advertising the producer may use the recommended price alongside the trade price. By this method he is able

[9] Margaret Wray, *The Women's Outerwear Industry*, London, 1957, p. 146.

to suggest a margin for the retailer with the intention of impressing him with an attractive business opportunity.

Thirdly, the producer's intention may be to increase the effectiveness of retailer advertising by giving retailers an opportunity to display the recommended price in company with their own cut price.

In countries where resale price maintenance has been outlawed, manufacturers have been aware that they are able to influence retailers to some extent by applying recommended prices. For this reason maintained prices have often been transformed into recommended prices. This has happened in many trades in Britain too. The chocolate and sugar confectionery industry, for example, told the Restrictive Practices Court, when their application for exemption from the Resale Prices Act, 1964, was being considered, that if resale price maintenance was abolished they (the big five companies) would publish recommended prices.[10]

Manufacturers sometimes introduce a recommended price as a basis for negotiating the retailer's buying price. This is the survival of the practice employed previously, when prices were negotiated on the basis of a certain percentage off the maintained retail price.[11]

There have been cases in Canada where some firms were accused of attempting to enforce recommended prices after the abolition of resale price maintenance in 1951.

There have also been cases where price recommendations have been discontinued because they have proved to be ineffective. Alfred Bird & Sons, for example, gave up recommending prices in 1965. Its sales manager was quoted as saying, 'There is no longer any sense in quoting retail prices when few grocers adhere to them or pay any attention.'[12]

Public policy

The question arises whether there is any need for a public policy dealing with the problems of recommended prices. Two lines of argument may be considered in this respect.

It may be argued that recommended prices mislead or confuse

[10] *Financial Times*, July 26, 1967.
[11] *The Economist*, May 20, 1967, p. 827.
[12] *Financial Times*, July 7, 1965.

the consumer. When the recommended price is shown together with the actual retail price on the price ticket, or in the retailer's advertising, it suggests a genuine price reduction, though the fact may be that recommended prices are set at an exaggerated level. This so-called 'dual pricing' or 'double pricing' is actually prohibited in the Republic of Ireland.[13]

The Federal Trade Commission has ruled in America that pre-ticketing of prices above the customary retail price level is an unfair method of competition, as it misleads the consumer about the value of the goods. 'Consequently a price-marking programme is likely to imply unfair competition if the suggested prices are not enforced and implies unreasonable restraint of trade if they are. Nevertheless, price suggestions are frequently used, particularly in apparel lines.'[14] In Sweden it is prohibited to advertise suggested prices without a reference that they may be cut.[15]

When investigating the prices of soaps and detergents in 1965, the Prices and Incomes Board found that suggested prices confused consumers, and recommended the termination of the practice:

> As far as the nature of the demand is concerned, the unit price is low; small variations in the price of a reasonably stable product are unlikely therefore to have much effect on the consumer. In other words, the consumer is not particularly price conscious. This apparent absence of price consciousness may be due in part to the confusion arising from the reductions made by retailers in the recommended price; the reductions are certainly regarded by many consumers as unreal and we suggest that the practice of recommended prices be terminated.[16]

The industry discontinued price recommendation in September 1965 in compliance with the recommendation of the Board. The Monopolies Commission reported on the household detergent industry in the following year. The report stated that the termination of price recommendation did not influence the general level of retail prices.[17]

The other reason for contemplating public measures against price recommendation may rely on evidence that it restricts price

---

[13] *Resale Price Maintenance*, edited by B. S. Yamey, London, 1966, p. 245.
[14] Ibid., p. 78.   [15] Ibid., p. 132.
[16] Cmnd. 2791, op. cit., para. 32.
[17] 'A Report on the Supply of Household Detergents', 1966, p. 13.

competition in certain cases and keeps prices above the competitive level.

The Board of Trade asked the Monopolies Commission in May 1967 to investigate whether recommended prices are, in general, consistent with the public interest. The terms of reference of the investigation are wide. The Commission is free to look into all practices designed to control retail prices after the abolition of resale price maintenance, such as suggested prices, and refusal to supply certain retailers; it may also investigate the practice of price leadership.

CHAPTER 11

Differential pricing

In an imperfect market the operator can follow, within limits, an independent pricing policy. He may not only set the prices of his products at various levels but may also sell the same article at different prices to different buyers. This latter policy is usually referred to as differential pricing or price discrimination.

Though these two terms are often understood as synonymous, it may be useful to distinguish between them. We propose to use the term 'discrimination' only with regard to those applications of differential pricing where the price differentials are not in line with cost differentials. Where relative prices are not based on relative costs, discrimination takes place because one class of buyers is favoured at the expense of the others. The price differentiation is discriminatory, for example, where different prices are charged in different markets, though the cost of production and distribution is identical.

When practising price differentiation, the businessman separates his buyers into distinct groups and charges each section the maximum price they are prepared to pay. The extreme form of price differentiation would be a pricing policy where every unit of a certain commodity is sold at a different price. Such a 'perfect price discrimination' is exceptional in practical life. Still, the Oriental bazaar comes near to this idea because every sale is made after a long haggling with the customer and, finally, many of them pay different prices for the identical article.

The obvious reason for price discrimination is that a higher profit can be made by separating the various markets from each other than by following a uniform price policy.

An essential condition of every price differentiation is that the various markets should be strictly separated from each other. Price differentiation is effective when goods sold on the cheaper market cannot move freely to the higher-priced market, or customers who are ready to pay the higher price cannot easily enter the low price market to take advantage of the better terms. The bases of price differentiation can be manifold.

Seasonal discounts

Seasonal discount schemes separate the market on a time basis. By offering goods or services in different time segments at different prices the seller is able to increase his total revenue. Seasonal prices may be introduced because of actual savings in production or distribution costs. When the National Coal Board sells household coal at a lower price during the summer months, for example, it obviously saves on storage costs, needs smaller marketing capital, and the ups and downs of production will be less marked.

In the book trade it is customary to bring out various editions at different prices. The basis of discrimination is quality and time. The hard-cover edition and a limited number edition for bibliophiles may be published first at two different prices. Some time later the paper-back edition is published at a low price. By using this method the publisher can separate the public into three groups according to their readiness to pay higher and lower prices for the different quality editions of the same literary work.

The cinema admitting people at a lower price in the afternoon than in the evening, tries to achieve a better utilization of its seating capacity by dividing the market into two price layers. The low-priced mid-week, night and off-season flights of air companies make better use of their planes and may appeal to rail travellers. Lower prices at lunch-time than in the evening in some restaurants, lower off-season prices at resorts, lower electricity off-peak charges, the cheap day or mid-week return ticket on railways, are all examples of price discrimination on a time basis.

Cash discounts

A variation on the time-based differentiation is the cash discount. In any business, prices may be calculated on a cash or on a credit basis. Most of the retailers quote cash prices, though the family grocer may be a notable exception who accepts payment at the end of the week or the month, seemingly without any extra charge. In fact, as he maintains a one-price system, his cash customers subsidize those who choose deferred payment. Retailers of household durables, on the other hand, usually quote cash prices and the customer pays an extra charge for credit sale or hire purchase. Where the business transaction takes place between the manufacturer and the wholesaler, or between the wholesaler and the retailer, a customary arrangement is that the buyer is free to pay his bill during a specified time without an extra charge, but if he pays on delivery or within a few days he gets a deduction called 'cash discount'. The economic justification of cash discount is clear. He who lends money is entitled to receive an interest and he who borrows money should pay for it. Cash discount schemes separate the market according to the ability of customers to pay without delay or at a later time.

Characteristics of the buyer

Certain characteristics of the buyer may be another reason for introducing a differential price system. It is a tradition, for example, in the medical profession that, for the same service, not all patients pay the same fee. Moral considerations encourage doctors to charge according to the ability of the patients to pay. Age is the dividing factor in other cases. Children pay less on railways and in swimming pools, students at exhibitions, and old age pensioners pay lower prices for certain services. In business, sometimes the status of the buyer in itself qualifies him to buy at a lower price.

Trade discounts

The price structure of an industry reflects the division of distributive functions among the producer, wholesaler and retailer. The manufacturer can quote prices in two ways. He may either quote prices directly or he may specify retail prices and percentage trade discounts. In the latter case a price list is issued by the manufacturer quoting fictitious retail prices, the so-called 'list prices'. The wholesale price (the price at which the retailer buys) and the producer's price (the selling price to the wholesaler) can be calculated by the deduction of percentage discounts from the retail price. These discounts are known as trade discounts or functional discounts. The application of trade discounts makes the administrative task of price changes more simple. Instead of reprinting the whole price list, the producer can notify dealers about a price change by simply announcing a change in the discount rates. Moreover, the use of discounts may be favoured by dealers, since discount rates facilitate the comparison of various margins offered by different producers. Their decision to stock or not to stock a product and, once stocked, what sales support to give it, chiefly depends on the margin offered.

The manufacturer often scrutinizes the trade status of distributors before deciding the trade discounts. He may hold the view, for example, that only genuine wholesalers are entitled to wholesale terms, and that those wholesalers who also do retail business should pay the same price as a retailer. Alternatively, he may decide that certain large-scale retailers are entitled to wholesale terms where they buy in bulk. In certain industries the list of buyers entitled to wholesale terms is a matter of agreement among a group of suppliers. They may also agree among themselves what the preferential terms should be. Such an agreement may form part of a wider price agreement. The General Report of the Monopolies Commission concluded that such preferential selling agreements do, in general, operate against the public interest, since a distributor who is refused admission to an approved list may be prevented from entering the trade.[1]

Loyalty discounts

Buyers sometimes receive discounts from a certain manufacturer on the undertaking that they will not buy supplies from competing producers at all, or that they will buy a major proportion of their purchases from him only. A similar discount may also be offered by a group of manufacturers as a means of securing the advantages of a stable market. The main argument against exclusive dealing arrangements is that they eliminate competition from producers outside the group. This arrangement has also often been made in conjunction with a common price system and other restrictive practices, such as resale price maintenance and aggregated rebate schemes. The Monopolies Commission has condemned exclusive

[1] 'Collective Discrimination': A Report on Exclusive Dealing, Collective Boycotts, Aggregated Rebates and other Discriminatory Trade Practices, Cmnd. 9054, 1955, para. 98.

dealing arrangements on many occasions. The Commission reported in 1951, for example, that of about 35,000 retailers selling electric lamps, 19,000 had signed an exclusive agreement with the Electric Lamp Manufacturers' Association, entitling them to a 5 per cent discount. The agreement had not shut out the 16,000 independent retailers; they could trade with lamps produced by the members of the Association without signing the agreement, or by outside manufacturers or both. Still, the Commission pointed out that the 5 per cent discount was a severe pressure on retailers to accept the exclusive arrangement and thereby impair the effectiveness of independent competition. Furthermore, independent manufacturers competed with each other by offering higher margins to retailers, rather than by lowering their prices. Consequently, the public was deprived of the benefit of price reductions. The Association's policy was more stringent towards wholesalers, inasmuch as members did not supply wholesalers at all unless the latter had signed an agreement not to sell any lamps produced by outside manufacturers. As a considerable number of wholesalers signed the exclusive agreement, the arrangement hampered the competition of independent manufacturers. Both arrangements were found to be against the public interest.[2]

Quantity rebates

A form of price differentiation is related to the amount or value of the goods purchased. Under a quantity rebate scheme the buyer is offered a lower unit price if he orders above a certain quantity or value. The rebate may be calculated either on the quantity or value of a certain individual line bought, or on the aggregated value of a number of items bought together.

Non-cumulative quantity rebates

Rebate schemes can be designed in such a way that every order qualifies independently for a price reduction whenever it is above a certain quantity or value. Taking a broader view of quantity rebates, two regular pricing practices should be mentioned. Retail prices of consumer goods marketed in various pack-sizes are often disproportionate to the quantity contained in the individual packs.

[2] 'Report on the Supply of Electric Lamps', 1951, paras, 155 and 287–289.

As a rule the shopper can economize by buying the larger size, since it is lower-priced in terms of quantity contained than the smaller one. The difference in unit prices can be considered as a quantity rebate.

The other common retail pricing practice that can be classified as a form of quantity discount is the so-called multiple pricing. As has been mentioned in Chapter 6, multiple pricing often involves a price reduction in exchange for buying more than one unit of the merchandise.

The same principles apply when a manufacturer offers a quantity rebate to the industrial buyer, or to the distributor, according to the size of the order of a certain article. By handling fewer orders instead of numerous small deliveries, the producer may make actual savings. Packaging, administration, accounting, selling, and transport costs may decrease. Further economies may arise from savings on storage costs, since large-scale buyers take over part of the stockholding function from the producer. Moreover, where quantity rebates boost total sales, production costs may also come down.

Aggregated quantity rebates

Some quantity rebate schemes grant a price reduction on all purchases during a specified period, usually a year. As against noncumulative quantity rebates these sorts of price reductions are usually called aggregated quantity rebates. Such schemes may disregard the size and frequency of individual orders or, alternatively, a minimum size for individual orders may be specified.

The structures of aggregated rebate schemes vary. As a rule a sliding scale is specified with several levels relating to the volume of purchase up to a ceiling, above which the rate of rebate does not increase further. Two main types of scheme have developed.

According to one system, the buyer is entitled to the same rate of rebate on his total purchases within the period as he gets on his last order. In other words, the whole quantity bought in a given period will qualify for the highest rebate rate. An example will illustrate the principle. An aggregate rebate scheme may specify that rebates are given on purchases of over 1,000 cases per year. The rate announced is 2 per cent between 1,000 and 2,000 cases, 3 per cent between 2,000 and 3,000, and 4 per cent for purchases over 3,000, this being the maximum rate. Under this scheme an annual purchase of 2,500 cases will qualify for a 3 per cent rebate, and on a purchase of 5,000 the buyer will earn 4 per cent on the whole quantity. It is obvious that there is a particularly strong incentive to continue buying from the company offering the rebate scheme whenever the total annual purchase is approaching a higher step of the scale, thus qualifying for the higher rebate on the whole quantity.

The alternative arrangement is the so-called 'layer system' where different rebate rates apply to each section of the quantity or value purchased. Taking the above example, in the case of an annual purchase of 5,000 cases, the buyer will get no rebate for his initial 1,000 cases, will earn 2 per cent for the second 1,000, 3 per cent for the third 1,000, and 4 per cent rebate on the remaining 2,000 cases. As compared with the other scheme, the layer system also rewards additional purchases but the incentive to go on buying is less strong, since the higher rebate rate is calculated only on a certain segment of the total purchase.

As we have seen in Chapter 7, American legislation has restricted the use of quantity rebates. The Robinson-Patman Act of 1936 outlawed those price concessions which are either not based on the differences in the cost of production and distribution or are not given to meet a competitor's lower price. Later on, the Federal Trade Commission ruled against several firms offering quantity rebates. American law discourages companies from applying price reductions unless they are able to prove the validity of actual cost reductions when selling different quantities. Cost allocation always entails some arbitrary element and it is particularly difficult to justify the existence of an aggregated rebate scheme, as the cost savings involved may be relatively small.

Collective aggregated rebate schemes

A group of sellers may agree to operate an aggregated rebate scheme collectively. Such an agreement is subject to registration under the Restrictive Trade Practices Act of 1956 and is adjudicated by the Restrictive Practices Court. These schemes are almost invariably linked with price agreements or at least with some common understanding on prices.

The Monopolies Commission has come upon aggregated rebate

schemes, partly in the course of its investigations into individual industries and partly while preparing its General Report on Collective Discrimination. In the General Report the Commission evaluated, amongst other restrictive practices, the effects of aggregated rebate schemes on the public interest.[3]

The essence of a collective aggregated rebate scheme is that two or more suppliers offer rebate terms to buyers on the aggregate amount or value of goods bought from them. The buyer can purchase his requirements from one or more suppliers and earns the rebate on the total amount of his orders.

Collective aggregated rebate schemes are often administered by the suppliers' trade association. The trade association keeps a record of sales by its members and calculates the amounts of rebate due to the customers at the end of the period specified in the agreement. The actual payment is made in a lump sum, either by the trade association itself or by the individual suppliers acting on the trade association's advice. In the former case, the trade association is reimbursed by the members for its payments.

The other form of customary arrangement is when payments are not made as deferred rebates at the end of the period, but are deducted from prices at the time of actual purchase. The rate of the rebate is determined either by the buyer's purchases in the previous period or by his estimated requirements in the current period. The former arrangement was discovered during the Monopolies Commission's general investigation into Collective Discrimination in the steel conduit and conductivity copper trades, and the latter in the salt and lead oxide trades. In the radio battery trade, the discount was based either on the previous year's purchase or on the previous two years', whichever was more favourable to the customer.[4]

Comparing these two forms of collective aggregated rebates, the payment as a discount from current prices proves to be the more simple to administer. The deferred rebate system involves extensive accounting work and cash payment. The buyer is also on safer ground with the discount on the current prices system, since he knows at once the final cost of the purchased items and can make his calculations accordingly.

[3] 'Collective Discrimination', Cmnd. 9054, paras. 189–213.
[4] Ibid., para. 196.

As a rule, rebates are paid only on goods bought directly from the manufacturers who are parties to a collective agreement. There are cases, however, where the retailer earns a quantity discount both on purchases directly from manufacturers and from the wholesalers. The Monopolies Commission found such an arrangement in the electric lamp trade. The payments were made by the Electric Lamp Manufacturers' Association, and the wholesalers, being also parties to the agreement, paid the amounts due to the Association.[5]

As in individual rebate schemes, the trade status of buyers may also be taken into account when designing a collective rebate scheme. In the steel conduit trade, for example, as reported by the Monopolies Commission, two separate scales of rebate were in existence – one for registered wholesalers and the other for manufacturers buying for their own use.[6] Similarly, exclusive buying undertakings, or the obligation to buy a substantial proportion of total requirements from the group, may also be a condition of participating in a collective rebate scheme.

The General Report on Collective Discrimination by the Monopolies Commission found only two cases (rolled brass and rolled copper) where the layer system was being adopted. In the great majority of trades the alternative system was in operation, that is, where the buyers earned the same rate of rebate on their total purchases within a period as they earned on their last orders.

During investigations by the Restrictive Practices Court and the Monopolies Commission into the economic effects of collective rebate schemes, four main arguments were advanced in favour of these agreements.

One line of defence was the claim that aggregated rebate schemes are necessary corollaries to price agreements and the only form of quantity discount appropriate to such agreements. It was argued that if members of a price agreement were free to offer quantity rebates individually they would in fact quote different net prices. Thus price competition would assume the form of quantity rebate competition and the price agreement would become void. It is true that the smooth functioning of a price agreement may be facilitated by a collective aggregated rebate scheme, but the claim that this sort of arrangement is the only one compatible with such agreements does not stand up to close scrutiny. Price agreements

[5] Ibid., para. 199.   [6] Ibid., para. 200.

are not weakened by the payment of individual quantity discounts when the rates are agreed among the parties of the group. Such arrangements were found by the Monopolies Commission in the paper trade and in certain building materials trades.[7]

Another argument in favour of these schemes was that they buttressed the position of small manufacturers who are parties to a common price agreement. If each manufacturer operated his individual quantity rebate system, many buyers would be induced to confine their purchases to large sellers who could offer a comprehensive range of products in any quantities. One may remark that it may not be necessarily beneficial to the public interest if small producers, who could not otherwise stand up to competition, are kept in business and it may be more economical to get supplies from large manufacturers rather than spread purchases over a large number of suppliers.

It is also said that collective aggregated rebates introduce flexibility into a common price system. Buyers have the advantage of being able to spread their purchases over a wide number of producers in the most convenient way and still earn the same amount of quantity discount as they would earn when buying from one supplier only. The advantage of this arrangement was emphasized to the Monopolies Commission by certain trades supplying building contractors. A particular contractor may undertake work in various parts of the country. In this situation the aggregated rebate system confers benefit on him because he is able to buy his supplies in the respective localities and still earn the same rebate as under central buying. Transport of these materials by the contractor is costly and some of them are easily damaged.[8] The fact that the buyer is free to place his orders with any number of producers within the group protects him against an eventual breakdown in supply. Furthermore, as buyers are likely to purchase each item from the manufacturer best equipped to produce it, this system promotes specialization within the group.

Finally, aggregated rebate schemes are sometimes defended on the ground that they are concessions given in consideration of the buying power of large buyers. The Cement Makers' Federation operated an aggregated rebate scheme when its common price agreement was looked into by the Restrictive Practices Court. The

[7] 'Collective Discrimination', Cmnd. 9054, para. 208.
[8] Ibid., para. 207.

rebate was given on the yearly quantity of cement bought from all members of the Federation. Purchase of more than 1,000 tons per annum qualified for a 1s. per ton reduction on the quantity in excess of 1,000 tons up to 10,000 tons. Between 10,000 and 25,000 tons the rebate was 2s. per ton, and over 25,000 tons it was 1s. 6d. per ton. (The average price of cement was 107s. per ton in 1959.) There was no serious attempt on the part of the Federation to justify the rebate scheme on economic grounds. The only argument advanced in defence of the scheme was the strong bargaining power of large purchasers and merchants *vis-à-vis* the Federation. The Court did not accept the argument and pointed out that the rebate created a privileged class, and any reduction of price to them was at the expense of the majority of purchasers who were not entitled to the rebate.[9]

The criticism of collective aggregated rebate schemes points out that the discounts given are often above the economies achieved by obtaining additional orders, and they benefit the large customers, who can compete on better terms against their smaller rivals. Moreover, it is costly to operate such a scheme because of the administrative expenses of a central office or trade association to settle the accounts of buyers.

The main criticism levelled against the aggregated rebate schemes, however, is that they impede competition from independent producers because they provide strong incentives to buy exclusively from the members of the agreement. The Restrictive Practices Court condemned the cement industry's scheme in these words:

> Apart from the absence of any economic justification for these rebates, they have the positive disadvantage of discouraging purchasers from buying cement from non-members of the Federation, thus making it more difficult for a member to resign from the Federation or for a new manufacturer to enter the industry without joining the Federation.

On many occasions the Monopolies Commission criticized aggregated rebates on similar grounds. On the other hand, the giant tyre scheme was passed by the Commission – partly because it was not strictly observed and partly because there was no

[9] Cement Makers' Federation Agreement, 1961, L.R. 2 R.P. 241.

manufacturer outside the group and so independent competition was not impaired.[10]

The incentive to buy only from members of a group is particularly strong when exclusive buying is required from customers to qualify for aggregated rebates. Such an arrangement was found in the copper trade by the Monopolies Commission. The Commission condemned the agreement:

> Both the loyalty and aggregated quantity rebates impede access to the market by independent producers because they provide a form of pecuniary pressure on buyers to confine their purchase to members of the associations. This is, of course, more pronounced in the case of loyalty rebates, but the inducement provided by aggregated rebates to buy from members of the associations rather than from non-members can be very substantial when a customer's purchases have brought him close to the point at which he qualifies for a higher rate of rebate. We conclude that both loyalty and aggregated quantity rebates and discounts operate against the public interest and we recommend that they should be brought to an end.[11]

The binding effect argument can, however, be overstated. Not every aggregated rebate scheme can secure buyers' loyalty. Once an initial purchase has been made from a member of the group a temporary binding effect exists, since it is advantageous for the buyer to patronize members until the end of the period. There is no long-term effect, however, since individual suppliers can compete with the group by offering similar prices. Aggregated rebate schemes can exert a long-term tying effect only in cases where there is an imbalance on the supply side. If, for example, independent suppliers do not produce sufficient quantity, large buyers are compelled to buy from members of the group. A long-term tying effect also exists when outsiders cannot offer a regularity of supply whereas the group can, or where the group is able to supply exclusive lines which are not available from independent competitors.[12]

---

[10] 'Report on the Supply and Export of Pneumatic Tyres', 1955, para. 532.

[11] 'Report on the Supply and Export of Certain Semi-manufactures of Copper and Copper-based Alloys', 1955, para. 319.

[12] B. S. Yamey, 'Aggregated Rebate Schemes and Independent Competition', *Oxford Economic Papers*, February 1960, pp. 41–51.

Selective price-cutting

Price-cutting on certain products, in certain geographical areas, or in respect of selective groups of buyers may serve various aims. The purpose of such a price reduction may only be to meet local competition, or originate price competition in a sluggish market with a view to increasing the firm's market share, or it may constitute an aggressive marketing policy to eliminate competition by defeating other operators. Outside investigators may often find it a delicate task to judge to which of these categories a particular pricing policy belongs.

The Monopolies Commission has investigated cases where selective price-cutting was used by dominant firms. Its report on industrial and medical gases revealed that Industrial Gases (Scotland) Ltd., a subsidiary of the British Oxygen Company, was used as a fighting company and probably contributed towards the withdrawal of its local rival from the Glasgow area, which gave up production of oxygen and acetylene in 1949. The Commission condemned British Oxygen's action: 'It is in our view contrary to the public interest that a monopoly such as B.O.C. should take advantage of its position to eliminate competitors by making local selective reductions in prices instead of extending to all consumers the benefits of any price reductions which may be possible.'[13]

Price discrimination can also be used to maintain market domination and to hinder the entry of new competitors. Suppliers of electrical equipment for motor vehicles, for example, charged a lower price for initial equipment supplied to car manufacturers and a considerably higher price for replacement supplies sold by the distributive trade. The difference could only partly be accounted for by differences in cost of bulk supply and individual packs, and the rate of profit on replacements was substantially higher than on initial equipment. In the Monopolies Commission's interpretation, the object of this policy was to keep new competitors out of the initial equipment market and they declared it to be against the public interest.[14]

Selective price-cutting was also practised by Lucas Ltd. in

[13] 'Report on the Supply of Certain Industrial and Medical Gases', 1956, para. 251.
[14] 'Report on the Supply of Electrical Equipment for Mechanically Propelled Land Vehicles', 1963, paras. 990–996.

respect of ignition coils in competition with AC-Delco. In this case the Monopolies Commission adopted a favourable view. Lucas was held to have reduced prices as a competitive action and not to suppress competition:

> It would in our view be . . . unrealistic to suggest that price differentiation for the purpose of meeting competition at the point where that competition is having most effect must be improper. . . . Although it may be difficult at times – particularly when one party is much more powerful than the other, to distinguish between price differentiation that intensifies competition and that which is intended to suppress competition, we do not consider that Lucas can be said to have abused its position in this respect.[15]

[15] 'Report on the Supply of Electrical Equipment for Mechanically Propelled Land Vehicles', 1963, para. 1060.

CHAPTER 12

Geographical price policies

A special category of differential pricing is based on the geographic location of the buyer. Some buyers live in the same town as the producer, others at shorter or longer distances up and down the country. Freight and insurance costs are involved in every transaction between the manufacturer and the industrial user or the distributor. It is a matter of pricing policy for the producer to decide how he will handle these costs. Similarly, the retailer who offers a delivery service to his customers must decide how to recoup his costs.

Most economists would argue that the correct method of pricing transport costs is that every buyer should pay exactly the actual costs from the producing plant to his warehouse. This is the only case where nobody is discriminated against and nobody is subsidized in respect of transport costs. Still, whenever a businessman is able to increase his turnover by charging disproportionately more for transport to some buyers and disproportionately less to others, he will feel that this is a reasonable course of action to take.

Ex-works pricing

The geographical pricing method under which each buyer pays for the actual transport cost between the factory and his own location is usually referred to as ex-works pricing. It is also known as mill-base, or FOB factory, or FOB mill pricing. FOB stands for 'free on board', a term which has long been used in the shipping business denoting the arrangement where the seller's responsibility for his goods ceases once they have been loaded into the ship. From this point of time the title of the goods is passed on to the buyer, who must meet all costs and bear all risks during the transport. The same principle applies when road, rail or air transport is used. Alternatively, the producer may charge a delivered price to his buyer which includes the actual freight cost. Under this arrangement he will retain the title of the goods in transit and will insure them, invoicing his exact costs to each buyer. Though this arrangement is, technically, delivered pricing, its effect is much the same as that of the ex-works system.

Though ex-works pricing is usually associated with manufacturing, it is also widely used by wholesalers and retailers. The retailer who obtains his supplies from a cash-and-carry wholesaler, buys in fact FOB warehouse, and the consumer who takes home his purchase from the retailer buys FOB retail shop. Similarly, if somebody buys from a retail store and the articles are delivered to his home by the shop and he is charged extra for the exact delivery cost, he makes an FOB retail shop purchase.

Ex-works pricing does not involve any price discrimination. The manufacturer gets the same price for his goods from every buyer and every buyer pays the exact costs of transport and insurance. By this method there are no special classes of customer who receive favourable treatment. If transport costs are not negligible, as compared with the value of the product, ex-works pricing tends to establish a monopoly position for the seller, based on location. Distant markets remain closed to him, since they are protected by high transport costs. In turn, the local seller is protected in the same way, since distant competitors have no access to his market. Thus, if freight is a substantial part of the total value of a commodity, its influence on the size of the market is important.

Ex-works pricing is likely to be practised when bulky low-value goods are sold locally, or high-value goods, whose freight charges are not relatively significant, are sold in distant markets. Especially where the high-value product is differentiated, it may be possible to market it at a distance and overcome the competition of local producers in spite of the transport charge involved. Where transport costs are substantial, the product standardized, and competitive producers scattered about the country, ex-works pricing is likely to sell only locally. But there is no limitation on the size of the market if all producers are located in the same area.

Where ex-works pricing is generally practised in an industry the market of each producer will be limited geographically, and producers will be priced out of distant markets. As the total price of the product increases with the distance, buyers will tend to place their orders with the nearest suppliers. Overall transport charges, therefore, will be kept at a minimum and the cross-haulage of goods will virtually be eliminated. It could be argued, however, that the ex-works pricing system ties operators to local supply and thereby restricts their choice. Under the ex-works pricing system the classic rule of industrial location will apply: where transport costs are a dominant factor, plants will be placed in locations where the sum of the transport costs of raw materials and finished products is the lowest. In some industries plants will be located near the source of bulky raw material, in others near to consuming centres.

Uniform delivered pricing

Under the uniform delivered, or single-zone, or postage-stamp pricing method the actual freight cost on individual transactions is completely disregarded. A single price is applied for the whole country, regardless of whether the buyer lives locally or at a great distance away from the producer, and the latter pays for the cost of transport. Each buyer gets the goods delivered to his door, or railway station, for the same stipulated uniform price, which includes the average freight of all transactions. The seller receives varying net prices from different buyers, depending on the transport cost paid by him on the deliveries. He absorbs freight costs on deliveries to distant buyers and overcharges freight to closely located customers. The difference between the overcharged freight and the actual cost of transport is sometimes called 'phantom freight'.

This pricing method involves discrimination in respect of most buyers. Only a few of them, located at an average distance from the producer, will pay the actual cost of delivery in the price; the rest will pay either too little or too much. Nearby buyers are overcharged and subsidize sales to more distant customers.

Uniform delivered pricing is not restricted to industry. Retailers who offer a free delivery service to the public also practise uniform delivered pricing. Shoppers in this situation have the choice of buying in the shop and taking the articles home or of having them delivered by the store free of charge. As both types of consumer pay the same price for the article bought, the cash-and-carry consumers subsidize those who require delivery. Sometimes retail shops charge a standard fee for delivery in a town. This arrangement can also be considered as single-zone pricing because discrimination exists in favour of those customers who live on the periphery of the town.

Many of the branded consumer goods with low freight charge content are priced according to the uniform delivered pricing system. Its greatest merit is simplicity, and its operation does not require costly paper work. It extends the boundaries of the individual manufacturer's market up to a national scale, ensuring a wide choice for the buyer in any locality. A further advantage of this pricing system is that the uniform price can be featured in nation-wide advertising campaigns. Against these advantages stands the substantial drawback that the total transport cost of an industry practising uniform delivered pricing is likely to be higher as compared with ex-works pricing, since buyers are free to get supplies from any seller without extra cost, regardless of the distance between them.

The point was made by the Monopolies Commission when it reported on the metal window industry. The Metal Window Association operated a uniform delivered price scheme in support of its minimum price agreement. The Association's defence was that to differentiate in price would involve additional administrative work and raise costs. The Commission did not accept this argument and pointed out that the scheme probably increased the aggregate transport costs, since it offered no inducement to the consumer to buy from the nearest source. The price agreement was finally approved by the Commission, subject to the submission of the price schedules to an independent body, but it suggested that the Association should consider allowing its members the option of quoting an ex-works price.[1]

It is interesting to note, however, that the Restrictive Practices Court gave an unqualified approval to the same scheme six years later on the following grounds: 'First, there is no public demand for ex-works contracts and customers do not desire to collect their own goods. It cannot be a detriment to deny someone something he does not want. Secondly, members have insufficient loading bays at their works to cater for the customers' lorries, so that there will probably be congestion and inconvenience for everyone con-

---

[1] 'Report on the Supply of Standard Metal Windows and Doors', 1956, paras. 244 and 249.

cerned. Thirdly, members for security reasons do not want strange lorry-drivers in their works. Fourthly, collection by customers would hinder members' dispatch departments and administration because they could never be certain when the customers' lorries would arrive, which ultimately would be reflected in higher costs. Planned transport leads to lower transport costs. Fifthly, it would be impracticable as a matter of accountancy to relate fixed prices in this industry to the actual cost of delivery. Sixthly, delivered prices enable more distant customers to have a wider choice of suppliers. Therefore, there is no detriment to offset the benefits conferred by the agreement on the public.'[2]

The problem of delivered versus ex-works price was also encountered by the Monopolies Commission when it investigated the chemical fertilizer industry.[3] Fisons argued that its uniform delivered price system helped to keep remote farms in business in accordance with official Government policy. Imperial Chemical Industries, on the other hand, claimed to operate a delivered price scheme for reasons of administrative convenience. Because of local traditions, both companies practised ex-works pricing, however, in Scotland and Northern Ireland. The majority of the Commission approved of the existing arrangements. They were aware of the relatively heavy transport cost element in the delivered price of fertilizers and the arguments against delivered prices, but were of the opinion that the general principles should not be applied too rigidly in this case. They did not think it wise to disrupt arrangements which, on the whole, had satisfied both suppliers and farmers and which had not been objected to by any Government Department. Professor G. C. Allen, however, dissented. He pointed out that fertilizer subsidies had been designed to accord with the delivered price system of fertilizer and thought it was against the public interest to obscure the fertilizer subsidies with a hidden subsidy of uniform delivered prices. Parliament, when determining agricultural policy, should be aware of the costs of sustaining remote farmers. He also stated that the uniform delivered price system distorted the pattern of production and costs and led to the uneconomic use of resources in the industry.

[2] Standard Metal Window Group's Agreement, 1962, L.R. 3 R.P. 198.
[3] 'Report on the Supply of Chemical Fertilizer', 1959, paras. 670–671 and 705–707.

Zone delivered pricing

A cross between ex-works pricing and uniform delivered pricing is the so-called zone delivered pricing system. Under zone pricing the market is divided into two, three or more parts (two-zone, three-zone, etc., price systems) according to the distance from the producing plant. Prices are uniform within each zone but higher in each subsequent zone as the distance increases from the production centre. When calculating the uniform zone price, average transport costs within the respective zones are taken into account. While in the case of uniform delivered pricing freight averaging takes place in respect of the whole country, here freight averaging applies separately in the individual zones. As actual transport costs are usually either below or above the zone price, buyers located below average distance within a zone subsidize those farther away.

Zone pricing can be found mainly where freight costs are substantial, and where a uniform delivered price would make the product too expensive in certain areas or where charging FOB prices would be too difficult administratively.

The glazed and floor tile industry has practised regional pricing in conjunction with its common price agreement, which was investigated by the Restrictive Practices Court. Prices were delivered prices and there was a 5 per cent surcharge on floor tiles and a 10 per cent addition to the prices of slabbed fireplace goods to Northern Ireland, Scotland, the Isle of Man and the Isle of Wight. The corresponding surcharges to the Channel Islands were 7½ per cent and 12½ per cent. The agreement itself was upheld by the Court on the grounds that it helped technical and commercial co-operation and standardization, and led to lower prices. The Registrar attacked both the application of delivered prices and the surcharges in respect of Scotland. He maintained that delivered prices are detrimental to customers who are near to the source of supply and to those who prefer to arrange their own collections. The surcharge system in relation to Scotland was described as arbitrary and illogical, since the cost of transport to Scotland was no greater than to certain parts of England but, nevertheless, the customer in Scotland had to pay more. The Court did not object to the system of delivered prices. The judgement stated that delivered prices were widespread in the building industry, collection by customers was troublesome and expensive to manufacturers, and if they had been common they could appreciably affect manufacturers' costs. Besides, the Court did not find evidence of resistance by customers to being charged delivered prices. The Court was in agreement with the Registrar, however, that the surcharge in Scotland was both arbitrary and illogical and detrimental to the public. Still, this detriment was not considered such as to outweigh the benefits of the agreement.[4]

Another example of zonal pricing can be found in the nationalized coal industry in respect of household coal. The country has been divided into sixty-three market zones for each of the five grades of house coal bought by merchants.[5] Industrial coal and that used for carbonization, however, are sold at pit prices.

Freight absorption pricing

Ex-works pricing limits the geographical size of the market. Market boundaries can sometimes be extended by the use of the so-called freight absorption or freight equalization pricing. This policy is a form of price-cutting in distant markets to eliminate the competitive transport cost advantage of a supplier situated near to the buyer. The delivered price is composed of two elements in the case of freight absorption pricing: the ex-works price plus a transport charge which would be the same as that of a competing producer situated nearer the buyer. The producer's net income on a certain good will vary according to the distance between his plant and the buyer's location and according to the proximity of the competing producer to the buyer. This pricing method is likely to be used by industries where products are standardized, transport costs are relatively substantial, and fixed costs are high.

The basing-point system

The most controversial delivered pricing method is the basing-point system or parity-point system of pricing.[6] All the geographic

---

[4] Glazed and Floor Tile Home Trade Association's Agreement, 1963, L.R. 4 R.P. 239.

[5] Report No. 21, National Board for Prices and Incomes, 'Coal Distribution Costs', September 1966, Cmnd. 3094, p. 5.

[6] For a detailed exposition see Fritz Machlup, *The Basing-point System*, Philadelphia, 1949.

pricing methods discussed so far can be operated by the individual firm, and when they are used throughout a whole industry it is the result of a separate agreement among the firms concerned. The basing-point system is, in contrast, an essentially collective pricing method which can only be adopted by a number of enterprises belonging to the same industry. Their co-operation may be based either on a formal or a tacit agreement. This pricing system ensures that identical delivered prices are quoted to all customers of the same locality by all suppliers.

Two main varieties of basing-point pricing have developed: single- and multiple-base systems. Under the single-basing-point system one particular location, usually an important production centre, is chosen as the base and all producers in the country add to their invoice price the same freight charge. This is calculated from the base to the buyer's town, irrespective of the actual distance between the buyer and supplier; thus price competition among producers is eliminated and the buyer can order from any supplier and will pay the same transport charges. It may happen that the producer and buyer are located in the same town and the basing-point is hundreds of miles away. Still, the customer is charged by the local seller the total amount of freights charged from the basing-point. The only place where this will not happen is the basing-point itself, where local buyers will not pay a transport charge at all. This will be the case even if a local buyer deals with a distant manufacturer as against a local one and delivery is made over a great distance. The actual freight charge paid by the seller can be more or less than the invoiced freight between the base and the location of the buyer. Accordingly, in some cases the producer will absorb costs and in others will earn a phantom freight.

An example will illustrate this. Let us assume that the single basing-point is London and an Oxford company buys from an Edinburgh manufacturer. The Edinburgh producer would charge the buyer with the transport cost only from London to Oxford, though his actual freight cost is more because of the longer distance between Edinburgh and Oxford. Consequently, the producer will make a loss on the freight; he must absorb part of the actual expense. When he receives an order from Glasgow, on the other hand, he will charge the London–Glasgow freight rate to the buyer but will only pay for the Edinburgh–Glasgow distance, and so will earn a phantom freight on the transaction. The actual and virtual transport charges will coincide only in cases of orders received exactly from half-way between London and Edinburgh. On orders from Edinburgh itself the producer will earn a phantom freight amounting to the whole transport costs between London and Edinburgh.

From the point of view of the London basing-point producer, the system will operate like ex-works pricing, since he will always charge his customers the actual freight cost. His competitive position will, however, be better than under ex-works pricing. The basing-point producer will have access to distant markets, since local producers will have to charge the same transport cost.

The design of a multiple-basing-point system includes two or more basing-points or governing-points. The actual quoted price includes the ex-works price and the freight cost from the nearest basing-point to the buyer's location. Actual and invoiced transport costs frequently differ under a multiple-basing-point system as well. Reverting to our previous example and taking Manchester as a second basing-point besides London, the Edinburgh producer would charge his Glasgow buyer not with the freight from London, but only from Manchester, as it is nearer to Glasgow.

Industries which have introduced basing-point pricing in the past show certain common characteristics. They produce standardized, non-differentiated products sold mainly on price appeal. As these products are of a bulky nature, freight constitutes a substantial element in their total delivered price. The industries in question are typically composed of a small number of large-scale plants scattered over a wide area, each of them representing substantial investment in capital goods and, therefore, operating with high overhead costs. When demand is slack and firms do not operate at capacity, unit costs rise sharply. In order to raise output they easily resort to price-cutting, and these cuts are almost certainly countered by competitors. In such a situation basing-point pricing may be used to stabilize prices and to avert the dangers of price-cutting.

The defence of the basing-point system of pricing is manifold. It is sometimes argued that the uniform price quoted by all producers in given localities is not a sign of collusion but the result of effective competition in an industry which produces standardized products. A second point frequently made in favour of basing-point pricing is that, in an industry with a high proportion of overhead costs, this pricing system helps to avoid devastating price wars in times of depressed market conditions. Furthermore, supporters of the basing-point scheme also refer to the danger of local monopoly where ex-works pricing is practised and claim that basing-point pricing widens the buyer's choice. Finally, legal abolition of basing-point pricing by the Federal Trade Commission in America was opposed on the ground that it would upset the existing deployment of industries. Under the basing-point system a certain location pattern has been established and a change would be costly for the economy.[7]

Critics, on the other hand, point out that basing-point pricing eliminates price competition and often promotes coercion in a given industry. The scheme facilitates collective retaliatory action against a producer who tries to increase his turnover by price-cutting. By lowering the base price in the offender's area to the level of the reduced price, his price advantage can be neutralized by competitors.

The other major criticism of basing-point pricing states that the average level of prices quoted under this system is higher than prices charged in the case of ex-works pricing. One obvious reason for this is that prices fixed under the scheme should be sufficiently high to give a reasonable return to all participants, including high-cost producers. The geographic extension of the market for all manufacturers partly raises the cost of salesmanship and partly increases aggregate transport costs in the industry. Because of the lack of incentive to buy from the nearest producer, a large amount of cross-hauling may take place in basing-point industries.

Industrial location is also adversely affected by the adoption of a basing-point pricing system. It encourages consuming industries to locate their plants near the basing-points and not near the producing centres in order to reduce transport costs. For those consuming producers whose plants are situated far from the basing-point of certain raw materials or industrial goods, the use of substitutes will be relatively cheaper, not because of a difference in the cost of production of the substitute, but because of the peculiarity of the pricing system. Producing firms may set up new plants in areas which would not be selected under competitive pricing conditions, and established plants are not moved in the

[7] Clair Wilcox, *Public Policies Toward Business*, Homewood, Ill., 1966, pp. 237–238.

wake of changed conditions under basing-point pricing. The consequence of the Pittsburgh Plus price system in America is, for example, that about 40 per cent of national steel capacity is located in the Pittsburgh area, while the region consumes only half that amount of steel.[8]

The cement industry provides an illustration of basing-point pricing in Britain. The Cement Makers' Federation's common price agreement was investigated by the Restrictive Practices Court in 1961. Each cement works, or group of adjacent works, and a few importing points, were basing-points in England and Wales. The net delivered price of cement averaged 107s. per ton in 1959. The basing-point prices were fairly uniform and not related to the costs of the particular works. When fixing prices, no precise formula was adopted by the Federation. Customers had the choice of collecting cement with their own vehicles at the works and being charged the ex-works price, or asking for delivery and paying the delivered price. Each works was treated as the centre of concentric circles with five miles radii from each other. Delivered price was the lowest in the inner circles, 2s. per ton above the ex-works price for bagged cement and 3s. per ton for bulk cement. The increase in the five to ten mile zone was 2s. 6d. per ton, for the ten to fifteen mile zone 2s. per ton. In the subsequent three circles, that is between fifteen and thirty miles from the centre, the price was only 1s. 6d. more in each successive zone, and over thirty miles the increase dropped to an extra 1s. per ton each five-mile circle. The concentric circles of various works intercepted each other at similar price ranges. The effect of this decreasing scale of transport charges was that each manufacturer tried to deliver as much cement as possible as near to his own works as possible, and the Federation claimed that cross-hauling had virtually been completely eliminated.

The Registrar suggested that the price structure subsidized distant customers at the expense of near ones. The scheme was said to distort the natural price pattern for cement which would emerge in a free market. Under the system a maker who did not operate long hauls had to charge his nearer customers more than an economic price, even though he had no distant customers to subsidize. The scheme was said to be arbitrary and artificial, and

[8] Walter Adams, *The Structure of American Industry*, New York, 1954, p. 180.

the distortion of the price mechanism it entailed had no economic justification. The Registrar refuted the claim that the scheme avoided the wasteful use of transport. He argued that if cross-freighting occurs in a free market, it indicates the existence of competition. Competition only arises when one maker charges a lower price than another. If a maker in one area is able to sell his cement in another at a lower price than the prevailing local price the public will benefit. The use of more transport by the maker who is more competitive does not put up the price. It was accepted by the Registrar that the scheme tended to promote sales near the works and lower transport costs, but any benefit was wholly outweighed by three considerations. First, the nearest customers had to pay more for their cement than would have been the case under competition. Secondly, the scheme discouraged low-cost works from absorbing some of their freight costs and extending their market. Thereby the scheme decreased competition. Thirdly, the subsidy to distant customers discouraged the building of new capacity in areas without cement works.

The Court was satisfied that the industry operated with a high degree of efficiency, both in respect of costs of production and costs of delivery, and that prices had been reasonable:

> As regards the geographical areas where expansion has in fact taken place, we see no reason for supposing that this has not been at sites where it was best justified from the economic point of view . . . there is no evidence that the common price scheme has resulted in the maintenance in operation of old works with high costs of production which could have been economically replaced by new works in some other locality.

The Court also held that there was no guarantee that, with a discontinuation of the existing system, cement would have been sold throughout the country at prices which corresponded more closely to the ex-works price plus actual costs of delivery; it found it difficult to forecast what alteration in the price pattern would take place. Concerning freight averaging, the Court held that the overall price charged for cement was not affected by this practice. It just reduced the price to more distant purchasers to the same extent as it increased it to the nearer located purchasers.[9]

The treaty of the European Coal and Steel Community – which was based on the Schuman Plan and came into force in 1953 –

[9] Cement Makers' Federation Agreement, 1961, L.R. 2 R.P. 241.

permitted basing-point pricing and prohibited only the use of abnormal basing-points. Companies were required to publish their prices and the High Authority was empowered to fix maximum and minimum prices in certain circumstances. The drafters of the treaty were well aware of the American experience with basing-point pricing; they even referred to American advisers on the subject. They intended to devise rules for effective competition and a proper allocation of resources. At the same time, they did not want to damage interests based on established practices. In respect of steel, the outcome was an essentially multiple-basing-point system, mitigated by the right of producers in certain cases to charge lower prices than the published ones to meet competition. In the Community's jargon this is called 'price alignment'.[10] The actual delivered price of steel falls between the upper limit of the basing-point price chosen plus freight, and the floor is determined by the lowest price quoted by a competitor.

Basing-point pricing is practised in the steel industry of every country belonging to the European Economic Community. Its significance, however, are not the same everywhere. In the Netherlands, Belgium, Luxemburg and Italy, the economic effects of basing-point pricing is not marked, since at least 85 per cent of the total steel output is produced within a 13-mile radius of the base-points. In France the basing-points are more scattered. Half of the steel output is produced within the 13-mile limit and the mean distance between the mills and the parity-points is 21 miles. In respect of tinplate the distance between the production centre and the basing-point is nearly 440 miles. The system is, however, most pronounced in Germany. Four basing-points only exist in the steel industry, one for each of the four kinds of rolled steel. Only 40 per cent of total output is produced within the 13-mile radius from the basing-points, and the mean distance between the basing-points and the mills is 42 miles. The economic effects of the basing-point system in Germany are meant to be mitigated by a price-equalization fund for rolled-steel products. A levy is paid into the fund by all steel consumers and those located farther than 140 miles away from the basing-point are compensated. This correction leads to further distortions in the price system.[11]

[10] William Diebold, *The Schuman Plan*, New York, 1959, pp. 275–277.
[11] J. E. Meade, H. H. Liesner and S. J. Wells, *Case Studies in European Economic Union*, London, 1962, pp. 259–263.

Basing-point pricing was first practised in the United States in 1880, when producers of steel beams agreed to operate a single-basing-point system. In those days Pittsburgh produced more steel than the rest of the country and, consequently, it was the obvious choice as a base. The scheme became known as the Pittsburgh Plus pricing system. The scheme was gradually extended to other steel products during the following decades and assumed a universal importance after the birth of the United States Steel Corporation in 1901. The Corporation came into being by large-scale mergers and became the dominant firm in the steel industry. From that time on the uniform base-price was simply set by the Corporation, the price leader, by publishing it periodically in the industry's journal. The uniformity of freight charges was secured by a publication of the Iron and Steel Institute which contained freight charges from Pittsburgh to every part of the country.

The scheme operated without much difficulty until 1920. In the early 1920's Chicago steel producers, with under-utilized plants, tried to establish Chicago as a separate basing-point, but had to retreat. Later, they reasserted their claim and western steel users also complained to the Federal Trade Commission against the Pittsburgh Plus scheme. The Commission started investigations and, in 1924, ordered the United States Steel Corporation to cease and desist from pricing on the Pittsburgh Plus basis.

In response to this order the Corporation increased the number of basing-points and thereby transformed the scheme from a single-into a multiple-basing-point system. Steel prices dropped sharply because of the smaller freight cost invoiced. This answer left United Steel in violation of the Commission's order, but no enforcement was attempted. The scheme was discontinued only in 1948, after the Supreme Court decision that the basing-point system was unlawful in the cement industry, and it was substituted by individual freight absorption pricing.

During the first decades of the century the practice of basing-point pricing spread rapidly in American industry and, by 1940, sixty industries used the system either in its pure or modified form.[12] Among others, the single-basing-point system was used in the glucose, malt, zinc, lead and copper industries, and multiple-basing-point schemes were applied in the gasoline, sugar, chemical

[12] Harold Koontz and Richard W. Gable, *Public Control of Economic Enterprise*, New York, 1956, p. 401.

fertilizers, corn products, gypsum products, linseed and lubricating oil, plate glass, etc., industries.[13]

Between 1945 and 1948 several basing-point schemes were declared unlawful in America, such as corn products (1945), milk cans (1946), cement (1948), and rigid steel conduits (1949). From 1948 on, business circles tried to put pressure on Congress to legalize the use of delivered pricing systems in cases where collusion could not be proved. President Truman vetoed the Bill in 1950. Basing-point pricing was not outlawed but a weakening of the Federal Trade Commission's policy set it. Earlier, the Commission generally charged basing-point industries with restraining competition by the concerted use of the scheme (unfair method of competition) under the Federal Trade Commission Act and with price discrimination under the Clayton Act, as amended by the Robinson-Patman Act. (Price discrimination exists under a basing-point system among buyers at different geographical locations, since the net return to the sellers varies according to phantom freight and freight absorption.) In the case against the American Iron and Steel Institute in 1951, the Commission condemned only the concerted action of manufacturers.

National versus regional pricing

The problem of geographic price policy presents itself in a different form when large companies own plants in various parts of the country. When plants are located in different regions, production and distribution costs are unlikely to be identical. Costs may vary because of the different technical and managerial efficiency of plants, the various degrees of utilization of plants, price variations in raw materials, differences in local wage rates, etc.

Such a company may follow a national price policy by charging an identical price for its products or, alternatively, may decide on a regional price scheme which will reflect the cost differentials of production in various plants. Regional pricing benefits consumers living in low-cost areas while the rest are relatively worse off. A national price system, on the other hand, disregards production cost differentials and discriminates in favour of consumers living in high-cost regions by charging them less than they would pay if the regional plant was owned by a local firm. Arguments

[13] Vernon A. Mund, *Government and Business*, New York, 1965, p. 247.

can be put forward both in favour and against these price policies.

If there is a substantial difference between the production costs of the various regional plants, a national price scheme may lead to an uneconomic employment of resources. High-cost plants may be kept in operation in the face of local competition by virtue of the internal subsidy system involved in national pricing. In the case of a regional price system, the same inefficient factory may be forced to close down, giving way to a low-cost rival. It can be argued, on the other hand, that regional schemes are difficult and costly to administer and may give rise to tensions, since consumers located near to regional boundaries are faced with different prices. Furthermore, a national price system may be defended on the grounds of equity. It is alleged that national pricing secures the maintenance of a reasonable service throughout the country, while under a regional scheme outlying areas suffer.

The merits and demerits of national versus regional price schemes were examined by the Monopolies Commission when it reported on Industrial Gases. The British Oxygen Company adopted a national price system and charged uniform prices in each of the eight districts supplied. The Commission approved of the company's policy.[14] The correctness of this decision has been questioned by critics.

Pricing for export

A further type of geographic price differentiation takes place between the home market and the export market. It often happens that the manufacturer is unable to place his goods at the same price abroad as in his own country, and he may decide to export at a narrower margin. An extreme form of exporting at a lower price is known as 'dumping'. The usual definition of dumping denotes the practice where the export price does not cover the full cost of production, but only variable costs plus a fraction of the overheads. Under this arrangement price discrimination works against the home buyer and in favour of the foreign customer. In an effort to protect their own industry, many countries have passed legislation against imports at dumping prices.

Under the Customs Duties (Dumping and Subsidies) Act, 1957,

[14] 'Report on the Supply of Certain Industrial and Medical Gases', 1956.

a duty can be levied on imported goods which are dumped or subsidized by the exporting country. Imported goods are regarded as having been dumped if the export price is less than the fair market price of the goods in the exporting country. Before an anti-dumping duty is imposed, the Board of Trade must be satisfied that actual dumping is taking place, and it is causing material injury to a home industry or will retard its establishment in this country. Applications from the home industries are publicized and the Board of Trade invites the alleged dumpers to argue against the case. Duties are imposed only as a last resort. A temporary duty was imposed, for example, on Irish butter between November 1961 and February 1962. Duty has also been imposed on a variety of barley from West Germany and on various chemicals.

CHAPTER 13

Organized commodity markets

Prices of basic commodities fluctuate according to market conditions. Their changing value involves financial risk for those who hold stocks and for those who enter into obligations which involves buying and selling commodities for the future. Organized commodity exchanges have been developed to provide markets for large-scale transactions in agricultural and mining products, and to give protection against risks derived from price fluctuations.

In London a centre of commodity trade is the London Commodity Exchange in Mincing Lane, in the City. Mincing Lane traces its origins as a trading centre back to the end of the tenth century. It was the site of the Royal Exchange, established in 1570 and destroyed in the Great Fire of 1666, and of the London Commercial Sale Rooms opened in 1811 and destroyed by bombing in 1941. The present Exchange was set up in 1954 and provides a meeting place where members of the various trade associations meet to conduct their business in primary commodities. The Exchange itself has no control over the methods or conditions of trading in the various markets. These are laid down by the respective trade associations. Trading in cocoa is regulated, for example, by the London Cocoa Terminal Market Association, and rubber trading by the Rubber Trade Association of London. Apart from cocoa and rubber, trading takes place on the Exchange in coffee, fish meal, jute, sugar, soyabean oil, spices, waxes, essential oils, etc. Copper, tin, lead and zinc are dealt with on the London Metal Exchange, established in 1877. Trading in corn is conducted at the London Corn Exchange and the Baltic Mercantile and Shipping Exchange. Corn is also traded in at Liverpool and Hull. Trading in cotton futures started in Liverpool in the 1860's. The two best known Continental commodity exchanges are the cocoa market in Amsterdam and the Hamburg coffee market. In America the first futures exchange was the Chicago Board of Trade organized in

1848, where futures business began in 1859.[1] The main products on the Chicago market are wheat, oats, corn, rye, cotton, soya-beans and lard. The other major centre of commodity trading is New York, where cotton, cocoa, coffee, and sugar are the principal commodities. Altogether there are 44 organized commodity markets in America. On 15 of these exchanges, futures trading is carried on in about 30 commodities.[2]

The rules of operation and organization of various commodity exchanges vary in details but follow certain general principles. Most members of the commodity exchanges are engaged in the production, marketing, or processing of commodities, and the rest are brokers who deal for others on a commission basis. The right of trading on the floor is usually reserved for full members and brokers, who do not pay commission after their deals. Associate members are usually entitled to deal through full members at a reduced rate of commission. At the London cocoa market members are classified into four groups: brokers, home members, U.K. associate members, and overseas members. The Rubber Trade Association of London divides members into the following classes: selling agents and importers belong to class A, brokers to class B, dealers to class C, and producers to class P. In 1967 members belonging to class A numbered 18, class B 14, class C 38, and class P 73. All these categories are restricted to U.K. individuals or firms. From 1967 onwards associate membership was established for firms trading in rubber and domiciled abroad. On the London sugar terminal market there are full, affiliated, associate, and overseas affiliated members. Full membership is limited to 63, of which there were 30 in 1967, while the number of other members was 186.

The Chicago Board of Trade, the largest grain futures trading centre in the world, has over 1,400 members.

The management of markets is conducted by committees elected from among the members. The London coffee terminal market, for example, is managed by a committee of 12 members, 8 of them representing the 35 floor members and 4 the associate members.

[1] Gerald Gold, *Modern Commodity Futures Trading*, New York, 1966, p. 11.
[2] Charles F. Phillips and Delbert J. Duncan, *Marketing*, Homewood, Ill., 1964, p. 478.

An important role of organized commodity exchanges is that they act as barometers for price movements in agricultural and mining products. Sales concluded on the exchanges are made public without delay for the information of floor members and for the use of operators at commodity exchanges abroad. Quotations made on the other exchanges throughout the world are also publicized. Thus, the principal world markets of commodities are in constant touch with each other by modern methods of communication, so that operators everywhere have up-to-date information about supply and demand conditions, and consequently prices at various markets cannot get substantially out of step with the rest of the world. Arbitrage dealings between the centres of the international market system tend to eliminate price differentials. By arbitrage dealings it is possible to make a profit, when price differentials exist on various markets. If the price of a certain commodity is higher on one market than on another, it pays to buy on the latter and sell on the former. As buying raises prices and selling depresses them, such deals will help to bring prices into line.

Transactions conducted on organized commodity exchanges fall into three categories: spot market deals, forward trading and futures trading. On the spot market, buying and selling takes place for immediate delivery. When a commodity is bought in a mutually agreed quantity, quality, and at an agreed price for delivery at a later date, the transaction is called a forward deal. By buying forward the buyer is freed from the costs of warehousing the commodity and the risk of deterioration of stocks until the delivery date, but he takes over the full risk of price fluctuations. Both spot and forward deals are trading in actuals, since virtually every deal is concluded with actual delivery. This is not the case on futures markets.

Futures trading

Futures trading is essentially trading in contracts incorporating transactions in certain quantities of goods some time ahead. Futures markets are therefore described as paper markets. Though physical delivery of goods is a possibility, in the majority of cases actual delivery does not take place. The total purchases and sales of futures contracts may well be in excess of the amount of total production of a commodity. As will be explained later, by selling and buying futures contracts, cover can be obtained against price risks which is the principal function of futures markets.

Commodities traded on these markets have certain common characteristics. First, such goods are of a durable nature which can be stored and, therefore, a definite relationship can be established between present and future prices. The quantity of commodities traded in can be expressed by number or weight and quality differences can be judged clearly. Based on these characteristics the commodities traded on futures markets are graded and can be bought and sold without examination. There is futures trading in cocoa and coffee but not in tea, as it is hard to standardize the grades of tea. Secondly, such commodities are important enough to occupy a large number of buyers and sellers. Concentration on either the supply or demand side diminishes the possibility of futures trading, since either dominant producers or dominant consumers can manipulate prices. This is the reason for not having futures trading in steel, aluminium and tobacco. Thirdly, as will presently be seen, the existence of normal price fluctuations is a prerequisite of futures trading.

On futures markets contracts are standardized to facilitate trading. They are made in respect of the 'basis' or 'contract grade', which is generally the most important grade of the commodity concerned. The price movements of this contract grade are representative of the whole commodity which is available in substantial quantities at any time. In some commodities several kinds of contracts are traded. On the London Wool Terminal Market, for example, two types of contract are available: the Bradford 64's Top Contract (the Merino Contract) and the Bradford 50's Carded Top (the Crossbred Contract). The seller is not obliged to deliver the contract grade but, depending on whether a superior or inferior grade is delivered, price adjustments take place in the form of premium or discount. This option makes it more difficult to corner the market by buying up supplies and then asking for delivery from those who sold futures. The premiums and discounts can be either fixed or periodically adjusted, or settled on the day of delivery. The minimum quantity and place of delivery is also part of the standardized contract. On the London coffee market, for example, the contract unit is 5 tons of sound native Uganda Robusta, and deliverable stocks must be stored in approved London warehouses at contract price, or in Bristol at a discount. In cocoa the contract is for 5 tons of Ghana Fair Fermented ex-store London, Liverpool, Hull, Avonmouth, Amsterdam or Hamburg. On the London Metal Exchange the minimum negotiable quantities are 25 tons for copper, lead and zinc, and 5 tons for tin. Deliveries take place from authorized warehouses. Qualities traded are also specified, such as: refined tin containing not less than 99·75 per cent of tin in the form of ingots or slabs, each weighing not less than 28 lb. and not more than 112 lb. The New York Cotton Exchange contract refers to 100 bales (50,000 lb.) and on the Chicago Board of Trade corn is traded in quantities of 5,000 bushels.

The standardized contract also specifies the maximum time a futures contract can run and regulates delivery dates. On the London Commodity Exchange and the London Wool Terminal Market the period of contract can be up to 18 months; on the London sugar futures market 15 months, while at the London Metal Exchange up to 3 months. Some standardized contracts may stipulate a precise day of delivery while others, and this is the usual case, secure the choice of any day within a certain period, such as within a month or within two months. Thus futures contracts are identical in quantity, quality and terms except for price and time of delivery. The standardization of contracts makes them interchangeable and easy to deal with. As the grade to be delivered and the delivery day is uncertain, futures contracts are not suitable for securing the supply of a certain commodity on a specified date. This purpose can be served by forward buying, as forward contracts are not standardized. The choice of deliverable grades and of the day of delivery makes undesirable manipulation with prices more difficult.

While trading in actuals is based on confidence, and no supervisory body guarantees the correct fulfilment of a contract, the rules of the organized commodity exchanges, and the clearing houses attached to them, do give such guarantee in respect of futures contracts. Contracts are made according to the requirements of the exchange and registered with the clearing house. Every buyer and seller is usually required to pay a deposit, which is kept by the clearing house until the maturity of the contract. They are also obliged to pay additional margins to the clearing house, if prices move against them as compared with the contract price. The standardization of contracts, together with their guaranteed fulfilment, facilitates speculation and hedging in commodities. The London Produce Clearing House Ltd., founded in 1888, is an independent company specializing in guaranteeing and clearing futures contracts. Contracts are registered with the Clearing House for a fee, and a Certificate of Guarantee is issued. An initial deposit and additional margins are required when prices change. Any individual or company can become a member of the Clearing House by paying an annual fee. Members can register contracts in their own names instead of in the name of a floor member through whom they conduct business. Rubber futures contracts are guaranteed by the Rubber Settlement House in London, established in 1922.

Speculation

Apart from producers, traders and industrial users of commodities, speculators also operate on futures markets. They study market trends and endeavour to make a profit by anticipating price changes.

The word 'speculation' has an ominous ring and it is often thought that the speculator makes his living in a sinister way. This is particularly so in relation to the Stock Exchange. Professor Galbraith writes:

> As already so often emphasized, the collapse in the stock market in the autumn of 1929 was implicit in the speculation that went before. The only question concerning that speculation was how long it would last. Some time, sooner or later, confidence in the short-run reality of increasing common stock values would weaken. When this happened, some people would sell, and this would destroy the reality of increasing values. Holding for an increase would now become meaningless; the new reality would be falling prices. There would be a rush, pell-mell, to unload. This was the way past speculative orgies had ended. It was the way the end came in 1929. It is the way speculation will end in the future.[3]

Such statements may or may not be valid concerning stock exchanges, but they cannot be uncritically applied to commodity exchanges. Potential abuses on commodity exchanges are usually eliminated or kept to a minimum by the obligatory rules of trading. The State may also control organized produce markets.

[3] John Kenneth Galbraith, *The Great Crash, 1929*, Boston, 1954, p. 174.

A number of American states have, in the past, prohibited futures trading. The Federal Government also regulated exchanges. The Cotton Futures Act of 1916 provided for federal classification of cotton deliverable on futures contracts. The aim of the Grain Futures Act of 1922 was to discourage price manipulation. The Acts were amended several times and finally incorporated in the Commodity Exchange Act of 1936. This Act put most of the exchanges under the general supervision of the Commodity Exchange Authority of the Department of Agriculture.[4] A Bill to ban trading in onions was passed in 1958 because of manipulation of prices.[5]

Speculators on organized commodity markets in general perform a useful function. They act as expert observers of supply and demand conditions and, by anticipating future necessary price changes, they make the process of price adjustment gradual. Their activities also make hedging possible. Because of their presence, futures markets are particularly sensitive barometers of price movements in commodities.

Speculation in prices presupposes normal price fluctuations. It is essential that supplies should not be varied rapidly, as this causes violent price fluctuations and, since future price movements cannot be anticipated under these conditions, speculation is discouraged. Statutory control of a commodity also eliminates speculation. If an important producing country, for example, intends to keep up the prices of a commodity by controlling the quantity entering the world market, prices will no longer be set by impersonal market forces. Stocks will build up in the producing country and foreign buyers will suspect that the price cannot be kept at a high level for long. They will run down their stocks in anticipation of a collapse of the market. Under such circumstances futures trading will shrink and speculators will keep out of the market. This happened in cotton after the last war as a result of government intervention by most of the cotton-producing countries, including the United States, Egypt and the Sudan.[6] Another example is provided by the Liverpool wheat market. The wheat

---

[4] Rayburn D. Tousley, Eugene Clark, and Fred E. Clark, *Principles of Marketing*, New York, 1962, p. 649.

[5] *Fortune*, April 1962, pp. 205–206.

[6] B. S. Yamey, 'Cotton Futures Trading in Liverpool', *Three Banks Review*, March 1959.

futures market in Liverpool was reopened after the last war in 1953 and remained open until 1958. Its failure was due to the operation of the Canadian and Australian wheat boards. These bodies introduced a 'price-to-be-fixed' method of trading. This system enables the purchaser to buy at an unfixed price for future delivery and has the right, later on, at any time to nominate the date on which the price will be fixed in accordance with the wheat boards' price of the day. Such a system eliminates the price risk for the buyer.[7]

Speculation can anticipate an increase or a fall in prices. If an operator presumes that prices will rise some time ahead, he will attempt to make a profit by buying now with the intention of selling later at a higher price. Conversely, an expected price decrease will elicit selling now and buying later at the lower price. In the jargon of stock and commodity exchanges, he who anticipates a price increase is called a 'bull' and he who contemplates a price drop is called a 'bear'. The operator may either sell goods he has bought previously, when he is said to be in a 'long' position, or he may undertake to deliver commodities he has not yet bought. The latter situation is described as selling 'short'. One who has bought a futures contract is not obliged to hold it and wait for delivery but can sell it before the maturity period is reached and make a profit on the price differential. Similarly, he who has sold a futures contract may cancel his obligation to deliver the goods by buying a similar contract before the maturity date. Every buyer has, however, the right to enforce delivery and every seller has the right to deliver goods if he so wishes.

'Straddle' operators help to secure a correct relationship between prices of futures contracts of different maturity. The prices of futures maturing in various periods depend on the supply and demand conditions. If there are more buyers than sellers for futures due in a certain month, the prices will go up. The straddle speculator makes a profit by buying and selling contracts of a different month of maturity. His buying and selling will influence prices.

Hedging

The possibility of delivery on futures markets ensures that price movements on the cash and futures markets are interrelated. As

[7] G. L. Rees, 'Britain's Grain Markets', *National Provincial Bank Review*, November 1966, p. 15.

a rule futures prices are above spot prices, with a margin corresponding to the costs of carrying stocks over the period involved. If a larger gap existed between the two prices, such as in the case of a prospect of a poor harvest, it would pay to buy on the cash market and sell the same commodity at the inflated futures price. As the delivery date draws near the difference between the two prices gradually narrows and they coincide on the maturity date. This price pattern, when futures prices are above spot prices, is usually referred to as 'contango'. The opposite situation is also conceivable, when for some reason futures prices are below spot prices. Such a 'backwardation' develops, for example, when there is a temporary shortage on the market in consequence of a dock strike or some transport difficulties, or the anticipation of a bumper crop, or in expectation of the collapse of a government marketing scheme. A further example of backwardation is connected with the relationship of the basis and other deliverable grades. It may happen, for example, that in the case of a fixed premium-discount system the price of an inferior deliverable grade is cheaper on the spot market than its futures price minus the discount. Under such circumstances it will be profitable to deliver this inferior grade rather than the basis. Consequently, futures prices will drop, reflecting the spot prices of the inferior grade and not of the basis. This kind of backwardation cannot develop in the case of periodic adjustment of discounts and premiums or where differentials are settled on the day of delivery.[8]

The connection between prices on the spot and futures markets makes hedging possible. The essence of hedging is that the operator is able to eliminate or limit his loss due to price fluctuations by dealing simultaneously in the spot and futures markets. In the case of a 'hedge sale' the stock-holding merchant or manufacturer buys cash and, at the same time, sells an equivalent amount on the futures market, thus protecting himself against the fall in price whilst he holds stock. When he sells the commodity later for cash he buys back the equivalent amount of futures. The loss suffered on one market will be offset by the gain in the other. If the price declines on the cash market he will lose on his cash transaction but will make a similar gain on the futures market, since he will be able to buy back futures at a lower price. Conversely, if cash prices have

[8] B. S. Yamey, 'Future Trading in Cocoa, Rubber and Wool Tops', *Three Banks Review*, September 1954.

risen he will make a profit on the cash deal and an equivalent loss on the futures market.

The producer of primary commodities can also cover himself against the risk of a price fall by selling futures before, and buying them back after, harvest. The possible gain on this futures transaction will be offset by the eventual loss resulting from the difference between the value of the crop when selling forward and the price realized when selling the harvested product. The following example will illustrate in more detail the use of a selling hedge as a protection against a price fall. A grower of grain may assume, in the spring, that prices will fall after the harvest in July. In view of this he may sell futures contracts representing the value of his crop for delivery in September. After the harvest the grower buys back the futures contracts he has sold before, and sells his crop. If grain prices have really gone down in the meantime, the grower will make a profit on his futures contracts, since he will buy them back at a lower price. The net effect of the operation will be that the grower will get the price ruling in the spring for his crop, and not the lower post-harvest price. This will also be the case if, contrary to his expectations, prices have gone up. He will have to be satisfied with the spring price since, though he will make a profit on the spot market, he will have to buy back his futures contracts at a higher price and the profit on the spot market and the loss on the futures market will cancel each other out. The cost of obtaining this insurance against a price decline is the commission payable to the broker and the fee of the clearing house. On top of that the grower has to forgo the eventual profit he *would* get in the event of an upward price movement.

In our example the grower sold September futures though the harvest took place in July. This is a reasonable course to follow. The maturity of futures contracts used for hedging purposes should be some time beyond the duration of the risk to allow time for liquidation. The nearer the maturity date the more restricted becomes trading in futures, while there is no difficulty in dealing with September futures in July.

The risk of a loss due to price fluctuations can also be eliminated by a 'buying hedge'. A manufacturer, for example, may accept orders for future delivery at a stipulated price but may buy the raw material later. Fearing an increase in price, he can cover himself by buying futures. When he buys the raw materials later he then sells his futures. If prices have moved up during the intervening period he will make a profit on the futures transaction, enabling him to cover his loss on the cash market. If prices have dropped, on the other hand, the manufacturer will lose on the futures deal and gain on the cash market because he had not bought his stock earlier at the higher price. Similarly, an importer who has sold commodities short may get cover against losses by buying futures.

It will be clear by now that hedging is made possible by the fact that various operators want to cover themselves against adverse price risks. Some manufacturers and traders want to avoid a fall in prices, whilst other businessmen seek insurance against price rises. Therefore, some operators sell and others buy futures contracts. The market is broadened by the activities of speculators who buy or sell futures according to their estimate of future price movements.

Backwardation

Whenever, both in selling and buying hedges, price movements in the actual and the futures markets are strictly in line, losses and gains will cancel each other out. Such a 'perfect hedge' cannot be achieved when spot and futures prices get out of line, and in such cases operators are left with a net loss or gain. Let us now consider the effect of backwardation on hedging.

Backwardation discourages hedging by the selling of futures because the operator cannot eliminate, but only limit, his loss due to price fluctuations. Somebody who holds or buys stocks and sells futures, while backwardation exists, already accepts a lower price for the futures contracts than the present value of his stocks. Prices of futures may go up or down later on but he will not be able to eliminate this loss any more. If prices move up the operator will make a gain on the spot market, but he will have to suffer a greater loss on the futures market when buying back his futures contracts at the higher price. His actual loss will be the same as he accepted when selling futures under the condition of backwardation. Conversely, if prices decrease further, his loss will remain pegged to the original amount, as he will be able, partly, to offset his greater loss on the actual market by buying back his futures contracts with a profit. Therefore, operators will make a selling hedge in such a situation only if they expect a further fall in prices. Backwardation therefore discourages stock-holding.

While backwardation discourages hedging by means of selling futures, it acts as a definite incentive to hedging by buying futures for those who are in a short position. They will not buy stocks at the higher current price, and carry them at a further cost, but will buy futures. Thus the operator will definitely secure the advantage of the lower backwardation price. The market may move up or down; in either case, he will gain the difference between the initial spot and futures price. Later on, the operator may require delivery on the futures market, or will close his position by selling futures contracts. The manufacturer who wants a certain quality on a certain date will choose the latter course and will buy his requirements on the spot market. If prices have gone up he will make a profit on the futures contracts when selling out. This profit will be partly offset by the loss he suffers by not buying on the spot market initially at a lower price. But, even after deducting this sum, he will end up with a net gain corresponding to the amount of backwardation on the date of purchasing the futures contracts. If prices have dropped, on the other hand, the manufacturer will make a profit on the spot market, from which his loss on the futures market must be deducted. As in the previous case, his net gain will equal the original amount of backwardation.

CHAPTER 14

Pricing in nationalized industries

Nationalization in Britain is a post-war phenomenon. Before the last war the Post Office was the only major industry owned by the state. By 1951 the railways, London Transport, long-distance road haulage, electricity supply, gas supply, some of the airlines, coal-mining, and the iron and steel industry, joined the list of state industries. After 1951 the returned Conservative Government de-nationalized the major part of road haulage and the iron and steel industry – with the exception of Richard, Thomas and Baldwin's. De-nationalization did not introduce, however, free competition in the industry, since price policy and planning remained within the purview of a statutory body, the Iron and Steel Board. In 1967 the Labour Government re-nationalized the iron and steel industry.

Though most of the nationalized industries are monopolies in the legal sense, they are in competition with alternative sources of supply. This is certainly true of the railways, which compete with the airlines, buses and private cars for passenger traffic, and with road hauliers for freight. The nationalized airlines compete, not only with rail and road services, but also with private and foreign airlines. On the home-heating and the industrial energy market, electricity, gas, coal and oil are rivals. Electricity supply for lighting purposes, on the other hand, is not exposed to competition, as electricity virtually has no substitute in this respect, except for the dwindling pockets of gas and oil lighting. Competition can also exist internally between the various services of the same industry. An obvious example is London Transport, with its underground railway and its bus services. The Post Office is in a similar situation where letter, telegram and telephone services are alternatives for each other to some extent. As in the case of private industries, the presence of competition limits the pricing freedom of nationalized industries, as prices cannot be manipulated without regard to the consumer's freedom to transfer his custom to competing services.

The level of prices a nationalized undertaking can maintain without incurring a loss depends, of course, on its efficiency, and this cannot be properly assessed if comparison with a similar business organization is lacking. With competitive industries the financial success of a company is itself sometimes the indicator of its relative efficiency, since consumers patronize those firms who offer them the best value. In respect of monopolies, either privately or publicly owned, the market test cannot be applied. They may be profitable but may not necessarily use the minimum amount of economic resources in producing their output, and they may be unsuccessful in satisfying consumers' needs. Where nationalized industries are organized into a number of quasi-independent regional units, like the gas industry, some comparison can be made in respect of their relative performance. But where a nationalized industry consists of only one monolithic organization, comparison of data is possible only between different operational periods. Neither of these two methods gives, however, an answer to the crucial question of whether the consumer would be supplied with a wider variety of goods or services at lower prices if competitive conditions existed. There are also considerable obstacles in the way of accurate international efficiency comparisons.

The commercial principle

It is usually contended that unhampered competition tends to bring about a better allocation of economic resources than when competition is restricted. To approximate to this ideal it is desirable that all firms, both privately owned and nationalized enterprises, should compete on an equal footing for their inputs, like capital, materials and labour. If this condition is fulfilled and competition is effective their prices will reflect the value of the amount of resources necessary to produce their output. Where any industry receives preferential treatment or a subsidy it will be able to quote a lower price. Demand for its products will increase and a larger amount of economic resources will be tied up in the industry than would be the case under the rule of the market. If state enterprises, for example, can borrow capital below the market rate their prices could be artificially lowered with a consequent expansion of demand for their services.

Nationalized industries should, therefore, follow commercial principles and pay their way without being subsidized by the taxpayer. They should pay the market price for their materials, labour and capital, and sell their outputs at prices reflecting their true costs. If these principles are not followed and prices are made lower as a consequence of a direct or indirect subsidy, an over-investment in the nationalized sector will follow at the expense of a corresponding under-investment in the economy elsewhere. The long-term national interest requires that the allocation of resources should be directed by realistic prices.

Following the private enterprise model also means that nationalized industries may raise their prices in order to provide capital for future expansion from inner sources. This is just what private industry does, where a substantial portion of capital financing comes from ploughed-back profits.

It also follows from the adoption of the competitive market model that every consumer should pay the price reflecting the actual costs of services provided to him. It is contrary to the commercial principle to select certain groups of consumers for privileged treatment. If some consumers pay less than their fair share, the rest subsidize them by paying more for the services consumed. Nationalized industries cannot be considered as an extension of social services and, if the state requires them to supply certain people at uneconomical prices, the state budget should foot the bill. Ideally these services should be financed by the government in the form of open subsidies and should not be mixed up with the operating results of state enterprises. In practice, however, the calculation of their value is a cumbersome task. Referring to rural electrification, the Herbert Committee stated:

> If it is thought in the national interest that some course other than a purely economic course should be followed, it is in our opinion the responsibility of the Minister acting on behalf of the Government to require that course to be adopted. Whether this need be by a formal direction or by the expression of Government wishes in writing is not, in our opinion, important, so long as it is known publicly that the Minister has taken a particular course and is answerable to Parliament for it. It is not for the persons running the industry to undertake

uneconomic schemes of expansion, whether in rural or urban areas, in the supposed national interest, if the effect is to subsidize one particular body of consumers out of the pockets of others.[1]

A further application of the commercial principle is that the Government should refrain from protecting declining nationalized industries; protection blocks the way of necessary changes in the economy. In the private enterprise field competition brings about the elimination or contraction of outdated industries. The same should be aimed at by a policy of non-interference in respect of public enterprises. However, these questions can be extremely complicated in practice, and powerful arguments may press towards a departure from strict commercial lines. The present energy policy in this country shows the complexity of the problem. It has been estimated that coal production is due to be run down by 30 million tons to about 140–145 million tons a year by 1970 in consequence of competition from oil, natural gas and atomic energy. Still, declining coal production is protected from the competition of other fuels in various ways. The import of coal is not authorized at present and foreign competition is kept away. A tax on fuel oil (since April 1965) also protects coal. At the same time government departments were instructed to favour solid fuel if the price difference was within the 5 per cent limit. The General Electricity Generating Board and the gas industry have also undertaken to use more coal, irrespective of pure cost considerations.

The 1961 White Paper

The surplus aimed at by state-owned companies is not identical with the profit made by private enterprise. It is not a payment for bearing risk but is designed to meet the capital commitments of nationalized undertakings in the form of depreciation, interest, and surplus for further investment. Before 1961 nationalized industries were expected to pay their way by earning revenue sufficient to meet all items chargeable to revenue, including interest, depreciation, the redemption of capital and the provision of reserves. In general they were required to average out the good and the bad years, to make up for previous losses by earning higher

[1] 'Report of the Committee of Inquiry into the Electricity Supply Industry', Cmnd. 9672, January 1956, para. 373.

profits later. In practice these requirements were not stringently enforced. Most of the nationalized industries charged customers less than would have been necessary to meet these obligations and either earned insufficient profits or incurred losses. They were often subject to pressure from public opinion, and sometimes even from Government circles, to keep their prices down despite rising costs and to set an example to private industry. It gradually became clear that this financial policy was incorrect, and this recognition paved the way for a new departure incorporated in a White Paper in 1961.[2]

The White Paper declared that it was the task of the Government to ensure that the nationalized industries were organized and administered efficiently and economically to carry out their responsibilities to enable them to make the maximum contribution towards the economic well-being of the community as a whole. The White Paper did not establish the principle that publicly-owned companies should be run on a purely commercial basis, but came down in favour of a stricter application of the commercial principle. Although nationalized enterprises have obligations of a national and non-commercial kind, they should not be regarded as social services absolved from economic justification. The idea of paying specific subsidies for unprofitable public services maintained because of social considerations was, however, rejected. It was envisaged that, instead of subsidies, the cost of commercially unprofitable activities must be taken into account when fixing the financial targets of industries.

The Government realized the danger that charging uneconomically low prices would lead to mis-allocation of resources, since too much of the total savings in the economy would be diverted into the nationalized industries. An unduly low rate of return on investment would require the continuous financial assistance of the Treasury; thus, instead of the consumer, the taxpayer would pay. Examples from the past were reminders of this fact. Accordingly, the previously fairly obscure area of financial targets was redefined more clearly in the White Paper. Instead of the former 'break even taking one year with another' principle a double objective was set for nationalized industries. They were now expected to earn a return on their capital investment which was

[2] 'The Financial and Economic Obligations of the Nationalized Industries', Cmnd. 1337, April 1961.

not substantially lower than in private industry and to pay their way over five-year periods.

The White Paper also recognized that nationalized industries had relied too heavily on the Government in the past for capital finance. Under the new policy companies were required to earn revenues high enough to build up adequate reserves to deal with contingencies, and to make a substantial contribution towards the cost of their capital development. Depreciation charges should be taken into account, not on an historical cost basis, but on a replacement cost level. Purely commercial considerations were, however, not introduced in every respect of capital requirements. It was considered that, in spite of substantial self-financing, the capital needed was too large to be raised in the open market without Government support. Thus the previous arrangements, under which nationalized industries resorted to the Exchequer for a proportion of their long-term capital requirements, remained in force and over half of their capital investment was financed by the Treasury in the ensuing years.

To achieve the objective set out in the White Paper a larger degree of pricing freedom was given to nationalized industries. It was recognized that they should be in a position to make upward price adjustments, especially where their prices were artificially low. In a way the White Paper marked a reversal of Government policy in respect of prices. For years the Government had used its influence to depress prices in the public sector; now a more realistic approach was adopted. The new policy did not mean, however, the discontinuation of Government control over prices. In the past the standing practice was that the chairmen of the Boards ascertained in advance the views of the appropriate Ministers, before a substantial change in the level of their prices was introduced. The Government expressed its wish that existing informal arrangements concerning price changes should be maintained in the future. The White Paper states, concerning any disagreement between the Boards and Ministers, that if a Board decides to modify its own proposals concerning a price change because of the views expressed by the Minister, the Board could require a written statement of those views and propose an appropriate adjustment of the financial objectives of the industry, where the modification would significantly influence financial performance. Before suggesting a price increase to the Minister to meet the financial obligations set for an industry, however, possibilities should be explored for the reduction of costs by better investment policy, elimination of unprofitable activities, improving productivity, etc.

Following the publication of the 1961 White Paper, the financial objectives of each nationalized industry were determined in the light of its own circumstances. Before 1961 most of the nationalized industries earned considerably less than 5 per cent per annum net on capital employed, while the comparable figure was considerably higher in private enterprise.[3] The new targets aimed at higher returns. The net return of the electricity industry, for example, was set at 6·75 per cent over the five-year period, to cover interest on all outstanding borrowing and a surplus to contribute to the industry's expansion. Over and above this figure, the industry was required to earn 5·75 per cent to cover depreciation. This total of 12·5 per cent gross return is lower than it would otherwise have been because of the obligation of the industry to supply rural areas. The gas industry is not under a similar obligation. Still, it received a fairly low 10·2 per cent target from the Government because finance for expansion was not necessary, as the industry was declining at that time.[4] Coal received the most preferential treatment because of its special position. Its financial target was set to break even, after calculation of interest and depreciation on a replacement cost basis.

The Prices and Incomes Board

With the setting up of the National Board for Prices and Incomes in 1965 (see Chapter 15) the pricing of nationalized industries has come under wider public control. The White Paper on Prices and Incomes Policy states that the Government regards nationalized industries as being under the same obligations as private firms to contribute to the general objective of price stability, while taking account of their financial and social obligations. The Government has the right to refer proposals for price increases to the new body and the reports on its findings are published by the Board.

[3] 'The Financial and Economic Obligations of the Nationalized Indusrties', Cmnd. 1337, April 1961, paras. 10 and 12.
[4] Report No. 7, National Board for Prices and Incomes, 'Electricity and Gas Tariffs', Cmnd. 2862, December 1965, para. 77.

The Board reported on electricity and gas tariffs (London Electricity Board and Scottish, South Western and Wales Gas Boards) in December 1965,[5] and on coal prices in February 1966.[6] Electricity and gas price increases were found to be justified – measured against the yardstick of the long-term trend in costs in these industries, and the financial targets set for them in 1961. The Board also approved of the increase in the pit-head prices of coal and suggested that the increases should be related more closely to the costs of individual production areas.

In the spring of 1967 the question of a price increase for the whole electricity industry arose, as demand for power had not been rising according to forecast. The consequence was that the return on capital was under 11 per cent in 1966-67, as against the 12·5 per cent objective set for the industry, and an even worse prospect was in sight for the future. The Minister of Power authorized the industry to raise tariffs to bring its rate of return back on target – without referring the question to the Prices and Incomes Board. An average price increase of 10·5 per cent was announced in September 1967. The announcement brought a wave of criticism against the Government. The Board felt by-passed and, as this was the first major price increase after the period of severe restraint of the prices and incomes policy, the unions felt that this whole policy was jeopardized. The Opposition attacked the Government for giving favourable treatment to nationalized industries and not subjecting them to the same economic disciplines which applied to all other commercial enterprises. A few days later the Government decided that every major price increase of the nationalized industries would go to the Board in the future, but refused to cancel the announced electricity price rises. Under the new arrangement the Board is called on to scrutinize the capital investment programmes of publicly-owned industry and is entrusted to carry out efficiency audits.[7] To enable the Board to carry out the new task, its staff was strengthened.

Within a short space of time, proposed increases of rail fares, London Transport Underground and bus fares, gas prices, Post Office charges and electricity bulk tariff rates were referred to the Board by the Government.

[5] Ibid.
[6] Report No. 12, 'Coal Prices', Cmnd. 2919.
[7] *Financial Times*, September 5, 1967.

Relative prices

It follows from what has been previously said that prices charged for the different products and services of a nationalized multi-product enterprise should correspond to relative costs. If certain services are under-priced, demand for them will unduly expand and, conversely, over-priced services will dampen demand. Low prices result in insufficient return or loss and, because of increased demand, an excessive amount of resources will be channelled into the production of the low-price services. The converse is true of over-priced services.

When relative prices are out of line with relative costs, discrimination and cross-subsidization takes place. This can take two forms. Uniform prices may be charged for different services in the same region, or for the same service in different regions, where production costs are widely different. Uniform prices are usually defended on the grounds of equity and administrative ease, since the proper allocation of fixed costs is cumbersome in the case of multi-product firms. The second type of cross-subsidization arises where different prices are fixed for certain services though cost considerations would justify a uniform price.

Social services

One can find many examples where nationalized industries do not set their prices according to costs but, mainly for social and historical reasons, subsidize various groups of consumers at the expense of others.

The railways are an obvious example of services maintained for social reasons. The railway network is substantially larger than could be justified on commercial grounds alone, and many branch-lines are maintained at a loss. As there is a standard passenger mile rate for the whole country, journeys on the uneconomic branch-lines do not cost more than elsewhere. The total deficit of British Railways amounted to £135 million in 1966. The Board's Chairman estimated that, out of the total loss, the cost of social services was about £100 million a year.[8] Apart from the maintenance of service branch-lines, suburban services and season tickets were sources of

[8] *Financial Times*, May 10, 1967.

substantial losses, but these are also regarded as socially desirable services.

The Post Office is also required to maintain a comprehensive national service regardless of costs, and, therefore, a considerable amount of cross-subsidization takes place between the various services. Letters are delivered for a uniform rate in the whole country. It has been estimated by the Post Office that, on the average, the handling of letters posted in rural areas, and those delivered in such areas, costs a penny more than urban letters. In remote areas the cost of delivering a letter might be as much as a shilling or more. Still, the Post Office believes that the uniformity of letter rates can be justified because the transport of mail between towns is a relatively small part of the total handling cost, and not only rural areas benefit from the uniform rate system but town-dwellers too.[9] On purely commercial grounds the inland telegram service should be closed down; it is being operated only for social reasons in favour of those who are not telephone subscribers and may need to send an urgent communication. Telephone kiosks are also making a loss at present prices, but the Post Office felt that it was not desirable to raise charges because of social considerations.

The provision of electricity in rural regions is obviously more costly than in urban areas, and a uniform price can be justified only on social grounds. In 1964 electricity was being supplied to 93 per cent of all farms in England and Wales.

Price differentiation

Cross-subsidization takes place in nationalized industries not only because of the maintenance of social services but also because tariffs are not differentiated enough to take account of the relative costs of supplying the various segments of the market. This does not mean to say that uniform prices are all-pervading in nationalized industries. There has been a gradual development towards a more refined tariff system since the early days of nationalization, and differentiation in prices now exists in many fields.

A characteristic feature of the inland postal tariff is, for example, that there is always a higher charge for the first weight step than

[9] 'Select Committee on Nationalized Industries', *The Post Office*, vol. 1, February 1967, p. 57.

for subsequent steps, since handling costs do not vary proportionately with weight. Another sort of price differentiation was introduced by the Post Office in 1961, when a rebate of up to 20 per cent was allowed on posting a quarter of a million items at one time. This concession rate was increased to 25 per cent in 1965. Postcards, newspapers and printed papers, on the other hand, are handled at a reduced rate, not because of cost considerations, but for historical reasons. Telephone charges are related to distance and duration of calls and a special cheap rate period is in operation between 6 p.m. and 6 a.m. every night and all day on Sundays.

There is a serious imbalance between prices of trunk and local telephone calls. On trunk calls the Post Office made over £54 million profit and on local calls nearly a £15 million loss in 1966–67. Telephone tariffs have been criticized because, despite wide differences in cost and demand from area to area, the telephone service charges uniform prices all over the country.[10]

Though a standard passenger mile rate is applied to the whole country, British Railways do practise differential pricing in more than one respect. First-class fares are 50 per cent higher than the second class, and special rates are in operation for various reasons. Of the 865 million passenger journeys in 1965, 550 million were made at fares below the ordinary level with mid-week, day, season and other cheap tickets.[11]

A large-scale experiment has been mounted by the Electricity Council to study the effects of tariff structure on domestic demand at different times of the day and year. It is desirable that retail tariffs should be lower in off-peak times and higher in the peaks. Restricted-hour tariffs (offering lower rates for electricity restricted automatically by time switches to certain off-peak hours) are already available to all domestic consumers, and a day and night tariff is in operation in two of the Board's areas. It was contemplated in 1966 that the experiment would last about 5 years. Any advantage derived from a new, more elaborate tariff system will, naturally, be considered against the increased cost of metering.[12]

---

[10] Michael Canes, *Telephones – Public or Private?*, Hobart Paper, London, 1966.

[11] British Railways Board, 'Information Sheet No. 5', January 1967.

[12] Electricity Council, 'Electricity – Progress and Plans', October 1966, pp. 18–19.

Marginal pricing

As the perfectly competitive market model fulfils the optimum condition of economic welfare, it has been suggested that its rules ought to be applied to public utility pricing. The application of this idea would mean that prices of nationalized industries would be equal to the marginal costs of production.

The difficulty is that public enterprises do not operate on a perfect market, and their average costs are, more often than not, above marginal costs. If prices were set at the marginal cost level this policy would often result in a loss. It has also been put forward that, in such cases, public companies should receive a subsidy from the state, while those nationalized enterprises whose marginal cost is above average cost and who consequently make a profit, should pay a tax. It is a mistaken idea to apply the rule of the perfect market under monopolistic conditions which would result in the taxpayer partly paying for the services of public companies instead of the consumer paying for them entirely. According to some opinions, therefore, the rule of the perfect market should be relaxed and prices should be, not equal to, but proportional to marginal costs.

The example of the coal industry shows that the marginal principle cannot be applied uncritically to nationalized industries. It is in the nature of the coal industry that production costs vary widely from pit to pit. Before 1957 there was a coal shortage and, therefore, a large number of high-cost pits remained in production. It was suggested that coal prices should be raised to the level of the marginal cost, that is, the production cost in the marginal high-cost pits. As marginal cost was above average cost, this pricing policy would have ensured large surpluses. At present, demand for coal is falling, the coal industry is contracting, and marginal cost is much lower than average cost. The introduction of prices based on marginal cost would lead to substantial losses.[13]

The first serious attempt ever made by a public utility enterprise to engage in marginal-cost pricing was the so-called 'Green Tariff' operated by Electricité de France in respect of high-voltage electricity. This was essentially a time-of-day pricing. Similar developments are taking place in the bulk electricity tariffs

[13] L. J. Tivey, *Nationalization in British Industry*, London, 1966, p. 146.

in this country. The Central Electricity Generating Board is in charge of producing electricity, and distributes it to the Area Boards which retail electricity to industry and to households. The Area Boards are charged by the Generating Board according to the bulk supply tariff. It has always been a two-part tariff and it has undergone progressive refinements over the years. Up to 1962 a fixed charge was paid by the Area Boards according to the kilowattage of their maximum demand, plus a running charge per kilowatt-hour supplied. When calculating the running charge, the local differences in the cost of fuel – mainly coal – used at the power stations supplying the area were taken into account. From 1962–63 the fixed generating costs were distributed among the Area Boards in proportion to each Board's contribution to the Generating Board's system peaks. At the same time, the running charge was separated into day and night rates. As consumption drops during the night and the lowest running-cost plants are able to satisfy demand, night unit cost is lower than day cost.[14] A new bulk supply tariff was introduced in April 1967 to reflect more accurately, in its prices, the actual costs of supplying electricity. This will be fully implemented by about 1970–71. The new tariff is, in fact, a changeover from average to marginal costing.

So far, running rates have been related to the average day and average night running cost of all stations operating during the period in question. Generating stations have, however, widely different running costs. Production starts with the lowest-cost station and, as demand increases, additional stations are called in, in the order of their running costs. The cost at the margin is, therefore, always higher than the average costs of the total generating at any one time. Based on the differences in marginal running costs, the new tariff contains three basic running rates: a peak period rate (in certain time-segments in December and January), a day running rate (relating to supplies between 7 a.m. and 11 p.m.), and a night rate. The adjustment for fuel prices in the different areas will be maintained, though in a different form than before. The new tariff splits the capacity charges into two parts: one related to the costs of providing the basic capacity and the other to the costs of plant capacity intended for use during peak periods only.[15]

[14] The Electricity Council, 'Finance for Power', 1963, pp. 25–26.
[15] Central Electricity Generating Board, 'News Letter No. 66', May 1966.

The 1967 White Paper

The system of five-year financial targets introduced by the 1961 White Paper had been criticized for making it too easy for companies in a monopoly position to meet targets by simply putting up their prices. The question of social obligations was also not fully settled in 1961, since state industries sometimes had to provide unprofitable services without obtaining any adjustment in their financial obligations. Some critics also pointed out that the simple return on investment criterion, modelled on private industry, was too narrow an objective for nationalized industries.

In November 1967 a new White Paper was published on the economic and financial objectives of nationalized industries.[16] It contains a re-definition of the principles to be taken into account by public enterprises in conducting their business.

Investment projects are required to show a satisfactory return, unless they are justifiable on social grounds or are provided to meet statutory obligations. Nationalized industries are expected to use the discounted cash flow techniques (an investment evaluation method where all future returns derived from a planned project are discounted to the present date and compared with the cost of investment) when selecting investment projects. In these calculations, as a rule, the cost of capital should be taken as 8 per cent. This figure is broadly in line with the average rate of return on low-risk projects in the private sector. This means that the Government will only approve those investment programmes in the future where the initial costs will be justified on the 8 per cent basis, or by some special social or wider economic justification. In appraising exceptionally risky projects, a higher test discount rate may be applied. Investments passing the test rate are, however, not to be undertaken automatically. The Government will consider and co-ordinate investment plans in the light of the general policy for a whole sector, like fuel or transport. In the course of the annual investment review discussions, the Government will approve only those investments which bring, relatively, the greatest returns. The economic value of investments cannot always be assessed by basing a judgement solely on the financial return to the industry concerned. Social costs and benefits should

[16] 'Nationalized Industries: A Review of Economic and Financial Objectives', Cmnd. 2427, November 1967.

be taken into account. A new underground line, for example, eases traffic congestion in the streets. Social cost-benefit studies of major projects will accordingly be carried out by the Government.

To eliminate undesirable cross-subsidization, and consequent mis-allocation of resources, it is required by the White Paper that, while covering overall costs, prices should be related to the cost of the particular goods and services provided wherever possible. Cross-subsidization can be justified only by statutory requirements or by wider economic or social considerations. Different prices may also be charged in industries where persistent spare capacity exists. Prices should be reduced in such cases to stimulate demand and to save investment in industries supplying competing services. To avoid cross-subsidization, differential pricing systems such as two-part and multi-part tariffs and quantity discounts are advocated. While covering costs, prices in general should be related to costs at the margin. Marginal pricing will not be applied, however, where its use would over-stimulate supply in the short-term, cause revenue deficits or conflict with the prices and incomes policy (see Chapter 15).

The pricing policy nationalized industries are expected to follow should not be 'rigid or doctrinaire'. Targets are set for periods of five years, as before, and provided industries observe the general principles set out in the White Paper, the Government intends to give management the maximum freedom to formulate a price policy to meet competition. The price policy of nationalized industries is, however, subject to the provisions of the prices and incomes policy, including the early warning system.

The White Paper remarks that it would be wrong if a nationalized enterprise could exploit its monopoly power by making unnecessary price increases to cover unnecessary high costs. Therefore, costs ought to be kept under firm control and it is the management's task to endeavour to reduce costs by employing improved methods to increase efficiency and productivity. It is particularly important to use manpower more efficiently and to look for possibilities of labour saving, since the cost of labour is likely to rise continuously.

Financial objectives for individual nationalized industries are fixed by the Government in the light of the principles incorporated in the White Paper. While setting the financial targets the Government takes into consideration the return on new investment, sound pricing, social obligations not covered by subsidy, efficient operation, and the aspects of the prices and incomes policy. Therefore, in spite of the common test rate of return on new investment, the financial objectives are different for each industry. These objectives can be expressed in terms of a percentage return on the net assets or as a fixed sum of money. It may be desirable in the future to set some targets for a shorter period than five years or to reconsider the previously set objectives of a certain industry before the end of the five-year period, if circumstances change.

Where a nationalized industry is required to supply uneconomical services or to undertake such investments because of wider social or economic considerations, the Government intends to make a special payment to the industry or to adjust its financial objectives appropriately.

The possible payment of a special subsidy is, undoubtedly, a definite advance towards tidying up state enterprise finances. The White Paper on railways, published in November 1967, proposed that grants totalling £35–£40 million should be paid by the Government as compensation for maintaining socially desirable services which are not commercially justifiable.[17]

After the publication of the 1967 White Paper, the economic and financial obligations of individual nationalized industries were announced in a series of individual White Papers.

[17] *The Economist*, November 11, 1967, p. 649.

CHAPTER 15

Prices and incomes policy

The post-war history of the British economy has been marked by a virtually permanent disparity between the growth of production and money incomes. As incomes have risen faster than output, prices have been increasing. Moreover, the country has suffered from periodic balance of payment crises leading to temporary restrictions of home demand. The growth of the economy has been much slower than that of many other industrial countries.

After the particularly severe foreign exchange crisis in the second half of 1964, the new Labour Government felt that an effective productivity, prices and incomes policy was needed to restore the health of the economy. On December 16, 1964, the celebrated Joint Statement of Intent on Productivity, Prices and Incomes was signed by the representatives of the Trades Union Congress, The Association of British Chambers of Commerce, The British Employers' Confederation, The Federation of British Industries, and The National Association of British Manufacturers. With the Joint Statement the Trades Union Congress and the employers' organizations undertook to co-operate with the Government in the running of an incomes policy, aiming to raise productivity, to keep increases in total money incomes in line with increases in real national output and to maintain a stable general price level. In order to realize the objectives of the Joint Statement, it was agreed that the general movement of prices and money incomes, and the behaviour of particular prices and incomes should be kept under permanent review.

The White Paper on the Machinery of Prices and Incomes Policy was published at the beginning of 1965.[1] The task of keeping under review general price and incomes behaviour was assigned to the National Economic Development Council, acting on reports submitted by the National Economic Development Office in con-

[1] Cmd. 2577, February 1965.

sultation with various Government Departments. To investigate particular cases of price, wage and other income behaviour, the White Paper proposed the setting up of a new advisory body, the National Board for Prices and Incomes. It was hoped that all parties concerned would give their support and voluntary co-operation in the investigations of individual cases, but the possibility of giving the Board statutory authority, if necessary, was indicated. To ensure that the findings of the Board were accepted, the Government intended to rely on persuasion and pressure of public opinion.

Following the recommendation of the White Paper, the National Board for Prices and Incomes (popularly known later as the Prices and Incomes Board or PIB) was set up by Royal Warrant in April 1965. Five full-time and four part-time members were appointed, representing partly management, partly unions and partly professions like law, accountancy and economics. The Board was headed by a chairman and two deputy chairmen appointed from the nine members. The Board's staff was recruited from specialists in the various fields related to business.

A further White Paper, published in April 1965, set out the principles expected to be taken into account by individual enterprises when framing their pricing policy and by the Prices and Incomes Board when examining individual cases suggested by the Government.[2]

In the interests of an effective incomes policy, management was expected to increase efficiency, avoid cost increases and, wherever possible, to stabilize or reduce prices. The White Paper emphasized that competition had an important part to play in stimulating economic expansion, that firms should earn sufficient profit to secure the necessary capital, and that efficient firms can reasonably expect to earn higher profits than their rivals. As it would have been impossible to lay down detailed rules which could have covered all the circumstances faced by individual firms when deciding the prices of their products, only the general principles governing price increases and price reductions were spelled out as a basis for judging whether particular pricing decisions were consistent with the national interest.

The criteria for price behaviour is described by paragraph 9 of the White Paper as follows:

[2] 'Prices and Incomes Policy', Cmnd. 2639, April 1965.

To keep the general level of prices stable, it is vital that price increases should be avoided where possible and that prices should be reduced wherever circumstances permit. Enterprises will not be expected to raise their prices except in the following circumstances:

(i) if output per employee cannot be increased sufficiently to allow wages and salaries to increase . . . without some increase in prices, and no offsetting reductions can be made in non-labour costs per unit of output or in the return sought on investment;

(ii) if there are unavoidable increases in non-labour costs such as materials, fuel, services or marketing costs per unit of output which cannot be offset by reductions in labour or capital costs per unit of output or in the return sought on investment;

(iii) if there are unavoidable increases in capital costs per unit of output which cannot be offset by reductions in non-capital costs per unit of output or in the return sought on investment;

(iv) if, after every effort has been made to reduce costs, the enterprise is unable to secure the capital required to meet home and overseas demand.

Paragraph 10 of the White Paper gives instructions concerning price reductions:

Enterprises will be expected to reduce their prices in the following circumstances:

(i) if output per employee is increasing faster than the rate of increase in wages and salaries . . . and there are no offsetting and unavoidable increases in non-labour costs per unit of output;

(ii) the costs of materials, fuel or services per unit of output are falling and there are no offsetting and unavoidable increases in labour or capital costs per unit of output;

(iii) if capital costs per unit of output are falling and there are no offsetting and unavoidable increases in non-capital costs per unit of output;

(iv) if profits are based on excessive market power.

The White Paper also outlined general criteria for pay increases and increases in other incomes. The norm for the average rate of annual increase of money incomes was fixed at $3-3\frac{1}{2}$ per cent.

The early warning system

The prices and incomes policy did not prove to be a success initially. By the time the Prices and Incomes Board was set up a pattern of wage increase well above the 3–3½ per cent norm had already been established. Simultaneously, claims for the introduction of a 40-hour week were also put forward by various industries. Wage increases ranging up to 7 per cent were granted. Retail prices were also moving upwards. After a while the need for strengthening the existing arrangements became apparent.

Therefore, in September 1965, the Government announced its intention to seek statutory power to introduce a compulsory 'early warning' system for prices and incomes. As legislation takes time and the Government was anxious to curb the rise of prices and wages as soon as possible, an arrangement was made with employers and unions to operate the early warning system on a voluntary basis. In return the Government undertook not to use its powers to operate a compulsory early warning system unless the voluntary arrangement did not work satisfactorily. The TUC agreed to set up its own machinery for vetting all pay claims by affiliated unions. The Confederation of British Industry accepted the new wage reviewing procedure but turned down the Government's request to act as a channel of communication between its members and the Departments in respect of prices.[3]

The new measure gave the Government an opportunity to review decisions on prices and pay before they were put into effect. The principles of the non-statutory early warning system were detailed in a White Paper published in November 1965.[4]

The early warning arrangement was not intended to cover each of the very large number of price changes, but only those related to goods and services of particular economic significance and those consumer goods which were important elements in the cost of living. The main target was to keep an eye on changes in manufacturers' prices for the home market. Wholesale and retail prices were included only in special cases, such as when the manufacturer was also the retailer. Some classes of goods were omitted altogether, such as goods whose prices were determined by frequent changes of supply-and-demand conditions, where imported materials played a dominant role in price formation, and industrial goods sold on the basis of individually negotiated contracts. Products representing over half of all consumer expenditure on

---

[3] Confederation of British Industry, Annual Report, 1965, p. 10.
[4] 'Prices and Incomes Policy: An "Early Warning" System', Cmnd. 2808, November 1965.

food and drink were subjected to the new measure. The range of goods, classified into 84 broad categories, are enumerated in Appendix A of the White Paper. A number of additions were made to this original list later to meet the needs of the prices standstill (see below).

Under the early warning system any enterprise wanting to increase the price of a product is expected to give at least four weeks' advance notice to the appropriate Government Department. On receipt of the notification about a proposed price increase, the Government Department may ask for further detail to judge whether the case would be consistent with the agreed criteria and whether reference should be made for investigation to the Prices and Incomes Board. If the firm is not contacted by the Government Department before the end of the four-week period, it is an indication that no action will be taken concerning the proposed price increase, though the White Paper emphasized that this does not imply any positive approval of the move. Where the Government notifies the firm that a more prolonged inquiry is needed, or the case shall be referred to the Board, the price increase is expected to be deferred until the completion of such investigations. The Government Department should arrive at a decision within another four weeks. In the case of a reference to the Board, the total time between the notification of the Government Department by the firm and the Board's report, during which period the price increase is expected to be deferred, should be no more than three months.

All the information received by the Government under the early warning system is treated as confidential. References to the Board are, however, publicly announced and reports published.

The prices and incomes standstill

In the first half of 1966 the country's economic situation failed to improve. As a consequence of a particularly serious balance of payments situation, the Government introduced a severe deflationary policy on July 20. At the same time a twelve-month standstill on prices and incomes, later popularly known as the 'freeze', was introduced to provide a breathing-space for the economy during which period productivity was expected to catch up with incomes, making British goods more competitive abroad.[5] Two phases of the standstill were envisaged. The first six months, that is, the second half of 1966, were marked as 'general standstill', when virtually no increases of prices and incomes would take place. The second six months, the first half of 1967, was called 'the period of severe restraint', when only for particularly compelling reasons would increases be allowed.

For the one-year period of standstill the criteria for price increases, set out in the White Paper on Prices and Incomes Policy in April 1965, were superseded by much more stringent principles. All firms, within and outside the early warning system, were expected to make every effort to absorb increases in costs. This was expected not only from industrial firms but also from wholesalers and retailers. Exceptions to the general standstill were made only in respect of imported materials, changes in supply for seasonal and other reasons, and action by the Government, such as increased taxation. In cases when a firm felt compelled to propose a price increase, and were unable to absorb increased costs, a most vigorous scrutiny was intended to be carried out. In respect of price reductions the criteria remains unchanged. Upon the insistence of the Confederation of British Industry, these criteria were widened for the period of severe restraint by allowing price increases where the receipts of an enterprise were not adequate to maintain efficiency and to undertake necessary investment.[6] As far as wages were concerned, the norm was zero for the period of standstill.

When introducing the standstill, the Government also intended to extend substantially the early warning system for advanced notification of price increases. A request for advance notification from all manufacturing firms employing over a hundred workers, and notification concerning all goods and services within and outside the original early warning system, was also contained in the White Paper.[7] The Confederation of British Industry, however, opposed the new measure, pointing out that such a wide obligation to report price changes was administratively cumbersome and ill-conceived. Therefore, it advised manufacturers to comply with the new request only for a short period of time, until the end of

---

[5] 'Prices and Incomes Standstill', Cmnd. 3073, July 1966.
[6] Confederation of British Industry, Annual Report, 1966, p. 13.
[7] Cmnd. 3073, op. cit., paras. 8–10.

August 1966, and thereafter to return to the former early warning system, or any extension of it which might have been negotiated with the Departments in the meantime. In a later White Paper the Government made it public that the general request for advance notification would progressively be discontinued and replaced by the former arrangement as extended to cover a wider field of items.[8]

The Prices and Incomes Act, 1966

In the meantime the Government went ahead seeking statutory reserve powers in the field of prices and incomes policy. The Prices and Incomes Act, 1966, received the royal assent on August 12, shortly after the imposition of the one-year standstill.

The Act changed the status of the National Board for Prices and Incomes from a royal commission to a statutory body. Its membership is now limited to between nine and fifteen. Members can be appointed by the Secretary of State either as full-time or part-time members. The Secretary of State was also empowered to appoint the chairman of the Board and one or more deputy chairmen selected from the full-time members.

The Secretary of State, or he and any other Minister acting jointly, may refer to the Board any question relating to prices, wages, and other incomes for investigation. The Board is required to report to the Minister or Ministers who referred the question to it. A significant new measure introduced by the Act is that the Secretary of State, or he and another Minister acting jointly, may instruct the Board to keep under continuous review any question related to prices and incomes and ask for a report at any time. While making its investigations into any price problem the Board is required to have regard to the same criteria as those set out in the White Paper on Prices and Incomes Policy, which are reiterated in Schedule 2 of the Act.

The Board is under obligation to publish its reports within three months of any reference, unless the period is extended by the Ministers concerned. All reports are to be laid before each House of Parliament.

Part II of the Act provides for statutory reserve power about

[8] 'Prices and Incomes Standstill: Period of Severe Restraint', Cmnd. 3150, November 1966, paras. 15–17.

advance notification of proposed price increases. This part can be brought into force for a period of twelve months by an Order in Council, subject to previous approval by each House of Parliament. Such orders are renewable for subsequent periods of twelve months. This part of the Act allows for a one-month period deferment of any price increase while the Government Department investigates the case. A further three months' delay is imposed on those cases which are referred to the Prices and Incomes Board regardless of whether or not there has been prior notification. Part II was activated for the first time in July 1967 and came into force from August 12, 1967, in conjunction with the Prices and Incomes Act, 1967 (see page 219).

Part III of the Act provides that price-restricting agreements entered into as a result of a recommendation by the Board and approved by the Secretary of State and the President of the Board of Trade shall be exempted for a limited period from the operation of the Restrictive Trade Practices Act, 1956.

Under Part IV the Government took power to fix wages and prices by Statutory Order, or to restore them to the July 20 level, the date when the freeze started. This part also provided an indemnity for employers who voluntarily withheld from their employees pay increases which fell due under contracts of employment made before this measure had come into force. Part IV lapsed after a period of twelve months, on August 11, 1967. The Government's intention was to use these powers only as a last resort in case the freeze was broken, and only after consultation with the employers and the unions. Therefore, at the beginning of the twelve-month period the Government relied entirely on voluntary co-operation. Later, however, the voluntary policy had to be discontinued and Part IV of the Act was activated.

Two events are memorable in this connection. At the end of September a county court, passing judgement in the Association of Supervisory Staffs, Executives and Technicians (ASSET) *contra* Thorn Electrical Industries case, decided that the company could not refuse to pay wage increases already agreed before the pay standstill. The other major event, which compelled the Government to bring Part IV into force, was the agreement between the Newspaper Proprietors Association (NPA) and the printing unions on the payment of a 2 shillings a week cost of living bonus to 25,000 workers at the end of September. The bonus was due under a 2½-year-old agreement. In a statement, NPA accused the Government of placing the employers in an impossible position by its refusal to activate Part IV of the Act, which would give protection to employers who breached contractual obligations because of the freeze. Part IV was in fact brought into force on October 6, 1966. It was described as 'unprecedented in peace or war' by the Leader of the Opposition and 'an unprecedented peacetime curtailment of the citizen's liberties' by *The Statist*.[9]

The new powers of the Government were used only once in respect of price increases, and on fourteen occasions in connection with wages. In October the Government imposed a standstill Order on certain dry-cleaning and laundry charges in response to complaints from the public about price rises. This move provoked a storm of protest, since the Government issued the Order without the promised consultation with the industry. Previously the Government had made it clear that it did not wish to use its powers to introduce a total freeze throughout an industry as it had now done. A number of applications for the increase of dry-cleaning and laundry charges were approved later by the Board of Trade.

Moderation

The one-year period of standstill on prices and incomes ended in June 1967. During the year average earnings rose by 2 per cent, while retail prices increased by nearly 3 per cent. In comparison with previous years, these figures suggested that the policy of standstill, combined with deflation, was fairly effective. The balance of payments also showed an improving tendency. The cost of the policy was, however, a 1 per cent drop in industrial production on the previous year and an unemployment figure of half a million people.

Already in the spring of 1967 the Government announced its new policy for the period after the end of the standstill. It called for a continued moderation of prices and incomes for a further twelve months following June 30, 1967.[10] This policy was designed to avoid widespread price and wage increases after July for which

---

[9] *The Statist*, October 7, 1966, p. 847.
[10] 'Prices and Incomes Policy after 30th June, 1967', Cmnd. 3235, March 1967.

pressure had been building up during the period of standstill and severe restraint.

From July 1967 the prices and incomes policy reverted partly to the system operating before the one-year freeze. Its voluntary character was newly emphasized. In respect of the early warning system, the existing arrangement was retained, but the general request for advance notification was finally and formally discontinued. At the same time the limited criteria concerning price and wage increases, valid during the freeze, were replaced by the broader considerations laid down in the White Paper on Prices and Incomes Policy. In respect of wages, however, an important difference was that, while before the freeze a norm of $3-3\frac{1}{2}$ per cent applied, the new norm was zero; no automatic entitlement to a minimum wage increase was created. In spite of this 'nil norm', some increases in wage rates took place in the second half of the year because of wage commitments carried over from before the freeze and because of new agreements.

Part IV of the Prices and Incomes Act, 1966, lapsed on August 11, 1967. In spite of the voluntary nature of the prices and incomes policy during the period of moderation, the Government wanted to secure some new statutory reserve power in this field. For this reason, as mentioned before, Part II of the 1966 Act was brought into force for a period of twelve months from August 12, 1967. It should be noted that the activation of Part II did not establish a system of compulsory notification in itself. This measure only provided power to do so, subject to a special Order.

The Prices and Incomes Act, 1967

To secure further reserve powers for the Government after the lapse of Part IV of the Prices and Incomes Act, 1966, on August 11, 1967, and to close some loopholes in the existing legislation, the Prices and Incomes Act, 1967, was enacted in July.

The new Act increases the Government's delaying power over proposed price and pay increase from four months, secured in the 1966 Act, to seven months, subject to reference to the Prices and Incomes Board. Under the new Act the Government has a month to consider whether the application for a price increase should be referred to the Board or not. If reference is made, there is a three months' delay imposed on the firm not to raise its prices. In case the Board opposes the price increase, the Government has a right to delay it for a further three months. After the lapse of seven months, however, the Government is powerless to do anything against the increase, and the applicant firm is free to implement it if it feels strong enough to defy public opinion.

The first major price increase after the freeze was announced by the electricity generating industry at the beginning of September (see Chapter 14).

Sterling was devalued on November 18, 1967. After the devaluation, the Government stressed that, in order not to erode the benefits of the move, a strict prices and incomes policy was to be followed. When presenting his 1968-69 deflationary Budget, the Chancellor of the Exchequer announced in Parliament on March 19, 1968, that the Government would seek statutory powers to limit rising incomes. It was envisaged that a $3\frac{1}{2}$ per cent ceiling on increases in remuneration of all kinds would be imposed until the end of 1969, coupled with powers to suspend and defer price increases.

The Prices and Incomes Board

The first references to the Board were made by the Government in May 1965, and by the end of the year the Board had received sixteen references and issued seven reports. Up to August 1967, in the period covered by its first and second General Reports, the Board had reported on 38 references, 18 of which were concerned wholly or partly with prices. At the time of the publication of the second General Report, 18 references were under investigation.

The White Paper on the Machinery of Prices and Incomes Policy suggested that the Board should work in two divisions: the Prices Review and the Incomes Review Divisions. This suggestion has never been put into practice because the Board found that price and income problems were inseparable. Proposed price increases were often originated by a wage rise and proposed wage increases had direct implications for prices. For this reason the Board encouraged the Government to make references of both prices and wages in particular industries jointly together.[11]

[11] 'General Report', April 1965 to July 1966, Cmnd. 3087, August 1966, paras. 26 and 88.

The examination of reference problems are usually assigned to a committee of three members, though the Board as a whole has retained responsibility for the final reports and recommendations. During its work the Board has also engaged the services of management consultants and outside independent specialists. It is the Board's practice not to publish the names of the consultants and their terms of reference. Outside consultants are employed only as fact-finders; they do not take part in the policy discussions and drafting of reports. Tasks of a particularly confidential nature are handled by the Board's own staff wherever possible.[12]

The Government retained full responsibility for all references to be made to the Board. Such references could be prompted by complaints from the public, from interested parties or independent bodies, or selected directly by the Government. The Board has been increasingly encouraged to suggest possible references, and its suggestions have often been acted upon. After investigating coal pit-head prices, for example, the Board drew attention to the different rates of increase in the price of coal at pit-head and to the domestic consumer, and suggested an investigation into the distribution costs of coal. The recommendation was accepted by the Government and the problem was returned as a reference to the Board.

During the first two years of its existence the Board looked generally into manufacturing and service industry prices. In the meantime the Department of Economic Affairs received thousands of complaints from consumers about retail prices. It was felt that retailers should be as involved as manufacturers in the prices and incomes policy and, therefore, some retail prices should also be scrutinized. In August 1967 the Government referred the question of distributors' costs and margins in the furniture, electrical appliances, and footwear trades to the Board.

The overall attitude of the Board has been that price increases are justified if it is not possible to absorb a long-run rise in costs or if the existing levels of prices are insufficient to generate finance for necessary investment in the industry. Increased demand has not been recognized as a valid reason for price increases, in accordance with the criteria laid down in the White Paper on Prices and Incomes Policy and incorporated later in the Prices and Incomes Act, 1966. The Board has met, however, the effect of decreased

[12] 'Second General Report', Cmnd. 3394, August 1967, paras. 61–64.

demand on capital-intensive industries in the references on news-print, fertilizers, cement, and aluminium semi-manufactures. In such industries unit costs rise in a period of recession. With the exception of aluminium semi-manufactures the Board agreed to price increases in these industries. In the case of aluminium semi-manufactures a price increase was not condoned because of the threat of competition from other materials.

The average time between reference and the publication of reports has been three to four months; five weeks and nearly a year being the lower and upper limits. The published reports have been criticized for their brevity and for not containing the evidence submitted by the parties concerned.[13] Studies prepared by outside consultants for the Board are not published either.

Though the Government is perfectly free to disregard the recommendations of the Board, it has usually accepted them and negotiated undertakings with the reference industries along the suggested lines. The main exceptions were industries concerning which the Board proposed major reorganizations, such as banks and laundries. The industries concerned were, on the whole, co-operative. The Road Haulage Association, however, contravened the suggested measure. In the interim report on road haulage rates in June 1965 the Board suggested, and the Association reluctantly agreed, not to recommend blanket rate increases to its members. In June 1966, after the final report of the Board, the Association 'advised' its members to negotiate rate increases ranging up to 9 per cent. At the request of the Minister of Transport, the Board produced a Memorandum deploring the Association's move and advising the industry's customers to be critical of the automatic passing on of cost increases. At the same time the Board suggested that trade association price recommendations should be registrable under the Restrictive Trade Practices Act, 1956.

The smooth co-operation between the Government and the Board was disturbed for a number of reasons. The Board pointed out that some of the references made by the Government were made for political reasons and cases were selected because certain issues were in the forefront of public interest and not because of their overall significance. The Board expressed its wish to investigate problems of longer-term interest, such as the effects of

[13] E. Victor Morgan, 'When the P.I.B. Should Mind Its Own Business', *British Industry*, September 16, 1966, p. 17.

new taxation schemes, and also its preference for investigating important industries.[14]

In certain cases, sponsoring Government departments were reluctant to see industries under their supervision investigated by the Board. For example, under the influence of the Confederation of British Industry and the car industry itself, the Government did not refer car prices to the Board in August 1967. This would have been the Board's most important inquiry ever, and it did not conceal its disappointment. This case revealed some conflict between the Board and the 'little Neddys', whose task is to investigate efficiency issues in various individual industries. (Little Neddy is the popular name for Economic Development Committees organized for various industries under the National Economic Development Council. They include representatives of management, trade unions, relevant government departments, and members of the NED office.) The reason given for the shelving of the car-price inquiry by the Government was that a little Neddy had been set up for the car industry to probe into the industry's problems. The Board was quick to point out that while the little Neddy reports were produced by interested parties the Board represented an objective, independent view.

A further policy clash between the Government and the Board came about when the general rise in electricity tariffs was announced by the Government in September 1967 without prior consultation with the Board (see Chapter 14).

There has also been disagreement in the interpretation of references by the Government, the Board, and by the interested parties. The Board met, for the first time, an industry with fixed common prices when investigating the suggested price increase of the cement industry in 1967.[15] As already related in Chapter 8, the Restrictive Practices Court had accepted the industry's agreement as not being contrary to the public interest in 1961. The Board was prepared to have a fresh look into the question of the price agreement but the industry insisted that the Court's decision could not be questioned. The cause of the disagreement was that the reference was drawn up in such an imprecise way that the industry could interpret it differently from the Board.[16] The issue

[14] Cmnd. 3394, op. cit., para. 75.
[15] 'Report No. 38, Portland Cement Prices', Cmnd. 3381, August 1967.
[16] *The Times*, August 11, 1967.

of the interpretation of a reference also arose when the Board looked into the question of bank charges. It was exposed to criticism for taking too wide a brief and suggesting substantial changes in the whole financial system.

During the first years of its existence the importance of the Prices and Incomes Board has undoubtedly grown. Its reports discussed not only price changes in various industries, but problems of efficiency, profits, and investments. The reports proved to be sources of new ideas and promoted industrial change. Its new role in relation to nationalized industries (see Chapter 14) increases the Board's influence in economic matters still further.

Prices and incomes policy in America

Prices and incomes policy is frequently referred to as 'wage-price guidelines' or 'guideposts' in the North American continent. In the United States the guideposts devised by the Council of Economic Advisers were first announced in 1962. In the following years, when the Council learned of an important actual or impending price increase, an invitation was sent to the industry to discuss the matter with the Council. In a number of cases price increases have been rescinded, reduced or delayed. Between 1961 and 1965 the United States economy exhibited a remarkable degree of price stability. The same cannot be said of the ensuing years. In 1966 and 1967 consumer prices increased by about 3 per cent each year, signalling an accelerating tendency in the second half of 1967. Consequently, the Economic Report of the President, published in February 1968, announced the setting up of a Cabinet Committee on Price Stability, charged with the responsibility of studying and recommending policies to achieve price stability. The Committee consists of the Secretaries of the Treasury, Commerce and Labour Departments, the Director of the Budget, and the Chairman of the Council of Economic Advisers. It is not the task of the Committee to get involved with specific current wage and price matters, but to enlist the co-operation of business and labour 'towards responsible wage and price behaviour'. The Committee intends to achieve concensus on appropriate standards to guide private price and wage decisions.[17]

[17] 'Economic Report of the President, Together with the Annual Report of the Council of Economic Advisers', Washington, February 1968, pp. 19–21 and 96–128.

EPILOGUE

The main issues of business and prices have been surveyed. To conclude the discussion, it may not be out of place to summarize briefly the possible future developments in this field.

There is an obvious need, first of all, for the further refinement of economic theory on business pricing. As we have seen, the management of large organizations has gradually been transferred from owners to professional executives, accompanied by a transition from 'classical' to 'managerial' objectives. It would be desirable to narrow the existing gap between the profit-maximizing concept and the variety of actual business goals.

Economic theory should also further develop the yardsticks against which actual market situations can be measured. The use of perfect competition as a welfare ideal is unrealistic. It cannot be said simply that competition is beneficial and monopoly detrimental to the public interest. A more sophisticated definition of public interest is needed when judging issues connected with market structures. The refinements of the concept of workable competition offers a possible way of dealing with this problem.

A further development is also in sight in respect of actual pricing practices. The time-honoured difference of opinion which has existed between accountants and economists in this area is on the wane. It is being increasingly realized that wherever the entrepreneur has an idea about the shape of the demand curve, marginal pricing may offer a distinct possibility for increasing net returns as against full-cost pricing. Consumer psychology also presents a field for unlimited experimentation and research. Many firms may find it rewarding to revise their established price structure based on the findings of tests into consumers' reactions to various pricing practices.

Public policy concerning prices is likely to be active in the coming years. The vast majority of the numerous restrictive price agreements have been dismantled since the passing of the Restrictive Trade Practices Act in 1956. Information agreements, which have often replaced price agreements, are, on the other hand, still not regulated by law. The Government has already announced its intention to bring these agreements within the scope of the act.

After the passing of the Resale Prices Act, 1964, resale price maintenance is becoming a thing of the past, though certain industries still stick to their guns, waiting for adjudication of their case by the Restrictive Practices Court. Price recommendation has often replaced resale price maintenance. The current investigation of the Monopolies Commission will clarify the issue whether price recommendation is in complete harmony with the public interest or not.

Finally, the question of the whole future of the prices and incomes policy looms large. It is still an open question what achievements one can expect from state intervention in this area. An expert report on the subject suggests caution as against being over-optimistic: 'A few countries have also established procedures for discussion between the governmental authorities and industry of proposed price increases, and have found this technique useful from both an economic and a political standpoint. We have the impression that, with the help of these procedures, it may be possible to avoid or to reduce price increases for some time, but that they are rather inefficient, in the long run, to suppress price rises resulting from persisting inflationary forces. Moreover, these procedures do not readily lend themselves to securing price reductions which may seem to be justified but which do not actually take place. They may even reduce downward price flexibility by making entrepreneurs reluctant to lower prices for fear of being unable to raise them again when conditions change.'[1]

---

[1] William Fellner and others, *The Problem of Rising Prices*, O.E.C.D., Paris, 1961, p. 71.

Index